Womanhood in
Radical Protestantism
1525-1675

Joyce L. Irwin

The Edwin Mellen Press
New York and Toronto

The Edwin Mellen Press
Suite 918
225 West 34th Street
New York, New York 10001

Library of Congress Cataloging Number 79-66370

ISBN 0-88946-547-9

Studies in Women and Religion, ISBN 0-88946-549-5

Printed in the United States of America

To my mother

and

to her mother—

two extraordinary examples of womanhood.

PREFACE

The demand in recent years for courses in women's studies has caused those of us involved in such courses to become aware of the relative inaccessibility of primary sources in this area. At the same time, the inadequacies of many secondary sources dealing with women's history make the encounter with the primary sources all the more desirable. For survey courses in women's history a few good sourcebooks are now available. The present volume seeks not to compete with these but to fill a need for more specialized sets of readings to be used by those prepared to explore a particular historical era in greater depth. It is my hope that this book will be useful to a wide variety of persons, whether their primary interest be the history of women, the history of the Reformation, or the history of Christianity.

In facing questions of editorial style, I wanted to ensure that the texts would be readable for the non-specialist yet also reliable for the specialist. Because many texts were being translated from German, French, or Latin into modern English, the early English texts were placed at a disadvantage, appearing more archaic by comparison. To retain the original text seemed desirable from a scholarly standpoint but a potential stumblingblock for many readers. As a compromise, I decided to modernize spelling on the assumption that to do so in no way affected the original meaning,

given the irregularities of spelling during the early
modern period. *Webster's Third New International Dictionary* has been taken as the standard for judging acceptable varieties of spelling. In cases where the
two punctuation practices were significantly at variance, I also modernized punctuation; nevertheless, many
cumbersome sentences are retained because of my unwillingness to alter the original sentence structure. Underlines are omitted except where emphasis seems appropriate; quotation marks have been added for clarity.

At various points in the preparation of the manuscript, I received valuable assistance from others. A
former colleague, Ingrid Edlund, and my brother and
sister-in-law, Galen and Jeannette Irwin, were of help
in some translation problems, though I take full responsibility for all translations offered here for the
first time. In my search for materials, I became indebted to the librarians of the University of Georgia,
particularly those of the Interlibrary Loan Office, as
well as to librarians at Yale, the New York Public Library, and Columbia University. LeAnne Thurmond performed
many tasks very reliably as my research assistant in the
early stages of the project. The secretaries of the History Department of the University of Georgia deserve sincere thanks for the original typing job, as does Una Crist
for the final copy. Finally, my appreciation is due to
Steven Ozment, Roland Bainton, and Franklin Littell for
their helpful suggestions and to Elizabeth Clark and
Herbert Richardson for their encouragement and editorial
advice.

                                          Joyce L. Irwin

Hamilton, New York
April, 1979

CONTENTS

GENERAL INTRODUCTION

Religions espoused by entire countries seldom
seek to overturn the social values of those countries.
State churches, having gained the endorsement of political leaders of a country, usually accept, and even
reinforce, the social and political status quo of that
country. Sociologists from Emile Durkheim to Peter
Berger have observed the importance of religion as a
force for social cohesion. As Berger has argued, the
meanings, ideas and values which hold a society together are sanctioned by religion. "By thus putting
under its sanctions the most important elements of
consensus, religion makes possible a moral community,
and thus makes it possible for society to exist at
all."[1]

Radical criticism of a society's moral consensus
issues normally only from religious spokesmen who have
not received majority support. Small, relatively new
religious sects are far more likely to reject prevailing social values and institutions than are large,
well-established churches. Whatever updating may be
necessary, Ernst Troeltsch's distinction between sects
and churches remains helpful in understanding the
variety of social teachings which have been advocated
in Christian history.[2] In their attempts to direct
the life of the entire society, churches enter into relationships of reciprocal influence with the State:

"The Church both stabilizes and determines the social
order; in so doing, however, she becomes dependent upon
the upper classes, and upon their development."[3] Sects,
on the other hand, usually renounce the aim of domi-
nating the world, concentrating their efforts instead
on the perfection of their own comparatively small
group. Whether they are indifferent, tolerant, or hos-
tile to the larger society, according to Troeltsch, they
are connected "with those elements in society which are
opposed to the State and to Society."[4]

      Within Christianity, the Bible has been the pri-
mary source of opposition to existing social norms.
The church of the apostles and, to a lesser extent, the
patriarchates and monarchies of the ancient Hebrews,
provided alternative models for Christians dissatisfied
with their social order. The radical sects of the
later Middle Ages—Lollards and Hussites, for example—
proclaimed the centrality of the Bible as the source of
religious truth and decried non-scriptural accretions.
Political and ecclesiastical hierarchies were among
the elements of medieval society which were considered
unscriptural by these sects.

      When, with the watchword "Scripture alone," the
Reformers placed the medieval *corpus Christianorum*
under attack, a total upheaval of the social structure
might have been expected. Certainly there were significant social dislocations, affecting particularly Roman Catholic priests, monks and nuns. Further, towns-
people began to play a greater role in their own political and religious affairs. But in spite of some
early confusion, it became evident through the Peasants'
War that religious reformation did not necessarily en-

tail radical social change. Luther's repudiation of
the peasants—for better or worse—helped to cement the
alliance of Lutheranism with the existing political
structure. The switch from Catholicism to Lutheranism
was more likely to take place through the personal decision of a prince than through the agitation of his
opponents. Whether or not any betrayal of Luther's
original beliefs occurred in the process of establishing the Lutheran state church structure, it appears
that he always envisioned a church which would be co-
terminous with the State.

     Luther's antagonism toward the Anabaptists re-
sulted not merely from his greater reverence for the
sacraments but also from his greater respect for government. Government is a "special ordinance and function
of God,"[5] not a necessary evil. Because of this positive view of government, both Luther and Calvin encouraged their followers to work for change "within the
system," whereas Anabaptists viewed such accommodation
to worldly powers as moral contamination. Hence the
term "Magisterial Reformation" has come into usage to
describe those reforming groups which gained acceptance by the magistrates of various political units,
whereas "Radical Reformation" designates those groups
or individuals who neither sought nor gained endorsement by the political establishment.

     With the vision of a society governed by the law
of God rather than of man, the Anabaptists sought to
recover the mutually supportive community structure of
the New Testament church. Groups such as the Hutterites, who found a sufficiently tolerant setting to begin to form such a community, shared their goods in

common and subordinated family bonds to the community
as a whole. Among other Anabaptist groups, the communal impetus was expressed through church government,
in which pastors were chosen by the congregation. Anabaptists opposed elaborate hierarchical structures in
the church, and, though the Hutterites had bishops,
most Anabaptists distinguished only between local ministers and apostles who wandered from place to place.
Even these leaders normally held another job which provided their means of support.[6]

    If the Anabaptists were less willing to accept
those institutions shaping the earthly community than
were Luther and Calvin, it might be supposed that they
would attempt a systematic reshaping of the fundamental
social institution, marriage and the family. Inclined
as they were toward a levelling of social distinctions,
they might be expected to eliminate the subordination
of female to male which constituted the most pervasive
of social hierarchies. It is presumably such expectations, along with a certain amount of corroborating
evidence, which have led some observers to conclude
that relations between the sexes were much more egalitarian among radical Protestants than in the larger
society. Sherrin Marshall Wyntjes wrote recently:

> The radical Reformation's insistence on
> freedom of conscience for all adult be-
> lievers eliminated distinctions based on
> sex, and the doctrine of baptism or re-
> baptism for all believers became an
> equalizing covenant. Anabaptist priest-
> hood included all members of the laity,
> both men and women....[7]

Similarly, Elise Boulding declared straightforwardly

that the Anabaptists "practiced complete equality of

women and men in every respect, including preaching."[8]

Perhaps such sweeping statements result from a
careless reading of more limited observations, which
nevertheless give the impression that Anabaptism and
other radical movements changed the status of women.
According to Vern L. Bullough, for instance, "Some of
the minor Protestant groups," in this case the Bohemian
Brethren represented by Jan Comenius, offered women
greater equality of education.[9] Julia O'Faolain and
Lauro Martines saw Anabaptism and radical sects as providing an occasion for women to achieve "some prominence as workers and even agitators."[10] Finally, in
examining Christian attitudes toward marriage, Roland
Bainton found that the emphasis on companionability
"came into its own most fully with the more radical
varieties of the Reformation such as the Anabaptists,
later the Quakers, and in no small measure the Calvinists, particularly the English Puritans."[11]

It is the intention of this book to present evidence which would allow the reader to evaluate the
above statements. The general trend of all these quo-
tations is the same, yet they refer to different religious groups, different time periods, and different aspects of women's lives. Such variety should alert us
to the complexity of the problem. What "radical Protestants" have in common is their opposition to the religious and/or political establishment. The attempt
to describe those who belong to the "Radical Reformation"—or, as it is variously known, the "left wing of
the Reformation" or the "Free Church tradition"—has
resulted in classifications into at least two major
strands, possibly with several subdivisions.[12] Grouped

together in a negative sense as outsiders to the mainstream of the Reformation, the positive orientation of
their thought is by no means united. The point of dif-
ferentiation between the two main categories, Anabaptist and Spiritualist,[13] is the source of religious
authority. Anabaptists are identified as relying fundamentally on the Bible, Spiritualists as relying on
the Spirit. The fact that George Williams found it
necessary to set up such subcategories as "revolutionary," "contemplative," and "evangelical" Anabaptists
and "revolutionary," "evangelical," and "rational
Spiritualists,"[14] is an indication of the difficulty
of making clear-cut identification of a particular
thinker's orientation. All Anabaptists had a place for
the Holy Spirit in their theology and all Spiritualists
held the Bible in some esteem.

As long as the danger of over-simplification is
recognized, the two categories may be used fruitfully
in the attempt to explain differences on many issues.
For those who believe that the Bible should be taken at
face value, the guidelines for religious life are at
once more clear-cut and more confining than for those
who may be led by the Spirit. Spiritualists may be
able to justify historical change through a claim that
the age of the Spirit has superceded the age of the
Law. A conception of historical progress is thereby
made possible, whereas an Anabaptist would view change
as positive only if it helped to recover the conditions of biblical times.

Because the Spirit may speak directly to and
through individuals, organized religious communities
may not be necessary for a Spiritualist. In any case

the aim need not be to restore the New Testament church.
Troeltsch, in fact, found the Spiritualists too individualistic to fall into either the church or sect type.
Indeed, the most noted sixteenth-century Spiritualists,
Caspar Schwenckfeld, Valentin Weigel, and Sebastian
Franck, are not known primarily as leaders of movements
but as individual thinkers. Yet this is not true of
the seventeenth century, where individualistic mysticism was often preached and practiced within sectarian
movements. Troeltsch himself, while refusing to abandon his categories, had to admit that several groups
such as the Labadists and the Quakers belonged in
both.[15]

Although the complexities of the problem increase
when the sixteenth and seventeenth centuries are taken
together, the study of women can only be enhanced by so
doing. The possibilities opened up by the early reformers are only self-consciously and consistently developed, as far as the role of women is concerned, by
thinkers of the seventeenth century. As indicated by
Bainton's statement above, the theme of companionability in marriage links Anabaptists, Puritans, and Quakers. Anabaptists focussed on religious or doctrinal
compatibility, whereas Puritans looked at all aspects
of the marriage relationship. Within the church, the
stirrings of female activity felt in sixteenth-century
sects reach their culmination with the women's meetings
of the Society of Friends. By extending our study to
include this culminating point we reach beyond what is
normally termed "Radical Reformation," leading us to
label the subject of our study "radical Protestantism"
instead. Whether Puritanism is properly defined as

radical could well evoke differing opinions because of
the wide variety of theological and political stances
among those of this designation. Should Puritans who
remained within the Church of England in the early
seventeenth century be termed "radical"? Does the Puritanism of Cromwellian England or of colonial Massachusetts, in which it was the established religion, belong to "radical Protestantism"? Recognizing the possibility of differing answers to these questions, I
nevertheless decided to include in the study Puritans
of all varieties, based on their common criticisms of
the Church of England. To do otherwise, I felt, would
be to introduce artificial distinctions based on political fluctuations rather than religious inclinations.

By the last quarter of the seventeenth century, a
new era in Protestantism had arrived: the age of Pietism.
Whatever its genetic relation to the forms of Protestantism preceding it, Pietism marks a new, even more problem-
atic blurring of the distinctions among state church,
sect, and mysticism. For this age a separate study of
the role of women is needed. Pietistic women such as
Jane Leade, Antoinette Bourignon, and Johanna Eleonora
Petersen may be only the best known of a large number
of interesting, religiously active women of the period.
Writings on marriage by such leading Pietists as
Philipp Jakob Spener and Nikolaus Ludwig von Zinzendorf
reveal a new attempt to integrate religious and sexual
purity. Yet the Pietist solutions to this problem are
too diverse for a simple, unitary picture of the situation.[16] Hence this volume ends at the point where
Pietism is said to begin, that is, with the publication
of Spener's *Pia Desideria* in 1675.

What, then, can be said about womanhood among
radical Protestants from 1525 to 1675? As with Pietist
views of marriage, the picture lacks unity. The status
of women necessarily entails many facets, including
their relations to husbands and children, to clergy and
male church members, to those who teach, and to those
who govern. Insights may be gained from many sources,
originating from both men and women, addressing the
question either directly or indirectly. In choosing
the word "womanhood" for my title, I was reflecting my
decision to present selections of a more theoretical
than biographical or sociological nature. I was less
concerned to accumulate data or to identify particular
women active in the groups under investigation than to
find expressions of attitudes concerning the status of
women. The resulting preponderance of male authors reflects the inescapable fact that comparatively few
writings by women from the period before the mid-seven-
teenth century have survived. Even fewer contain any
conscious reflection on the writer's womanhood. The
present study does not presume a direct correlation between the actual status of women among sectarians and
the expressed male position regarding their role. It
does assume, however, that male attitudes had significant influence in determining which role options would
be open to women.

The organization of texts into chapters was also
shaped by the available materials. Comparison of the
lengths of various chapters results in some significant
insights. First, the chapter on women's education is
relatively brief. The radical sects often drew their
members from the lower, less educated classes in so-

ciety. Anabaptists in particular took pride in their
simple, unsophisticated style of life. Learning was
considered a luxury with all the dangers of physical
luxuries, prone to corruption if not used carefully.
Ultimately it was useless, perhaps even an obstacle to
faith. Gabriel Ascherham's statement, "We have had
universities for fifteen hundred years, but they had
only prevented people from finding their salvation,"[17]
expresses the typical Anabaptist distrust of higher education. If this was the opinion on education for men,
it is obvious why there are no Anabaptist writings debating the question of higher education for women.

   If this book had attempted to cover all elements
of European society in this period, however, this chapter would probably have been the longest. Just as for
men the education of the middle class was a central
factor in setting the stage for liberation from clerical domination, so too for women education was the tool
whereby a woman could rise to a higher status. Recently it has been argued that Renaissance education placed
women under the tutelage of men, resulting in a greater
dependency than during the Middle Ages, when aristocratic girls were trained by other women.[18] While it
may be true that women were not the primary shapers of
humanistic culture, it must also be admitted that men
took women more seriously as students than before.
Noblewomen were expected to be well-enough educated to
engage in interesting conversations with men of the
court. Hence their learning had indeed a somewhat
decorative intent, to be combined with other feminine
charms and skills which might delight men and enhance
court society. Because femininity entailed modesty

and chastity, certain studies were not appropriate,
such as ribald poetry and any literature which might
appear to condone illicit love. Education of girls
was limited by consideration not only of morality but
also of propriety. The study of history and oratory
was sometimes discouraged lest it lead women to engage
in public speaking or teaching.[19] Nevertheless, the
opening of the door to classical learning through the
study of Latin should not be underestimated. From
Latin to Greek and from there to the numerous languages studied by women such as Anna Maria van Schurman, humanistic education, once undertaken by women,
was destined to exploit to the fullest those areas
considered acceptable. In so doing, these women could
not fail to exert some influence on society, whether
they were in positions of leadership or not. The very
existence of highly learned women could not help but
demonstrate an intellectual capacity of which many
people, both male and female, had been unaware.

     If education is the key to upward mobility,
whether of social classes or of sexes, the lack of
higher education among Anabaptists, combined with a
frame of mind bordering on anti-intellectualism, could
not be advantageous for women. This is perhaps one
explanation for the failure of Anabaptist women to exploit the anti-hierarchical biases of their sects in
their favor. In spite of democratic tendencies, the
women remained entirely subordinate to the men, both
in the home and in the church. One wonders how a
strong education might have led them to change the
situation.

     An answer to such speculation might focus on the

Puritans of the English Civil War period. The educational environment for Puritan women was considerably
better than for sixteenth-century Anabaptists. Puritans
did not share the scorn for university education. The
founding of Harvard in 1636 is perhaps the best demon-
stration of their respect for theological education.
Although women were not admitted to the universities,
nevertheless, as potential mothers of boys who would
later attend a university, they could not be left ignorant. In some cases they attained, through tutoring,
quite an impressive level of knowledge. Few used their
knowledge outside the home; yet during the English Civil War period women emerged for the first time in no-
ticeable numbers as preachers and prophets. It is safe
to assume that increased attention to women's education
was one factor underlying this new state of affairs.

       With the intermixture of religious and political
concerns during the English Civil War period, some women made their influence felt in the political arena.[20]
From such material it might have been conceivable to
gather selections for a chapter on women in public life.
Yet such a chapter would have been seriously out of
balance, lacking documents from other periods and
groups among the radical Protestants. If the subject
was found worthy of discussion at all, there was general agreement that women should not take positions of
leadership in public life. Such sentiments among radical Protestants were significantly different from those
in society at large. Yet had this book attempted to
survey the role of women in Reformation society as a
whole, such a chapter would have to have been included.
John Knox's *First Blast of the Trumpet against the*

Monstrous Regiment of Women may be an indication that
many would have preferred it otherwise, but in actual
fact women of the nobility held positions of great
power in the sixteenth and seventeenth centuries.
Queens Mary and Elizabeth of England, Mary of Scotland,
Christine of Sweden, and regents Catherine and Marie de
Medici are but a few of the leading ladies of the age.[21]
Because radical Protestantism gets its identity from
its opposition to the establishment, however, one cannot
expect to meet such women in the present volume.

　　The longest chapter, by contrast, is that concerning women as wives. To say that reformers, both
radical and mainstream, felt that women's place was in
the home hardly seems either surprising or interesting.
Certainly for the vast majority of women this was merely an affirmation of the status quo. Yet the seriousness with which reformers went about discussing marriage and family relationships indicates that for them
it was no overworked, matter-of-fact subject. If early
Protestants wanted to gain acceptance for clerical marriage, they had to demonstrate that marriage had some
virtues over celibacy. At the outset scholastically-
trained minds like Luther's might see its chief value
in being a remedy for sin. The longer the Protestant
ministers lived with their wives, however, the more
they realized that companionship had more than physical
benefits.

　　Attention to this subject attained its greatest
concentration among the Puritan writers of the seventeenth century, who made use of writings from the sixteenth century by Heinrich Bullinger and Martin Bucer.
The Reformed tradition thus seems to have matured in
this respect earlier than the Lutheran, where the sub-

ject gains prominence only in the Pietist period.
Bainton's linking of Anabaptists and Puritans on this
topic is subject to question, however, because of the
wide disparities among the Anabaptists themselves.
Some, reflecting their medieval heritage, saw celibacy
as preferable to marriage, which should be entered into
only to avoid fornication. Others emphasized the need
for spiritual unity beyond mere physical unity. In
practical terms this often meant that an Anabaptist
should not marry or remain married to a non-Anabaptist.
This might be interpreted broadly as companionability,
but the prohibitions against marriage with outsiders
seem to indicate more concern for the Anabaptist cause
than for marital harmony.[22] The lack of a consistent
Anabaptist position on marriage may well reflect the
secondary nature of the question for them. More than
for Puritans, who lived comparatively settled lives,
the demands of the faith conflicted with those of the
family.

        The difference between Anabaptist and Puritan or
Quaker positions on marriage might best be explained
in terms that have less to do with theology than
chronology. The claim has been made that romantic
marriage emerged for the first time in the seventeenth
century. According to Herbert Richardson, romantic
marriage was created in the context of a major social
revolution in the seventeenth-century Western world.

> In this revolution, a major reversal of
> the traditional relation between persons
> and social institutions was effected.
> Whereas before the seventeenth century
> men assumed that social institutions are
> stable and should be defined in terms of

> enduring essences for functions that
> should never be altered by individuals,
> after the seventeenth century men be-
> gan to assume that social institutions
> should be reconstructed to meet the wishes
> of individuals.[23]

Such an interpretation relieves us of the difficulty of finding a complete explanation within the religious arena for the rich development of Puritan
thought on marriage and the family. To be sure, a
theological downgrading of sacraments and outward forms
may have forced the radical thinkers to find meaning in
the spiritual relationship. But further explanation
must be sought in the mood of the time. As feudal
culture came to an end, the merits of courtly love
were re-evaluated. Was it better "to love a woman as
a woman" or "to make her one's idol?", asked the char-
acters of Marguerite d'Angoulême's *Heptameron*.[24] The
same question was a subject for discussion in Castiglione's *The Courtier*. As humanistic learning made the
women intellectual companions of the men, marriage
based on shared love came to be more attractive than
the often imaginary delights of chivalric love. To
what extent women outside the nobility benefited from
the more nearly egalitarian views of marriage seems to
have depended on the country. According to writers of
the time, women of France were freer than those of Germany, while the women of England easily held their own
against the French women.[25] Although such cultural
differences may require further explanation, they con-
stitute another factor to be considered in noting differences between Anabaptists and Puritans.

Independent as theology may wish to be from both
cultural and historical influences, it can never

achieve such a supratemporal status. Societal influence makes itself felt even among religious groups
which are fundamentally at odds with society. In times
of social change, however, churches usually follow
rather than lead. This, I think, is true for the cause
of women in the sixteenth century. In humanist circles
and in the *querelle des femmes* among French writers,[26]
the question of the role and capabilities of women was
addressed directly. In Protestant circles of the same
time the issue was dealt with mainly as a side effect
of the new theology, coming into its own only in the
seventeenth century.

As women were attracted to the new theology, they
became active in the movement, usually without question-
ing the woman's assigned subordinate role. For Anabaptists, though, even a subordinate role could bring recognition when the woman was called upon to bear witness
to the faith in martyrdom. At least to those who sym-
pathized with the cause, steadfast women unwittingly
testified for their sex as well as their faith. Unfortunately, to those who considered the cause heretical, their perseverance could be construed as the folly
and delusion to which women were said to be dispropor-
tionately subject. Very gradually, however, and
through the subtle influences of changing social relations in the larger culture, ministers came to recognize that women—far from being the first to stray—
were the most faithful church members. By the early
eighteenth century in America, women far outnumbered
men in church membership, which Cotton Mather explained
as a result of the perils of childbirth: "They are
saved through childbearing, inasmuch as it singularly

obliges them to continue in faith, and charity, and
holiness, with sobriety."[27] Numerous funeral sermons
were preached and published in praise of the lives of
virtuous women.[28]

Most of these pious women did not self-consciously question their female role, nor would they have received the same praise had they done so; but in those
cases where women did seek to expand the permissible
boundaries of female activities, it is likely that they
had begun simply with genuine devotion to the religious
cause. When they observed the need for expanded or improved ministry, they sometimes stepped in to fill a
gap or set a situation right. Such a description would
apply to Anne Hutchinson and the female preachers who
held devotional meetings for other women. When their
teachings were recognized as worthwhile, men began to
attend, and debate ensued over the right of women to
teach. A parallel situation has been observed by Anne
Firor Scott among women of the American South during
the nineteenth century. First becoming involved in
charitable organizations out of religious fervor, they
developed leadership capabilities which led them eventually to question their subordination to male clergy.[29]

In both the early modern and the nineteenth-cen-
tury American setting, women of the churches were unlikely to be among the early champions of feminism.
Rather, such leadership came primarily from those who
were prepared to reject or reinterpret the traditional
view of the biblical position on women. Early women's
rights advocates such as Elizabeth Cady Stanton sharp-
ly criticized what they considered to be the biblical
degradation of women;[30] such efforts as *The Woman's*

Bible had to be disavowed by the movement as a whole
before churchwomen would affiliate themselves. Similarly, imaginative sixteenth-century claims to women's superiority such as those of Agrippa of Nettesheim and
Lucretia Marinella, were an affront to pious women who
regarded the biblical subordination of women as binding.[31]

The presence of the Grimké sisters among the early women's rights leaders, however, alerts us to the
one religious group in which the religious and feminist
causes were successfully harmonized. The Society of
Friends to which the Grimké sisters belonged was the
one religious organization emerging during the period
1525-1675 in which equality of the sexes was conscious-
ly advocated and consistently practiced. Why was it
that this group was able to endorse such equality,
whereas isolated voices to the same effect in other
churches died out? Arising toward the end of our time
period, they undoubtedly benefited from the efforts of
those who had paved the way. But most important was
their attitude toward biblical interpretation. As re-
presentatives of the Spiritualist approach to theology,
they could be led by the Spirit or the Light Within in
their understanding of the meaning of Scripture. But
further, according to their theology, Scripture itself
was a product of an age which had been outgrown. In
the Age of the Spirit, many of the limitations of the
previous age (the Age of the Law) had been overcome.
Finally, to the extent that each believer entered this
Age, the Inner Light became the vehicle of spiritual
truth. Such a doctrine could scarcely be conceived to
to apply to only one sex.

As the importance of the Inner Light in Quaker
doctrine enhanced the resources of Spiritualism for
raising the status of women, Spiritualist approaches
in general were far more helpful to this cause than
Anabaptist methods. As George Williams pointed out,
the Anabaptists "looked steadily into the *past*, finding
their own image and ecclesiastical blueprints in
the Bible and the martyr church of antiquity. The
Spiritualists gazed mostly into the *future*."[32] In fo-
cussing on the future, the reader of the Bible is allowed to pay less attention to St. Paul's instructions
on silence to women of his own time and more attention
to the promise that in Christ "there is neither male
nor female" (Galatians 3:28). The tension between a
literalism which seeks to restore the outward characteristics of the early church and, on the other hand,
hermeneutical principles which seek to rediscover the
spirit and promise of the gospel was in the early
modern period and remains today the key to resolving
the issue of women in the church.[33]

To use the Bible as a guideline for establishing
communities holier than the State, then, by no means
guarantees unity among those who might attempt this.
Evaluated as a step on the path toward greater extension of liberties, an appeal to a biblical standard
may prove either progressive or retrogressive. In a
time such as the Renaissance in which men were gaining
respect for women's intellects, an emphasis on biblical
passages forbidding women to teach could only be viewed
as retrogressive from a feminist perspective. If the
defense be offered that such was the majority view of
the time, this in any case prevents most of our radical

Protestants from laying any claim to a special place
in the history of the move toward female emancipation.
The main biblical verse which could aid in such a movement was that of Acts 2:18 which legitimated prophesying by women. But to emphasize this verse is to move
toward a spiritualistic stance in which the historical
revelation and the activities of the early church take
a second place behind the immediate workings of the
Holy Spirit. In such cases women might be led by the
Spirit to break through the inhibitions normally imposed on those of their sex. If change was to be proposed from a religious rather than secular or rational-
istic position, only the spiritualistic approach could
offer a new role for women.

WOMANHOOD IN

RADICAL PROTESTANTISM

1525-1675

CHAPTER ONE

WOMEN IN THE BIBLE
———————————————

Throughout the pages of this book, biblical passages are used to support various viewpoints regarding
the proper role of women. This chapter, then, is by
no means an attempt to compile a complete biblical theology of womanhood as expressed by radical Protestants.
It is rather a sampling of a few of the ways in which
theological interpretation of such key events as the
Fall, the Incarnation, and the Resurrection expressed
the interpreter's attitudes toward women.

To blame women for bringing sin into the world
was an idea at least as old as Christianity. Indeed,
as John Brinsley will not let us forget, St. Paul himself pointed out that it was not Adam but Eve who was
deceived. Early Christian thinkers concluded that,
since Eve brought about the Fall, her sex was cursed
and degraded far more than that of her husband. For
Tertullian, Christ's death would have been unnecessary,
it would seem, had woman never been created:

> God's judgment over this sex continues in
> this eon; its guilt must also continue.
> You are the gate of the devil, the traitor
> of the tree, the first deserter of divine
> Law; you are she who enticed the one whom
> the devil dare not approach; you broke so
> easily the image of God, man [*hominem*];
> on account of the death you deserved,

even the Son of God had to die.[1]

The Church Fathers do not present a uniform picture of the nature of woman before the Fall. On the
one hand, there is the necessity to affirm that woman
was a part of the creation which God declared good.
On the other hand, expressing ascetic tendencies typical of the Hellenistic age, they saw woman as an object
of lust and, therefore, a tangible reminder of the
lower carnal nature they were attempting to overcome.
The ideal of celibacy, even though espoused by women
as well as men, often combined a strong element of
misogyny with the basic requirement of chastity. Yet
if a woman rose above her feeble female nature to a
life of virginity, a theologian such as Jerome might
shower encomiums on her.[2]

The possibilities for theological ambivalence toward women were inherent in the creation story: "So
God created man in his own image, in the image of God
he created him; male and female he created them" (Gen.
1:27 RSV). This verse could lead, on the one hand, to
the conclusion that the first human was androgynous
or, on the other hand, to the belief that only the
male was imbued with divine likeness. Most thinkers
took a middle position, affirming a divine likeness in
woman in one sense but denying it in another. Never
is woman so unambiguously the image of God as is man,
but in combination with her husband (according to
Augustine) or through her intellectual nature (according to Thomas Aquinas), she may properly be called the
image of God.

Seen against this patristic and medieval back-
ground, radical reformers of the sixteenth and seven-

teenth centuries may not have been more, but they were
seldom less patriarchal than their predecessors. The
Anabaptist Hubmaier reverted to imagery already rejected by Augustine, who wrote of the custom of earlier
theologians to identify "man as the mind, but the woman
as the sense of the body."[3] Augustine himself, however, in order to distinguish woman from beasts, preferred to differentiate between rational and carnal
movements within the soul itself, comparing man to the
former, woman to the latter. This model was adopted
by such medieval writers as Peter Lombard and Bonaventure.[4] Hubmaier, on the other hand, preferred the
earlier model, equating woman with body and man with
soul. Conceiving of human nature as tripartite (flesh,
soul, spirit), he asserted that free will, used properly, can make the soul into spirit, but, used improper-
ly, "it becomes an Eve and carnal."[5] To his credit,
however, Hubmaier recognized in Christ the overcoming
of this scheme, leaving each individual responsible
for his or her own sin.

Another Anabaptist, Menno Simons, used a combination of scientific theory and biblical interpretation
to deny Eve's antitype Mary any genuine role in bringing the Redeemer into the world. Medieval Catholicism
had increasingly enhanced the role of Mary in making
possible the conquest of sin through Christ. By means
of the popular cult and scholastic defense of her Im-
maculate Conception, womankind received a theological
counterbalance to Eve. But Catholicism, the Protestant Reformers charged, had herein gone beyond biblical
warrant; Mary, though indeed a virgin who gave birth,
was not otherwise different from any other woman and

played no redemptive role. If this is true, how could
Jesus have been born without original sin? Most Protestants would reply that the miraculous power which
caused Christ to be born of Mary without an earthly
father also preserved him from the taint of heredi-
tary sin. For Menno Simons, and Melchior Hoffmann
before him, this explanation was insufficient. If Mary
had been the source of Christ's physical nature, he
would necessarily have inherited the sinfulness that
inheres in human flesh. But, says Menno, relying on an
oversimplified Aristotelianism[6] and his reading of certain Scripture passages, woman is merely a passive
field in the generative process; she contributes no
seed to the child. Just as a seed is nourished by the
soil in which it grows yet remains distinct in substance, so a child is nourished in its mother's womb,
but can only be said to be *in* her, not *of* her. Mary
was, for Menno, the true and natural mother of Jesus;
but in saying this he makes physical motherhood of
little consequence. There is in Menno no implication
that the woman's flesh is more sinful than that of man;
yet the belief in woman's naturally inferior position
is integral to his treatment of the Incarnation.

     An interesting contrast is provided by Caspar
Schwenckfeld, who shared Menno's belief that Christ
could not have had ordinary human nature. Yet instead
of minimizing Mary's role Schwenckfeld exalted her, in
this respect resembling Roman Catholic writers. In
order to be worthy to produce the "celestial flesh of
Christ," Mary's flesh was elevated and sanctified
above that of the rest of mankind. That this enhance-
ment of Mary's role in the Incarnation reflects a

generally positive attitude toward women on Schwenckfeld's part is evident from his letters to female followers, in one of which he stressed the faithfulness
of women at the time of the Resurrection.

It was left, however, to thinkers from other traditions such as Renaissance humanism and Dutch Calvinism to refute the scientific element of Menno's arguments by substituting Galenic embryology for that of
Aristotle. According to Galen, the woman contributed
seed as did the man, a theory which lent itself well
to feminist arguments. The occult philosopher Agrippa
of Nettesheim,[7] writing an exaggerated account of the
glories of women, oversimplified the Galenic position
just as much as Menno had oversimplified Aristotle,
with the result that now the male role was of little
significance:

> Do not we see that in the procreation of
> mankind, nature preferreth women before
> men? Which is chiefly perspicuous, be-
> cause the woman's seed alone, as Galen
> and Avicen say, that is the matter and
> nutriment of the child, not the man's,
> because it entreth into the woman as an
> accident into the substance.[8]

A more moderate position was taken in the following century by the Dutch physician Jan van Beverwyck
but with the same purpose of exalting womanhood. In
Concerning the Excellence of the Female Sex (1639),
Beverwyck spoke out against the Aristotelianism of theologians who denied woman a fertile seed. Appealing
to Galen, Beverwyck asserted the indispensability of
Mary's role in the Incarnation:

> The Lord Christ was called the Son of
> Man; but this he could not be except be-
> cause of his Mother. And if women were

> not persons,[9] then men would be born
> out of those who are not persons, which
> would be illogical. Besides that we
> have, as far as both our body and our
> mind are concerned, more characteristics
> of the mother than of the father.
> Athenaeus confirms such through our
> Galen...[10]

Beverwyck and Agrippa, however, do not properly
belong under the heading "radical Protestants," Agrippa
having been radical but not Protestant, Beverwyck Protestant but not radical. A more legitimate bearer of
this designation is the theosophist Jakob Böhme (1575-
1624), whose works influenced many later Pietists.
More than any other writer of the time, he seems to
have anticipated, if unintentionally, the present feminist demand for reconsideration of the sexual identity of God. For Böhme God is dialectical, containing a
negative, inward-looking principle and an affirmative
principle emanating outward to creation. While the
Father, Son, and Holy Spirit are aspects of the former,
a female spirit of Wisdom is the likeness of God which
mediates between God and man, making God visible to
man, man to God, and God to himself. Man can also enter into erotic union with Wisdom, which is his highest
essence. Adam, in fact, was created in such union and
was therefore, like God, androgynous. This original
unity of masculine and feminine elements was lost when
Adam's thought turned from God and Eve was taken out
of his rib. This, rather than the eating of the apple,
was the primary Fall. To be sure, to equate the creation of woman with the Fall might from one perspective
be considered a denigration of woman; but this is better understood as an expression of sexual asceticism.
The feminine element is integral to creation, but

physical sexual activity is a perversion of the original purity. An indication that Böhme's theology was
understood to be favorable to women is the fact that
women were leaders in spreading Böhme's influence in
the later seventeenth and early eighteenth centuries.
Jane Leade founded the Philadelphians, a Böhmenistic
theosophical society, in England, and Johanna Eleonora
Petersen, along with her husband, promoted this society
in Germany.

On the basis of the examples discussed, it may be
permissible to draw a preliminary conclusion regarding
the receptivity of various theologies to an ennobling
view of women. The line of division between Anabaptist
and Spiritualist appears to coincide with the division
between a traditional, subordinationist attitude toward
women and a more positive, even reverse-subordination-
ist view. In such categorization, Agrippa—mystic,
astrologer, occult thinker—would justifiably be included with Schwenckfeld and Böhme as part of a spiritualistic tradition open to the exaltation of the feminine. Anabaptists Hubmaier and Menno Simons, and Puritan John Brinsley, as upholders of the centrality of
Scripture, were more readily disposed to endorse the
subordinating tendencies expressed in many biblical
passages.

Such attempts at classification, nevertheless,
must remain flexible and merely suggestive. Only with
some distortion can biblical interpretations be labelled
"literalistic" or "spiritualistic." Indeed, it might
be argued that medieval allegory was more basic to
Hubmaier's thought than was biblical literalism.
Furthermore, external factors must be considered.

Puritanism, a broad-ranging movement, can be represented not only by John Brinsley but also by John Owen, who
found a much more positive biblical view of women. What
separates Brinsley from Owen is not a basic theological
stance but rather historical circumstances. The social
tensions and divisions of the 1640s had calmed considerably in succeeding decades. The women most visible
to Owen were no longer the Eves—the troublemaking theological deviants foremost in Brinsley's mind—but the
Sarahs, the good, pious women who were the mainstay of
the church. Thus, while the extent of rigidity or
flexibility in biblical interpretation may sometimes
determine the rigidity or flexibility of a theologian's
sex-role attitudes, the social circumstances of the
time are often just as important. As with almost any
other issue, the literal text of Scripture itself pre-
sents numerous possibilities.

A.   Balthasar Hubmaier, *On Free Will,* from George
     Huntston Williams, ed., *Spiritual and Anabaptist
     Writers* (Philadelphia: The Westminster Press,
     1957), pp. 118-120, 121, 130-131.

     [Balthasar Hubmaier (1485?-1528), early Anabaptist leader
     and head of a large congregation in Moravia, concurred
     with other Anabaptists on all major issues except that of
     the proper attitude toward civil authorities. Whereas
     others advocated nonresistance, Hubmaier encouraged armed
     intervention against the Austrian government. It was his
     political involvement which earned him death at the stake.

     His theology reflects to some extent his nominalist train-
     ing under John Eck, Luther's opponent at the Leipzig Dis-
     putation. The freedom of the will, which Hubmaier was
     defending in this treatise, was a concept characteristic
     of nominalists, as well as of Anabaptists. Similarly, his
     allegorical interpretation of Adam and Eve as representing
     flesh and soul has more in common with medieval than with
     Reformation exegesis.]

It is to be noted that man must be considered in
three states or forms: first, as he was before the Fall
of Adam; then as he became after the Fall; thirdly, as
he should be when restored....

Before Adam's transgression, all three substances
in man—flesh, soul, and spirit—were good. When God
looked at all of the things which he had made, they were
found good, especially man made in the image of God
(Gen. 1:26). The three substances in him were entirely
free to choose good or evil, life or death, heaven or
hell....

After our first father, Adam, through disobedience,
had transgressed the command of God, he lost this freedom for himself and all of his descendants. As when a
nobleman receives a fief from a king and then acts
against the king, the latter takes the fief away from
the nobleman and from all of his heirs, for they all
must bear the guilt of their forefather, so the flesh,
by the Fall of Adam, lost its goodness and freedom ir-
revocably, and became utterly nought and helpless, even
unto death. It can do nothing except sin, strive against
God, and hate his commands. From this comes the grievous
complaint that Paul makes to the Romans (ch. 7:5ff.)
against his wretched and accursed flesh. That is why it
must return, according to the curse of God to earth,
whence it came, or it cannot inherit the Kingdom of
Heaven. So also it is with the blood, for the two are
of one will (Gal. 5:13ff.; Gen., ch. 3; I Cor. 11:27),
as Paul writes (I Cor. 15:50): Flesh and blood cannot
inherit the Kingdom of God. And Christ says to Peter
(Matt. 16:17): Simon Bar-Jonah, flesh and blood have not

revealed it unto thee. When Eve, who is a figure of
our flesh, wished to eat, and did eat the forbidden
fruit, she thereupon *lost* the knowledge of good and
evil, yea, she lost the power of even wishing and doing
good and had to pay for this loss by death; as soon as
man is conceived and born, he is conceived and born in
sin (Ps. 51:5). He is in sin from the first moment of
his life, right up to his ears in sin, and when he had
completed his earthly course, he must die and become
dust....

The reason that the fall of the soul is partly re-
parable, however, and not fatal, even here on earth,
but the fall of the flesh is to a certain extent irre-
parable and deadly, is that Adam, as a type of the soul
(as is Eve, of the flesh), would have preferred not to
eat of the forbidden tree. He was also not deceived by
the serpent, but Eve was (I Tim. 2:14). Adam knew very
well that the words of the serpent were contrary to the
words of God. Yet he willed to eat the fruit against his
own conscience, so as not to vex or anger his rib, his
flesh, Eve. He would have preferred not to do it. But
when he was more obedient to his Eve than to God, he
lost the knowledge of good and evil, so that he could
not wish nor choose anything good (Ps. 14:1; 33:13; 53:
1). Neither could he reject or flee from anything evil,
for he no longer knows what is good or bad in the sight
of God. Everything has lost its savor for him, except
what is savory and pleasing to his Eve, that is, his
flesh. He has lost the real sense of taste....

From the foregoing things it is plainly and surely
to be seen that man received two wounds in the Fall of

Adam: an inner one, that is, ignorance of good and evil,
because Adam was more obedient to the voice of his Eve
than to the voice of God; the other wound outward, in
deed and action in such a way that man cannot perfectly
execute or obey the commandments of God, because of the
innate depravity of his flesh, but rather in all his
doings is an unprofitable servant (Luke 17:10). And
this fault or lack originates from the fact that Adam
did not rightly master his rib, Eve, according to the
command of God, but, contrary thereto, ate of the tree
forbidden to him under penalty of death.

The first wound is healed by the wine poured on it
by the Samaritan Christ (Luke, ch. 10), that is, by the
law, through which man is taught anew, by new grace,
what is really good or bad in the sight of God. The
second wound is healed by the oil, that is, the gospel
which thus deprives these sins or faults of their ven-
omous destructive power, unless we presumptuously pursue
them. Therefore Christ, the true Physician, mingled in
the New Covenant both wine and oil, that is, law and
gospel, and made of them a wholesome plaster for our
souls, which he wanted to make righteous and well again.

Here one can take hold with both hands of how
Christ made the Fall of Adam for us no longer damaging
or damning. He, through the woman's seed, crushed the
head of the old serpent, took out the fang, and made
its poison harmless to her (Rom. 16:20; I Cor. 15:30f.).
So now no one can any longer complain about Adam and
Eve, nor try to excuse or palliate his sin by Adam's
Fall, since everything has been adequately restored,
healed, made whole, which has been lost and wounded and
had died in Adam. For Christ, through his Spirit, has
won for our spirit from God his Heavenly Father that its

prison should no longer be harmful to our spirit; and
through his soul he recovered for our soul the capacity
to be taught and illuminated again by his divine Word,
as to what is good or evil. Yea, through his flesh, he
earned for our flesh that after it has moldered to ashes,
it will be resurrected in honor and immortal (I Cor. 15:
35ff.). Henceforth, each soul that sins must bear its
own sin. It is guilty—not Adam, nor Eve, nor the flesh,
nor sin, nor death, nor the devil. For all these, by
the power of God, have been captured, bound, overcome.

B.   Menno Simons, *Reply to Gellius Faber* (1554), from
*The Complete Writings of Menno Simons (c. 1496-
1561)*, trans. Leonard Verduin, ed. John Christian
Wenger (Scottdale, Pennsylvania: Herald Press,
1956), pp. 767-771.

[Menno Simons (c. 1496-1561) became the leader of Anabaptists in East Friesland through his activities as an
underground evangelist between 1536 and 1544. Prior to
this time he had remained within the Catholic Church, in
spite of doubts about transubstantiation and infant baptism. He dissociated himself from the violent excesses
of the followers of Melchior Hoffmann in Münster and is
therefore given much credit for channeling the Anabaptists
into a more constructive movement.

Hoffman, nevertheless, provided Menno with one of the
central theological ideas which differentiated him from
all mainstream reformers and many other radicals. Concerned that salvation could not be complete if Christ had
not been truly perfect, Menno followed Hoffmann in concluding that Christ had not inherited Mary's sinful
flesh.[1] The issue was debated with the Reformed thinkers John à Lasco and Gellius Faber in 1544. In 1552
Faber published a booklet against several points of Anabaptist theology, provoking the reply from Menno presented
here in part.[2]]

*Now they urge against this that God in the begin-
ning created man and woman and blessed them saying, Be*

fruitful and multiply. By this they say, a woman is become as much a contributor to the birth, and supplies as much from her body to the fetus, as the man does. And they conclude that Christ was promised out of the woman, and is called woman's seed, fruit, and son, in the Scriptures. Abraham's seed, a seed and fruit of the loins of David. Therefore He must, as to His humanity, be of Abraham's, David's and the woman's seed. They refer us to the philosophers, to sensible women, and to creatures. I am heartily ashamed of the fact, the Lord knows, that I have to use such human argumentation (they force me to it) in this glorious and holy transaction of God.

Reply. Seeing they try to sustain the matter with the reference to Gen. 1, appealing to God's and nature's ordinances, therefore they should speak of both husband and wife as they now become one flesh, for the ordinance referred to requires carnal contact for human procreation. This the Jews also assumed when they said of Christ, Is this not Joseph's son, the carpenter, and is not his mother's name Mary?

If now they counter that the Holy Spirit performed the function of a father, then I reply, that Christ's birth did not follow the formula of Genesis 1, and that in that representation the Holy Spirit was the father of Christ.

But if they say that not the Holy Spirit, but the Father Himself functioned in Mary, through the Holy Spirit, then I reply, that they thereby acknowledge once more, as above, that the birth of Christ was not in accordance with God's ordinance in Genesis 1. Also they grant then that the man Christ, who purchased us with His precious blood, is not God's first-born and only be-

gotten Son, but a created creature of Mary's flesh. And
how this agrees with the confession of the holy apostles
and prophets, I will let their own writings make out.

I say, moreover, that we do not go to the philosophers, nor to the sensible women, who are not agreed,
nor to the evidence from the creatures (to which they
point us) but to God's grace. We will go to the Lord's
own Word, the true fountain of all wisdom, and to the
dependable witnesses of the Holy Spirit. And in it we
seek diligently how much a natural mother, according to
the ordinance of God and Genesis 1, contributes and supplies from her flesh through conception.

That both man and woman are by the saying, Be fruitful and multiply, made competent by God unto procreation
is too plain to deny. But each in his own ordained
place: the man a sower and the woman as a receptive
field, prepared by God unto procreation, without which
it is impossible for fruit to be born.

That this is God's ordinance, the Scriptures teach
everywhere. Paul says, Even as the woman is of the man,
so also is man by the woman. Notice first that he says
that the woman is of the man; and then that he is not *of*
the woman but *by* [Dutch, *through*] the woman. I Cor.
11:12. At another place he says that Rebecca conceived
of Isaac. Ponder what this means. So also Sarah, says
he, received power by faith to receive seed (from her
husband, that is), to carry it, and that therefore
from one (Abraham is meant), and he as good as dead, so
many were born.[3] The Lord visited Sarah, Moses writes,
as He had promised and she conceived and bare a son to
Abraham. Notice carefully, it was Abraham's seed she
received, and to Abraham she bore a son; so also Bilhah

conceived and bare Jacob a son. A nation and a company
of nations (God said this to Jacob) will come of you
(note, He says of you) and kings shall come from thy
loins (notice again, He says thy loins).[4] Gen. 35:11.
Levi, says Paul, was still in the loins of his father
Abraham (he does not say in the matrix of the mother)
when Melchisedec came to meet him. Heb. 7:10. I also
am a mortal man (writes the author of Wisdom) like unto
the rest, born of the generation of the first created
man, formed in flesh ten months long, congealed in
blood of *man's* seed (notice this). Wisd. 7:3. Job
says, Hast thou not poured me out as milk and curdled
me like cheese? Job 10:10.

I do certainly think that we can gather from these
passages that the father is the real origin of his
child and the mother the prepared field, as has been related. Even as a field does not receive its own, but
the sower's seed, to sprout, feed, and increase it and
bring it to fruition so that it is called, although
sown upon it, that field's seed (as indeed it is), so
also the woman conceives seed, not of her own body but
of that of her husband, to nurture it from her own
flesh after God's ordinance, to carry it, and at the
proper time bring forth the fruit. The fruit is then
called the mother's seed, fruit, and son, no less than
the father's from whom she at the first received it,
exactly as the before-mentioned sown seed is called the
seed and fruit of the field for the reason given.

My reader, in this sense, I believe and confess
that Christ Jesus also, God's only begotten and first-
born Son and eternal Word, is Mary's or the woman's
seed, offspring, generation, fruit, and son, marvelously

sown in her virgin body by the Holy Spirit, just as
Isaac was a seed, offspring, generation, fruit, and son
of Sarah, John of Elisabeth, and Joseph of Rachel.

And I say that if the learned ones' proposal in
this matter were correct (a thing which I do not at all
grant, nor for the afore-mentioned reasons can grant),
then the mother would have ten times as much right concerning the child; for the mother's function, not the
father's, is fraught with great distress nine or ten
months long, she must nourish it of her own body, and
give it birth not without danger and peril, and nurse
it moreover a year or two with milk from her own body.
And yet disregarding all this the jurisdiction over the
child is in all the Scriptures assigned, not to the
mother, but to the father, as may be seen in the cited
passage in all clarity.

My reader, take note. If the position of the
learned ones were correct, then half the flesh necessarily of the children of Shelah, the son of Judah, was
Canaanite because of the Canaanite woman; of the children of Moses, Midianite because of the Cushite woman;
of the children of Joseph, Egyptian because of the
Egyptian woman. This is beyond dispute.

Nor could the man Christ Jesus then have been more
than half a man, that is, insofar as the woman's part
and portion according to the learned ones' representation goes; which half a man, this is too clear to deny,
then came not merely from Judah to whom the promise
pointed, but also in part from Levi and in part from
the Canaanites through Rahab, and in part from the
Moabites through Ruth.

Now notice, my reader, how very sadly the learned

ones pervert God's ordinance touching the seed, fruit,
and son of the woman, and how they vilify the Christ,
God's only begotten and first-born Son, asserting that
His most holy flesh was of Mary's flesh for the reason
that He is called in Scripture seed, son, and fruit of
the woman. They do not perceive how emphatically both
nature and Scripture teach us that the first origin and
seed of the human fruit is originally of the father and
not of the mother; a thing that is evident also from the
fact that the carnal function of the seed remains intact
until senescence, but the maternal function of the field
does not extend beyond fifty years or less, as may be
seen.

But as to the fruit of David's loins, I say first
of all that that promise was made literally not of Christ
but of Solomon. Nathan, David, and Solomon are my witnesses. Thus spoke the Lord by Nathan to David, as he
was planning to build the Lord's house, saying, When
thy days are fulfilled and thou shalt sleep with thy
fathers, I will set up thy seed after thee, which shall
proceed out of thy loins, and I will establish the throne
of his kingdom forever. I will be his father and he
shall be my son. If he commit iniquity (a thing that
can never be said of Christ), I will chasten him with
the rod of men and with the stripes of the children of
men. II Sam. 7:12-14. This is literally the way this
passage goes. And that David understood these words of
the prophet as applying literally to Solomon his own
words show plainly. My son, said he to Solomon, it was
in my mind to build a house unto the name of the Lord
my God, but the word of the Lord came to me saying, Thou
shalt not build a house unto my name, because thou hast

shed much blood upon the earth in my sight. Behold a
son shall be born unto thee, who shall be a man of rest
and I shall give him rest from all his enemies round
about, for his name shall be Solomon, and I will give
peace and quietness unto Israel in his days. He shall
build a house for my name and he shall be my son and I
will be his father, and I will establish the throne of
his kingdom over Israel forever. I Chron. 22:7-10.

So also Solomon understood the promise, as his
message to Hiram shows when he sent him word saying,
Thou knowest how that David my father could not build
a house unto the name of the Lord his God for the wars
which were about him on every side until the Lord put
them under the soles of his feet. But now the Lord my
God hath given me rest on every side so that there is
neither adversary nor evil occurrent. And, behold, I
propose to build a house unto the name of the Lord my
God, as the Lord spake unto David my father saying,
Thy son, whom I will set upon thy throne in thy room,
he shall build a house unto my name. I Kings 5:3-5.

Moreover, in the Psalms it is written, For thy
servant David's sake turn not away the face of thine
anointed. The Lord hath sworn in truth unto David; he
will not turn from it: Of the fruit of thy body will I
set upon thy throne. If thy children will keep my
covenant and my testimony that I shall teach them,
their children shall also sit upon thy throne for ever-
more. Psalm 132:10-12. Read also Psalm 89.

And so, my reader, these clear, plain passages
show plainly that the afore-mentioned promise made to
David in the old literal system was not made in reference to Christ, but to Solomon.

I say in the second place, that the prophet Isaiah prophesied of Christ saying, Unto us a child is born, unto us a son is given, and the government shall be upon his shoulders, and his name shall be called Wonderful, Counselor, The mighty God, The everlasting Father, The Prince of Peace. Of the increase of his government and peace there shall be no end upon the throne of David and upon his kingdom to order it and to establish it with judgment and with justice henceforth and even forever. Isa. 9:6,7.

And the angel said to Mary, And the Lord shall give unto him the throne of his father David, and he shall reign over the house of Jacob forever, and of his kingdom there shall be no end. Luke 1:32,33.

Faithful reader, take note. Since these two faithful witnesses, Isaiah and Gabriel, assign David's kingdom and throne so clearly to this promised king and Messiah Christ, saying that He shall sit in it and rule over it forever, and since it is evident that in this world He had no kingdom, yes, was poorer in the fleshly things than are the foxes and the birds, and since we know that God's promise made by the mouth of the prophet and the angel is true, therefore we have to understand this of another rule, kingdom, and throne than that of David; unless we say that the aforementioned witnesses erred in regard to their promise and did not speak the truth. If then the promised rule, kingdom, and throne are not David's literal or earthly rule, kingdom, and throne, but if they are spiritual, then verily also the king that is to sit on it and rule it is not David's literal or physical fruit, but a new and spiritual fruit even as the afore-said rule,

kingdom, and throne are new and spiritual. Otherwise
one half of the throne must be taken literally and the
other half spiritually. This is too evident to be denied.

In the third place, I say that the reader must
notice that Christ is, in the Scriptures, called the
fruit of the loins of David and the seed, fruit, and
son of the woman in no other sense than as to the promise and tribe to which He was born as to the flesh, or
with the flesh; and, that He is entitled to a real
mother according to God's ordinances of Genesis 1. For
if He were as to His humanity of Mary's flesh, as the
learned ones say, then He would not be the true Son of
God nor a genuine son of Mary, for then he would have
been made or born as to His whole human substance from
Mary's flesh and not come forth originally and born
from God His Father—which would not only be against
the essential qualities of the terms, father, mother,
and son, but also against God's ordinance, against nature, and against all the Scriptures, as was said.

In this way the promise of the fruit of the loins
of David is fulfilled in the old order in Solomon and
in the new spiritual order in Christ, a common thing in
Scriptures, as can be seen literally in the case of
Isaac (Gen. 21:22), David (Psalm 27), and Samson (Judg.
13:5), in a literal sense; but plainly referred to
Christ by the apostles and Gospel writers in the new
dispensation.

C. Caspar Schwenckfeld, "On the Enmity between the
    Woman and the Serpent," *Corpus Schwenckfeldianorum,*
    XII, 612-614, 616f.

[Caspar Schwenckfeld (1489-1561) represents the second
major category of radical reformers, the Spiritualists.
Attracted by Luther's writings in 1518, Schwenckfeld began to spread the Reformation in his homeland of Silesia
as a lay preacher and devotional writer. In the course
of time, however, he came to a more inwardly based spirit-
uality than that of either Luther or the Anabaptists, denying the importance of external forms and ceremonies,
though not necessarily rejecting them altogether.

In his doctrine of Christ he also stood alone. Sharing
Menno's concern that Christ be thought of as uncontami-
nated by creaturely flesh, he did not pursue Menno's logic
to the point of denying Mary a role in the Incarnation.
Instead, Christ's spiritualized "celestial flesh" was made
possible, Schwenckfeld argued, through the sanctification
of Mary's own flesh. Similarly, each believer is progres-
sively divinized by feeding spiritually on Christ's
celestial flesh.]

Elizabeth testified after she was filled with the
Holy Spirit. She called out loudly and said, "Blessed
are you, Mary, among women and blessed is the fruit of
your womb." And "how does it happen to me that the
mother of my Lord comes to me?"

Note that Elizabeth calls the Lord Jesus "a blessed fruit of the body of Mary, who is blessed among
women." And beyond that she calls Mary a mother of
the Lord. But who told her this? Luke answers and
says the Holy Spirit has revealed this to her, who is
also filled with the Spirit; Him we should certainly
believe.

Luke testifies in chapter 2[:7] when he says
that Mary brought forth her first-born son in Bethlehem and wrapped Him in swaddling clothes and laid Him
in the manger because there was no room in the inn.
And in Acts 1[:12-14] it says, "When they were all
together with one accord in the upper room (after
the Lord had ascended into heaven) they prayed and

made supplication together with the women and Mary the
mother of Jesus, etc."

Mary the mother of the Lord testifies of her son
whom she had conceived by the Holy Spirit; she had carried and given birth to Him and thus she herself called
the Lord Jesus her son when she said, "My son, why have
you done this to us?" Consider the lovely song, the
Magnificat, how delightfully she sings of God's works—
how He had regarded her with grace and done great things
to her and how she also remembered Abraham and the
fathers and also their noble seed which she now bore
under her heart.

John the Evangelist testifies in John 2[:3-5].
When wine was lacking at the wedding he shows how the
mother of the Lord spoke to Jesus, and soon thereafter
it says His mother spoke to the servants, etc. As
Jesus was dying on the cross, He commended this same
John to His mother, and he took her to himself and
cared for her faithfully as his dear mother. John 19
[:25-27].

Paul testifies to the Galatians in the third chapter where he interprets the promise made to Abraham and
says that the seed of Abraham is Christ, who was conceived by the Holy Spirit in His mother's body. She
carried Him, nourished Him and gave birth to Him as her
genuine first-born son, as Matthew testifies. [Matth.
1:21].

The unbelieving Jews testify in John 7[:41] where
they interpret the prophecy of Micah and say Christ is
to come out of Galilee. Does not Scripture say Christ
is to come from the seed of David and from the town of
Bethlehem, where David was? This is also the testimony

of the high priests and scribes among the people.
Matth. 2[:5-6].

Only restless Hoffmann and his erroneous followers, who still persist, deny such clear truth and err
therefore because they know neither Scripture nor the
power of God.

It is true, however, that a cursed nature cannot
produce a blessed one. But the blessed fruit of the
blessed Virgin's body, our Lord Jesus Christ, testifies
that her nature had previously been reformed, restored,
and sanctified through Him who ordered lodging in her
and took His manhood from her body. The angel Gabriel
told her openly, and thereafter Elizabeth, full of the
Holy Spirit, that she was blessed among women, which
previously was never written or heard concerning any
woman. All women conceive in the passion of lust. At
the will of a man they bear a sinful seed and by nature
an accursed fruit and children of wrath. Only this woman Mary, the highly praised virgin, was chosen above
all the rest. God's word was made flesh and man in
taking on the seed of Abraham, namely in the blessed
body of Mary. And she received from the Holy Spirit
God's son, God and man, her whole son, as the Evangelist
Luke describes it all at length with many words.

If then some of you don't believe this, one must
commend it to God the Lord. Should it not then be
true? God, who is trustworthy, has promised it; he has
also accomplished it. If it is not true among them, it
is nevertheless true among us who believe and enjoy the
promise. And certainly it is all described plainly and
clearly enough if we just didn't have untrained senses
and could address spiritual matters in a spiritual way.

Yes, if we weren't satisfied to take our own manner and
error for truth but rather with prayer to come before
the Lord and go into His school. How indeed could the
son of God, Jesus Christ our Lord, dwell physically in
the body of the Virgin and take her flesh and blood
for nourishment, if she were still a cursed daughter of
Eve, an unsanctified sinner? Concerning this Luke
writes profusely, "Through the enmity openly shown by
this woman, who was to bring forth the seed, it is
clear that God has no fellowship with sinners, and the
spirit of God does not dwell in a body subjected to
sin, nor will He dwell there."

But one should ask those who do not want to believe such clear testimony of Holy Scripture from
whence the Son of God took His flesh and blood, if it
is not the flesh and blood of the blessed Virgin Mary
the mother of the Lord. If it is not the fruit of the
body, what kind of flesh can it be? He surely didn't
bring it with Him from heaven, as the Valentinians
hold. For God is a spirit, does not have flesh and
blood, and beyond the six days' work of creation he
did not create anything new. They say that all things
are possible to God and that he created the flesh of
Christ anew. To this should be answered that God's
omnipotence is not contrary to His creation and order,
much less contrary to His promise, which God confirmed
to the fathers with an oath. Thus it is certain that
God the Lord rested on the seventh day after He had
created all His works and created nothing new thereafter. The flesh of Christ is found, as far as His
human nature (though not His origin) is concerned, in
the work of creation. For the woman, the blessed Vir-

gin Mary, is indeed the Mother of the Lord, from whom
He took His humanity, created in Adam.

* * *

God's eternal and only-begotten Son had to become
man from the substance and nature of the Virgin Mary,
from her flesh and blood, in order that God be true and
the promise made to the fathers for our salvation be
fulfilled. How could He otherwise be of the seed of
woman? Genesis 3[:15]. Of Abraham's seed? Genesis
22[:18]. How could He be David's seed? 2 Sam. 7[:12].
And a fruit of his body? Psalm 132[:11]. And a true
son of Mary and a blessed fruit of her body? Luke 1
[:35]. But He is also according to both natures the
only true, natural son of God, which He is by the conception of the Holy Spirit in the body of Mary. The
origin of this child is not from a physical father, for
Mary remained a virgin and remains so in eternity. Instead He was from God His heavenly Father, who through
His spirit made use of His heavenly mastership in this
work. The spirit of the Father is an originator,
founder, preparer and also overseer of this new holy
and natural flesh which the word of God assumed. Mary
also received in one person the second nature of God
and her son, since the flesh of Christ was spiritually
and divinely prepared and born in Mary and of Mary's
flesh and conceived by Mary through the working of the
Holy Spirit under the shelter of the power of the Most
High. Thus one should make a great distinction between
His flesh and that of Mary His true mother. For Mary's
flesh was born from her ancestors according to natural

processes. But not so with Christ, for in Mary the
process stopped. God the Father undertook a new way
with Mary and produced something new on earth, as Jeremiah says (ch. 31[:22]). That is, that a woman should
conceive a man without a man, that Mary the Virgin
should become impregnated through the Holy Spirit, carry and give birth to God's and her son. Christ is a
promised son of a woman, of Abraham, David and Mary;
even though he comes from them according to the flesh
it occurs in a marvelous manner. Not only is Christ a
wondrous son, but His mother is also a wondrous virginal mother. He is truly seed to a woman (Gen. 3[:15])....
He came not in corporeal manner but in supernatural,
spiritual and divine manner from Mary and the fathers,
not created but born in the body of Mary through the
spirit of the fathers. The substance of Mary, flesh
and blood, came into the hands of the Holy Spirit, who
undertook a new work previously unheard of. And through
His heavenly mastership He raised up in Mary a new, holy
flesh as a sanctuary and temple of the word of God.
This divine birthgiving of the holy, new, promised,
supernatural flesh of Christ the son of God is incom-
prehensible and inscrutable to reason; only true faith
can grasp it when it looks to the promise and fulfill-
ment wherein one recognizes the gracious will of God
toward himself. There is, as I have said, a great difference between Christ's flesh and that of Mary, although according to their substance they are both
flesh. For the flesh of Mary is a sanctified flesh according to the natural processes from the ancestors;
but Christ's flesh is not according to the natural processes from the ancestors, but a promised new flesh,

holy in nature. Therefore it could also see no decom-
position. It could not remain in death. Rather it is
a flesh of the word of the Father, a sufficient sacrifice for our sins.

The natural holiness of this new flesh above all
other flesh proves the origin of Christ from God.

D.   Letter of Caspar Schwenckfeld to Sibilla Eisler,
      April 6, 1561, *Corpus Schwenckfeldianorum*, XVII,
      615-6.

[Among the followers of Caspar Schwenckfeld were, it
would seem, an inordinate number of women. Several of
the women carried on quite extensive correspondence
with Schwenckfeld and, by their work in preserving and
copying his letters, made possible the vast collection
of his writings now available to us in the *Corpus
Schwenckfeldianorum*. Unfortunately, the letters of
the women were not accorded such painstaking care, so
that writings from their own hands are rare. Much,
however, concerning their outstanding character and
talents can be discerned from the respect and erudi-
tion with which Schwenckfeld addresses them. His appreciation for the efforts of these women was no doubt
the impetus behind this, his last letter to Sibilla
Eisler of Augsburg, who, with Catharine Ebertz of Isny,
was one of the most active and devoted of his followers.]

Dear sister in Christ: There is not time today to
write much, except to meditate upon the joyful resurrection of our dear Lord Christ and how he consoled
and cheered his disconsolate disciples and the beloved
women. The latter remained more faithful to the Lord
Christ than the men, leaving him neither at the Cross
nor at his burial. And soon after the Sabbath they
again sought his body and wanted to anoint it. Thereby they themselves were anointed with the heavenly
ointment of the Holy Spirit. Oh how heart-warming to

reflect on Mary Magdalene who loved the Lord so fervently and to whom he also appeared first, in the form of a gardener. She asked him to show her where he had laid the body of Christ and she would go after it. Oh, the wretched fetching and dragging of a dead body; indeed she could hardly have carried it.

But the love of Christ often promises more than is in one's power, and faith makes all things possible. When the Lord called her by her name, which had been written by God in the book of the living, and said, "Mary," her heart leaped for joy in her body. She was filled with joy greater than any tongue can tell, so that she wanted also to embrace the Lord; but he did not want to let Magdalene touch him again physically. But when he should ascend to the Father and become like Him in glory and splendour, then Mary with all the elect would touch him spiritually. For then he would also live in their hearts. From this we have a strong argument against the corporeal eating of the body of Christ and against the false teaching that the godless also eat and touch him. The Lord did not even permit this to the blessed Mary. Now no more. Commend yourself to the grace of Christ. Greet all dear friends.

E.   Jacob Böhme, *Drey Principien Göttliches Wesens*
      [*Three Principles of Divine Being*] (1619),
      translated from *Sämtliche Schriften* (Stuttgart,
      1960, facsimile reprint of 1730 edition), II,
      103-153 passim.

      [In the seventeenth century, Jacob Böhme (1575-1624) advanced a spiritualistic theology comparable to that of Schwenckfeld in its deviation from the theologies of all organized religious groups. A shoemaker and the son of poor peasants, Böhme experienced mystical revelations

which he eventually began to write down, beginning in
1612 with his *Aurora oder Morgenröthe im Aufgang*. De-
nounced as heretical by his Lutheran pastor, Böhme was
forced to cease writing for a time. When he published
his next work, persecution again ensued. Yet at his
death he was given a Christian burial. He retained his
belief in the traditional doctrines of Christianity, but
his explanations of such doctrines as the Trinity and
creation were hardly orthodox. The theosophic termi-
nology carried over from such sixteenth-century nonconformists as Paracelsus and Valentin Weigel also
worked against him. Slight though his effect on
Lutheranism may have been, his writings nevertheless
exerted great influence not only on the Philadelphians
and Quakers of his own century but on such later
philosophers as Hegel and Schelling as well.]

X. 7. No one should presume that the human being
before his fall had bestial, rather than heavenly, members for propagation. Nor did he have bowels, for such
a stink and movement[5] as the human has in his body is
not fitting for the Holy Trinity or for Paradise, but
rather for the earth, which must return into its ether.
The human being was created immortal and also holy,
like the angels. And although he was indeed made from
limbus,[6] he was nevertheless pure.

X. 18. So Adam and all men would have walked the
earth completely naked, as he did then. His clothing
was the clarity in the power of God; no heat or cold
would have affected him. His vision day and night was
through opened eyes lacking eyelashes. In him there
was no sleep, and in his disposition no night: for in
his eyes was the divine power, and he was complete and
perfect; he had the limbus and also the matrix[7] in himself. He was no man and also no woman, just as we will
be in the Resurrection. The knowledge of marks will

remain in the figure, but the limbus and the matrix
will not be separate as now.

XI.11. Since Adam was created an image and complete likeness of God and had all three principles[8] in
him like God himself, so his mind and imagination
should have seen only into God's heart, and his desire
and will should have been set therein. And just as he
was a Lord over all, and his mind a threefold spirit
with the three principles in one essence, so also his
spirit and the will in the spirit should have stood
free in the one paradisical, heavenly essence. And
his mind and soul were to eat from God's heart and his
body from the power of the heavenly limbus.

XI.12. But because the heavenly limbus was revealed through the earthly and was in the fruit in one
essence, and Adam likewise, so it was fitting for Adam
(as the one who had received the living soul out of
the first principle, breathed in by the Holy Ghost, il-
lumined by the light of God, and standing in the second
principle) not to grasp after the earthly matrix.

XI.24. Because Adam was drawn out of the fierce
essences, he had to be tested to see whether his essences, from which his imagination and desire proceeded, could endure in heavenly quality, and whether he
would eat of the Word of God. Which essences would
conquer in Adam—the paradisical or the fierce?

XII.10. For Adam was tempted forty days in Paradise, in the garden of Eden before the tree of temptation, to see whether he could direct his inclination
to God's heart and eat only of the word of God. God

wanted to give him (his body) to eat of the heavenly
limbus that he might eat in the mouth and not in the
body. He was to give birth out of himself to the child
of the virgin, for he was no man and also no woman; he
had the matrix and also the man in himself and was to
give birth out of the matrix to the virgin, full of
modesty and chastity, without rending his body.

XII.40. Now the human had also the spirit of the
world, for he was of the world and lived in the world.
Thus Adam was now the chaste virgin (understand the
spirit which was breathed into him from God); and the
spirit which was inherited from the world out of nature
was the young man. These were now both together and
rested in one arm.

XII.41. Now the chaste virgin was to cling to
God's heart, to have no other imagination and not to
let herself lust after the beauty of the shapely young
man. But now the young man burned toward the virgin
and he desired to contaminate her. For he said: "You
are my dearest bride, my paradise and crown of roses.
Just let me into your paradise; I want to conceive in
you that I may receive of your essence and enjoy your
gracious love. How gladly I would taste the friendly
sweetness of your power! If I might just receive your
beautiful light, how full of joy I would be!"

XII.44. Then the chaste spirit out of God spoke
in Adam as the virgin: "My dear love and companion, I
see plainly your desire. You would like to mingle with
me. But I am a virgin and you are a man. You would
stain my pearl and shatter my crown. Moreover, you

would mix your sourness with my sweetness and darken my
bright light.   Therefore I will not.   My pearl I will
lend you and with my clothing adorn you; but I will not
let you possess them."

XII.61.   This, therefore, in brief is the reason
we speak of Adam's fall into the highest depths.   Adam
lost the virgin through his desire, and in his desire
he received the wife, who is a cagastric[9] person.   And
the virgin waits for him still to see if he will enter
into the new birth where she would accept him again
with great honors.

XIII.1.   I can scarcely write for vexation; but
because it cannot be otherwise we will for a while wear
the clothes of the woman but live in the virgin.   And
even though we receive much affliction in the woman,
the virgin will still cheer us.   We must drag ourselves
with the woman until we send her to the grave, when she
shall be a shadow and figure.   And the virgin shall be
our bride and precious crown, who will give us her
pearls and beautiful crown and clothe us with her
jewels....

XIII.2.   Now when Adam went into the garden of
Eden and the three principles carried on such a struggle in Adam, his tincture[10] became very tired and the
virgin departed.   For this world's spirit of desire had
overcome in Adam, and therefore he sank down into sleep.
In this hour his heavenly body became flesh and blood,
and his strong power became bones.   Then the virgin
went into her ether and shadow, but into the heavenly
ether, into the principle of power.   There she waits on

all children of Adam to see if anyone will again accept
her as bride through the new birth.

XIII.3. But what was God to do? He had created
Adam out of his eternal will. But because it could not
be that Adam would give birth to the virgin in paradisical manner, God placed the Fiat[11] of the great
world in the middle. For Adam had now reverted again
to the Fiat as a half-broken person because he was half
killed by his desire and imagination. If he was to
live, God would have to come to his aid; if he was to
bring forth a kingdom, there would have to be a woman
to propagate like all other animals. The angelical
kingdom in Adam was gone. Now it would have to be a
kingdom of this world.

XIII.6. But the text says, "God looked at everything he had made, and behold, it was all very good."
Now if creation was good at that point, it must later
have become evil that God would say, "It is not good
that man should be alone" (Gen. 2:18). If God had
wanted them to have bestial propagation like all animals, he would surely have made man and woman right
away. But that God was disgusted at this is seen from
the first child of the woman—Cain the fratricide—as
also from the curse of the earth....

XIII.18. Reason says, "If Eve was merely created
from Adam's rib alone, is she not much less than Adam?"
My dear reason, it is not so. The fiat, as a sharp at-
traction, took from all essences and properties, from
each power of Adam. But it did not take from him more

members in substance, for the image was to be in the
limbus of a human of male sort, yet not with this de-
formity. Understand the basis of this correctly: he
was to be and indeed was a man, and had a virginal
heart, wholly chaste in the matrix.

XIII.19. Eve was certainly created out of all
Adam's essences, and thus Adam had a great rift; so
likewise the wife might come in complete perfection to
the image of God. This proves to me again the great
mystery which the virgin attests to again very dearly:
that the Son of the virgin let his side be pierced in
the regeneration and poured his blood out of his sunken
side; that he also let his hands and feet be bored
through and on his head a crown of thorns pressed, from
which his blood flowed. He let his body be whipped, so
that his blood flowed everywhere. Thus the Son of the
virgin lowered himself to help the sick, broken Adam
and his weak, imperfect Eve, to instruct them and bring
them again to the first glory.

XIII.20. Therefore you should know that Eve was
created out of all Adam's essences, but no more ribs
or members from Adam were broken. This is shown by
the wife's timidity and weakness, and also the command
of God, where he said, "Your will shall be subjected
to your husband, and he shall be your lord." Therefore,
because the man is whole and complete except for a rib,
the wife is his helper; she stands by him and shall
help him carry on his business in humility and subordination. And the man should recognize that she is very
weak, made from his essences, and should come to aid
her in her weakness and to love her as his own essence.

Likewise the wife should place her essences and will in
those of the man and be friendly toward her husband so
that the man desires his essences in the wife and the
two are of one will. For they are one flesh, one bone,
one heart; and in one will they bear children which
are not of the man nor of the woman alone but of both
together, as if they were from one body....

F.   John Brinsley, *A Looking-glasse for Good Women*
       (London, 1645), pp. 1-4.

> [England in the 1640s witnessed the proliferation of
> numerous sects demanding the radical restructuring of
> religion, government, and society. There is evidence
> that women were attracted to these sects in greater
> proportions than were men.[12] To feminists and psy-
> chologists of our own day, such a phenomenon would
> suggest a discontent rooted in women's otherwise re-
> stricted opportunities. However, for John Brinsley
> (1600-1665), Puritan minister, the explanation was
> found in the Bible: because women are more susceptible
> to deception than men, they are more likely to follow
> demagogic preachers.]

I Tim. 2:14:"And Adam was not deceived, but the
woman being deceived was in the transgression."
    This text is Scripture, and such a portion of
Scripture, as is but too proper for the times wherein
we live. Other apology, I shall need none for my
taking it up, handling of it in this place.

                          * * *

    "And Adam was not deceived." No? How came he
then to fall? How came he to adventure upon the eating of that forbidden fruit, the core whereof yet
sticketh in the throats and hearts of all his posterity to this day?

<u>Ans</u>. To this is answered variously: Six or seven
resolutions (such as they are) I find returned to it by
the Jesuit Estius.[13] I shall only single out two or three
of them, such as I find most approved of by Orthodox
Expositours.

1. "Adam was not deceived," that is (say some)
not formally, not properly, *Proprie nemo decipitur,
nisi a decipiente* (saith Estius). Properly and formally no man is said to be deceived, but by a deceiver,
who must be such a one as hath *animum fallendi,* a mind
and purpose to deceive; so was the woman deceived by
the serpent (or rather by Satan in the serpent) intend-
ing to deceive her. But so was not Adam deceived. The
woman in tendering the apple unto him, she had no purpose to deceive him. *Hoc fecit decepta, non decipiens*
(saith the foresaid author). This she did being herself deceived, not with an intention to deceive her
husband. No, that which herein she did, was only out
of a desire to make him partaker of her supposed happiness. As for deluding, deceiving of him, it was far
from her thought. And hereupon (say some) it is said,
that "Adam was not deceived." But this seemeth a little too acute, and curious.

2. More plainly and simply (in the second place)
"Adam was not deceived," that is, not primarily; he
was not the first that was deceived. So some expound
it, by borrowing a word from the verse foregoing, which
they conceive should here again be repeated *apo tō koinō,*
"Adam was first formed," *prōtos eplasthē,* but "Adam was
not first deceived," *ouk prōtos ēpatēthe,* "but the
woman...."

3. "Adam was not deceived," viz. not immediately
by the serpent. So was the woman deceived, giving ear
to Satan, speaking in and by the serpent, she was deceived; but so was not Adam deceived. Deceived indeed
he was; but it was by the means of the woman, handing
those suggestions unto him, which she had received from
the serpent, withall soliciting and inticing him; to
whom he yielded, partly *Ex amicabili quādam benevolentiā,*
out of a loving and indulgent affection towards her, and
so was overcome, even as Samson was by his Dalilah, and
Solomon by his wives.

These two last resolutions (being in effect one and
the same) we may safely pitch upon. "Adam was not deceived," viz. so as the woman was deceived: not firstly,
not immediately, so was the woman deceived; and being
so deceived, she was the instrument to deceive her husband. So it followeth: "But the woman being deceived,
she was in the transgression."

"The woman was deceived." So she was both properly, and primarily, and immediately. How deceived? By
what means? By what agent? By what instrument? By
what arguments and suggestions? You may read them all
in that third of Genesis, which I shall have occasion
to reflect upon anon. For the present I shall only
enquire. Why Satan singles out the woman? why he
first sets upon her, to deceive and seduce her?

A. For this take a double reason: Satan
looked upon her as a fitting object, and a fitting instrument: A fitting object to work upon, and a fitting
instrument to work by.

1. A fitting object to work upon, in as
much as she was the weaker vessel, less able to

withstand the stroke of his temptations. Had he en-
countered with the man, there might have been more
probability of resistance, less hope of prevailing.
Therefore he singles out the woman, as apprehending
more hopes of prevailing there, by reason of the natural infirmity of her sex.

2. As fit to work *upon*, so to work *by*; a
fitting instrument, being herself deceived, to deceive her husband, by conveying the same suggestions
unto him, who would the less suspect what came through
her hands, of whose cordial and entire affection he
was so fully persuaded. Such instruments Satan often
maketh use of in seducing the others: unsuspected
instruments; such was the woman to her husband. And
hereupon Satan singles out her, that she being herself deceived might be the instrument to deceive him,
which accordingly came to pass; so it followeth in
the text.

B. The woman being deceived, she was in the
transgression; *en parabasei*, "in the transgression."
The phrase here imports two things.

1. Hereby she became a transgressour;
Obnoxia facta est Transgressioni. So Erasmus, "she
became obnoxious, guilty of the transgression of the
law of God"; a truth, but not the whole truth.

2. She being hereby made a transgressour,
she became also the author and original of transgression. So Beza, *Causa transgressionis fuit*, "She
was the cause of transgression"; *en parabase*, put for
eis parabasin. So Ambrose renders it well, *Facta est
in Praevaricationem*. She became the means and instrument to seduce her husband, and so to draw him into

the like transgression, a truth which for the doctrinal part of it is so clearly held forth by the Spirit
of God in that third of Genesis, that it admits of
no further, either confirmation or illustration.

G.   John Owen, *An Exposition of the Epistle to the
         Hebrews,* ed. Edward Williams (Boston, 1812),
         IV, 172-173.

> [John Owen, prominent Puritan minister and theologian
> of the English Civil War and Restoration period, has
> not achieved the lasting fame that one might have
> forecast during his lifetime. After receiving an M.A.
> from Oxford in 1635, he was ordained, but ceased
> his studies toward the Bachelor of Divinity in 1637
> when he could not conform to the Laudian requirements.
> In 1643 he wrote a book against Arminianism; three
> years later he switched from Presbyterianism to
> Congregationalism. Through sermons before Parliament
> he gained the attention of Cromwell, under whom he
> served in various official positions. During the
> Restoration he held to his Puritan principles and
> refused to support plans to unite with the Church of
> England.
>
> His *Commentary on the Epistle to the Hebrews* was
> written during the period 1667-1683, when he was
> serving as pastor of an independent congregation.
> Among the members of his congregation were some
> prominent women, one of whom, Lady Abney, had pro-
> vided protection for him and his family during the
> time of persecution. It was no doubt his close
> friendship and pastoral concern for women[14] that
> led him to emphasize Sarah's role as an example for
> faithful women.]

Hebrews 11:11: "Through faith also Sarah herself received strength to conceive seed and was delivered of a child when she was past age."

     1. Here he proceeds to the instances of his

faith with respect to the promise made him, that in his seed all the nations of the earth should be blessed. And these also are two;—that which concern-eth the birth of Isaac, by whom the promise was to have its accomplishment; and—what he did by faith in offering up the son of the promise at the command of God.

In the first of these, Abraham was not alone, but Sarah his wife was both naturally and spiritually no less concerned than himself. Wherefore the apostle in the midst of his discourse concerning Abraham and his faith, in this one instance introduceth Sarah, with great propriety, in conjunction with him.

2. *Kai autē Sarra,* "and," or "also, Sarah her-self"; as Abraham was the father of the faithful, or the church, so she was the mother of it, so as that the distinct mention of her faith was necessary. She was the free woman from whence the church sprung (Gal. 4:22-23), and all believing women are her daughters (I Pet. 3:6; see Gen. 17:16). Her working and obedi-ence is proposed to the church as an example, and therefore her faith also may justly be so (I Pet. 3: 5-6); besides, she was equally concerned in the di-vine revelation with Abraham, and was as sensible of great difficulties in its accomplishment as Abraham, if not more; to which we may add, that the blessing of the promised seed was confined and appropriated to Sarah no less than to Abraham (Gen. 17:16): "I will bless her, yea, I will bless her, and she shall be a mother of nations." Herein her faith was necessary, and is here honorably recorded.

3. Something may be remarked in the very pro-

posing of this instance:

i. It is the faith of a woman that is celebrated. Hence that sex may learn that they also may
be examples of faith to the whole church, as Sarah was;
and it is necessary for their encouragement, because
of the special concernment of their sex in the first
entrance of sin; because of their natural weakness,
subject in a peculiar manner to various temptations,
which in this example they are encouraged to conflict
with and overcome by faith. Whence it is that they
are heirs, together with their believing husbands, of
the grace of life (I Pet. 3:7).

ii. Here is a single commendation of the
faith of Sarah, even in that very instance wherein it
was shaken; yea, being awakened by reproof (Gen. 17:
13-14), and receiving a fuller evidence that it was
the Lord who spoke to her, she recovered herself, and
rested by faith in his power and truth.

iii. The carriage of Sarah is twice repeated by the Holy Ghost, here and I Pet. 3:6; and
in both places only what was good—her faith towards
God on her recovery after the reproof, and her obser-
vance of her husband, whom, speaking to himself, she
called *Lord*—is mentioned and proposed without the
least remembrance of her failing or miscarriage; and
such will be the judgment of Christ at the last day,
concerning all those whose faith and obedience are
sincere, though accompanied with many failings.

CHAPTER TWO

WOMEN AS WIVES
_____

There is no doubt that the Reformation brought
changes in attitudes toward marriage. Whether these
changes improved the status of women is less clear.
There is no general agreement even today on whether
the exaltation of married life benefits or restricts
women. Furthermore, although Reformers exalted marriage in their attacks on clerical celibacy, some
would argue that the effect of this was cancelled out
by their denial of the sacramental nature of marriage.
To be sure, such a denial made divorce more feasible,
but, as we will see, it did not necessarily entail
lower esteem for the sanctity of marriage.

The attack on clerical celibacy was part of a
more fundamental criticism of the Roman Catholic distinction between clergy and laity. Reformers had
ceased to believe—largely because of the moral fail-
ures of the clergy—that the clerical estate was in-
trinsically holier than any other. The "priesthood
of all believers" made all Christians, at least in
theory, equally capable of being God's instruments on
earth. Presumably one could serve God equally well
whether minister or carpenter, married or unmarried.
The layperson already married at the time of the
Reformation could now be raised from a second-class

to a first-class Christian.

      This theoretical egalitarianism applied less
uniformly to those who had previously chosen the celi-
bate life. Although Luther did not intend to prohibit
monasticism, so long as it was not considered a means
of earning salvation, he nevertheless considered only
one person in thousands capable of remaining chaste
while unmarried. A moral life, he felt, was much more
likely within marriage, where lusts could be tamed,
than outside it. The combined effect of the new theology, popular anti-monasticism, and governmental se-
cularization of church lands eventually brought the
closing of most monasteries and convents in Protestant
territories. With them, the major medieval outlet for
literarily and spiritually creative women vanished.
Although at the end of the sixteenth century the diaconate was revived in a few places for charitable work
and nursing, this was generally open only to widows
over sixty and did not offer the same range of leadership opportunities as had the nunneries.

      On the other hand, women who had lived in con-
cubinage with priests could now gain a socially respectable position. Wives of Protestant ministers
had unusual opportunities for Christian service and
influence. Some—notably Katherine Zell—chose a
more active form of ministry than others, but all no
doubt felt the domestic tasks they performed for
their husbands were their contribution to an important movement. And their husbands often paid tribute
to their service; Calvin, for instance, wrote on the
death of his wife:

      I have been bereaved of the best companion

> of my life, who, if our lot had been
> harsher, would have been not only the
> willing sharer of exile and poverty,
> but even of death. While she lived,
> she was the faithful helper of my
> ministry. From her I never experienced
> the slightest hindrance.[1]

If the attacks on vows of celibacy had the effect of elevating marriage, the assertion that it was
not a biblically based sacrament might seem to have
the opposite effect. Catholics, in attempting to show
that the sanctity of marriage was being undermined,
have pointed to various recommendations of early Reformers to place matrimonial cases under civil jurisdiction and to legalize divorce under certain circumstances.[2] In 1525 Zwingli's Zurich removed jurisdiction in marital cases from the bishop of Constance to
a special marriage court under municipal authority.[3]
Luther also had spoken of marriage as an "external,
secular matter,"[4] but he at other times called it a
divine institution, an "ordinance and creation of
God."[5] This apparent contradiction is best explained
in reference to his "two kingdom theory": just as secular rulers have no religious jurisdiction but are
placed in their offices by God, so marriage belongs
to the civil realm but as part of the order of creation is willed by God.

Whereas this tension of the sacred and the secular remained intentionally unresolved for Luther,
Anabaptists and radical Puritans focussed on the secular nature of marriage, often to the point of denying
ministers any role in marriage ceremonies. In the
Middle Ages, clandestine marriages—entered into
either secretly by the couple alone or with witnesses

but no priest——were frequent, but by the sixteenth
century it was increasingly common to legitimize such
marriages afterwards by an ecclesiastical ceremony.
Anabaptists refused to submit to such a ceremony, even
though they eventually found a place for a blessing by
the leader of their religious community. Because Anabaptism was officially disapproved, however, their
marriages were left in a legally questionable position.

By the end of the sixteenth century, two Dutch
provinces (Holland and West Friesland) had introduced
civil marriage as a legal recognition of the contract
which the partners had previously made privately in
clandestine marriages. This did not replace a church
ceremony for the Dutch Reformed; church orders in Holland continued to outline marriage rites. But soon
radical Englishmen, many of whom lived in exile in
Holland, began to insist that marriage was a purely
civil matter. The Brownists and Independents, who
systematically discarded everything lacking biblical
support, could find no warrant in Scripture for the
church to be involved in marriage contracts. Many
members of John Robinson's Independent congregation
in Leyden were united in matrimony in accordance with
Holland's civil ceremony. When they left Leyden for
Plymouth colony, they took the practice of civil marriage with them. As other less radical Puritans came
to the New World, they, too, adopted this custom, and
within a few years all New England colonies forbade
marriage by any other than the magistrate or court
official.[6]

The less marriage was considered a religious
act, the more it was thought to be dissoluble. The

early German and Swiss reformers, in contrast to the
Roman Church and the Church of England, had recognized
certain grounds for divorce (not merely separation)
with the right of the injured party to remarry. Adultery was the most commonly mentioned, with desertion
frequently added, though the reformers were by no
means condoning such actions. Heinrich Bullinger's
influential *Der christlich Eestand* (1540) was written
to try to stem the tide of marital infidelity, but,
should adultery occur, Bullinger would defend the
right of the wronged spouse to divorce and remarry.
Martin Bucer, both in his 1530 commentaries on the
gospels and in his 1550 *De Regno Christi,* took a more
radical position, denying that adultery was the only
scripturally based reason for divorce. Christ, he af-
firmed, had not abrogated the Old Testament law, according to which divorce for hardness of heart was
permissible.[7]

Differences in religious belief were not generally considered sufficient justification in themselves
for dissolving an existing marriage. But in Calvin's
Geneva the argument for divorce on grounds of desertion could be applied in the case of one who had to
flee a region for religious reasons. Many Anabaptists,
notably Hutterites, went further than Calvin by actually advocating the desertion of a non-Anabaptist
partner.[8] Such teachings were sometimes exploited by
those seeking an easy divorce, but they no doubt resulted from a strong religious concern for the purity
of the faith and the attempt of Anabaptists to separate themselves from ungodliness in all its forms.
For John Robinson, on the other hand, the civil nature

of marriage meant that religious differences between
husband and wife should be no impediment to the duties
of marriage.[9] In some of the English civil war sects,
however, desertion of an "unbeliever" is again en-
countered (see selection V-D below).

Among more moderate Puritans there was no uniform teaching on the admissibility of divorce. Some
few, following the teaching of the Church of England,
tended to view marriage as indissoluble; most would
allow divorce for the same reasons as the continental
reformers: adultery and desertion. But the strong emphasis on companionship as a major reason for marriage
—typical of the Reformed tradition as far back as
Bullinger, Calvin and Bucer—eventually led Milton to
an explicit recognition of incompatibility as grounds
for divorce. Though this position had not been defended before Milton, it was a logical extension of
previous teachings. Puritans denied that marriage
was a sacrament, not because God's grace was not necessary to matrimony but because they saw grace operating
at all stages of the relationship, from the original
betrothal onward throughout married life. As James T.
Johnson nicely states, such a theology of marriage can
support either indissolubility or divorce:

> The Puritans argue that Christian marriage
> is indissoluble only because God is work-
> ing through the mutual love of the spouses
> to support their union. Those Puritans
> who argue for divorce for incompatibility
> accept this point but assert that in mar-
> riages where there is no mutual love, God
> is not working because he never intended
> this couple to be together in marriage.[10]

Such a concept of marriage as made in heaven becomes even more explicit in the Quaker George Fox.

Just as religious truth is known through the Inner
Light, so true marriage is revealed to a couple and
their friends by the Power of God. Only when all see
and feel the "Wisdom and Power of God" should the marriage be declared in the General Meeting "as they are
moved"; afterwards, "as they are moved," they may, or
may not, declare it to the magistrate.[11] If marriage
is based on such spiritual power and guidance, it will
be a recovery of the true original marriage in the
Garden of Eden and, because created by God, will be
indissoluble.

The Quakers, then, as the least sacramental
group under consideration, have one of the most spiritual views of marriage. To deny the sacramental nature of marriage did not, for any of the reformers,
indicate a lowered estimation of the sacred obligations of marriage. Nor did those who allowed divorce
advocate it; rather they sought to remedy the abuses
which already existed and to make the married state
more meaningful and spiritual.

In so doing they injected a measure of freedom
and mutual respect into the marriage relationship
which benefited married women. Both Calvin and Bucer
had accorded women as much right to divorce their
adulterous husbands as vice versa. According to
Milton, this right was so widely granted a century
later that there was no need to translate Bucer's
chapter of *De Regno Christi* on this subject. In
fact, Milton, as we will see, represented a certain
backlash against the movement for sexual equality,
feeling it was time to present the male side.

The long Protestant disquisitions on marriage

and family life, from Bullinger through Richard Baxter,
emphasize the mutual concerns of the partners and
their reciprocal obligations. But no matter how many
nuances are introduced into the understanding of matrimonial companionship, no theologian of our period ever
denied that the husband was the head of the household
and the wife his subordinate. Given this fundamental
guideline, however, the range of sensitivity to women
as wives varied dramatically, as we will see in the
following selections.

A.   "Meister Heinrich Gresbecks Bericht von der
      Wiedertaufe in Münster [Report on Anabaptism
      in Münster]," from *Berichte der Augenzeugen
      über das Münsterische Wiedertäuferreich,* ed.
      C. A. Cornelius (Münster, 1853), pp. 59-68.

      [Whether the Anabaptist uprising in Münster reveals
      the logical culmination of Anabaptist teachings or
      an aberration from the movement as a whole has long
      been debated by theologians and historians. The
      question might be raised more specifically regarding
      the Münsterite teachings on marriage. Certainly the
      forced polygamy which was introduced in Münster for
      a time was atypical. But it may reveal certain sig-
      nificant attitudes. For instance, among Anabaptists
      the cause of the faith took precedence over marriage
      bonds, especially those entered into prior to es-
      pousal of the true faith. Secondly, biblical prece-
      dents, in this case the more patriarchal practices
      of the Hebrews, reinforced the already common ten-
      dency to subordinate the wife. Finally, pressed by
      the immediate threat of a declining population, the
      preachers resorted to an emphasis on procreation as
      apparently the only reason for marriage. Thus, far
      from advancing the cause of women, they eliminated
      the marital aspects of fidelity and sacrament which
      had softened the primarily procreationist position
      of Roman Catholicism.

      Many Münsterites, however, were opposed to the intro-
      duction of polygamy, among them the more pacifistic
      Anabaptists who had predominated before the millenar-

ian, theocratic reign of John of Leiden. One treatise
of the pre-polygamist period, for instance, *Confession
of the Faith and Life of the Christian Congregation at
Münster,*[1] defends the Münster Anabaptists against
charges the writer considers slanderous, including
that of the practice of polygamy. He denies that any
have deviated from monogamous marriage, the only holy
and divinely ordained form. Another critic of the
radical regime was Heinrich Gresbeck, a citizen of
Münster but one who subjected himself to the regime
only out of fear. His account, therefore, while that
of an eyewitness, is of one who was not party to the
innermost workings of the city's leadership, and who
eventually provided vital information to the enemy
for an attack on the city. But the most adamant opponents of the innovations regarding marriage, as
Gresbeck indicates, were those women who had the
least to gain from a change in status.]

Now John of Leiden had discussed the estate of
marriage with the preachers and the twelve elders,
saying that a man should have more than one wife. So
the prophets, preachers and twelve elders decided this
secretly and were in agreement. The prophets and
preachers found in the Bible "grow and multiply." Also, some of the patriarchs such as Abraham, David and
Eliakim and others had more than one wife. Thus they
wanted to proceed and take on the married state. The
prophets and preachers proclaimed the state in their
sermons, saying it was God's will that they should
take on marriage, for it was pleasing to God that men
should populate the earth. God wanted to erect a new
world with his people and thus it was God's will that
each brother have more than one wife and populate the
earth....

Also the prophets, preachers and twelve elders
charged that a man with a young or old woman who was
infertile should take another who was fertile, for

such was God's will. If this one then became pregnant,
the man should have nothing more to do with her until
she was delivered. If he cannot contain himself without his wife for the length of time that she is with
child, he may take another. If the man takes another
wife and she too becomes pregnant, he should also
leave her alone. If the man can actually not refrain
from women, he may take yet another, or as many wives
as he wishes in order that they may populate the
earth....

     So the prophets, preachers and twelve elders
said in their sermons to all women, maidens, virgins,
widows, all who were marriageable, whether noble or
commoner, religious or lay, that they should all take
husbands. And the women who had husbands who had fled
from us outside the city should also take other husbands, for their husbands are godless, have fled from
God's word and are not our brothers. "Dear brothers
and sisters, you have lived all this time in paganism
in marriage, and it has been no true marriage." In
this way the preachers announced to the common people
in the sermon that they should take husbands. Part of
the wives were willing to do this, another part not; a
part of the virgins and other maidens were also willing, part not....

     Thus as marriage had progressed so that a man
should have as many wives as he wished, some were
pleased and others not. Many were even killed over
this issue, as you will hear. Because of this marriage decree many a person in the city strove unto
death. As soon as they had taken on marriage, each
was against the others to the very end. Once a woman

was found lying drowned in the water, floating on top
of the water with her clothes still on. The woman had
drowned in this place. So the people did not know how
she had drowned, whether the prophets and preachers
had had her drowned or whether she had drowned herself. Part of the people wanted to say the prophets
had had her drowned. Part wanted to say the woman had
drowned herself because of the marriage decree. The
woman lay in the water unbound. So the people in the
city believed that she had drowned herself because
she was struggling against the marriage decree. How
it was with the woman I cannot report. Her home was
not in Münster. No one knew where she came from. So
they pulled her out of the water and buried her.

There were also those in the city who could not
endure because of marriage, and there was great discontent in the city among the women where two or
three women had one man in common in one house. There
was always scolding and squabbling among the women.
The first wife wanted to be close to the man all the
time, and the other women, whom the man had taken in
addition to the first, also wanted to be with him and
to keep as close to him as the first woman did. They
could not endure each other, so they never had peace
together, and every day a complaint came before the
prophets and preachers and the twelve elders. Finally they proceeded to take part of the women who were
the first wives of their husbands and chop some of
their heads off so that others would be mindful that
they should live in peace with other women or concu-
bines. In this way they coerced their first wives,
whom they had had for ten or twenty years and with

whom they had had little children and who thus now
lived in discontent. These first wives had to keep
quiet and not dare say anything or they would be taken
and their heads chopped off....

So the prophets, preachers and twelve elders
took counsel what they should do with these women so
that they might be in peace together. They had the
preachers say in their sermons that all women who were
forced into marriage and took men but would like to be
free of them should come to the town hall and give
their names. They would be separated again, for the
preachers had erred regarding marriage. How clever it
was of John of Leiden, Stutenbernt,[2] and the twelve
elders, and also part of the other preachers, to say
that the preachers had erred regarding marriage. By
this they meant the preachers whom they had sent to
Soest, Warendorf, Coasfelt, and Osnabrück. They wanted to pretend they had not consented to or approved
the marriage decree and instead to ascribe it to the
other preachers. They knew well that the other
preachers had found their deaths and been executed
in these cities. So they thought they would redeem
themselves concerning marriage. Thus it happened
that they set the people apart again at the end of
the first summer that the town was occupied, when the
preachers had been expelled.

"Since now the preachers have made a mistake
with marriage, you should come to the town hall and
give your name. You will be separated from one another. No one should be coerced; marriage should be
free. Whoever likes should enter it; whoever does

not may leave it." But it was too late when they had
this announced, for all the women in the city had men
and some of the women had been executed because of
marriage. "For a man can live a godly life with a woman, and he can also live a godly life without women,
as can also a woman live a godly life without a man."
How they turned that around as they became tired of
the many women and then said that marriage was not
godly! But they had gotten in so far that they could
not get out again.

     So they gave the women a week to sign their
names. Several hundred women, young and old, gave
their names.... These women who gave their names were
told a time when they should come back. When these
same women returned, each of them, young and old, was
asked whether she too had been forced to her lord.
The women were accustomed to call their men lord.
Whoever could prove that she had been forced into marriage was allowed to separate. Many women in the city
had been forced thereto who did not dare to give their
names because they feared that the prophets and
preachers had something else in mind. They feared
they would have to go to the courtyard in bare skin
and have their heads chopped off. Had they known that
they were to be separated once more they would have
signed up by the hundreds. After it had happened that
the women were again separated from the men, the
preachers gave a sermon regarding these women and condemned them, saying they belonged to the devil, body
and soul. This reputation and "benediction" they had
to carry with them afterwards.

B.   Menno Simons, *The True Christian Faith,* c. 1541,
        from *The Complete Writings of Menno Simons (c.
        1496-1561),* trans. Leonard Verduin, ed. John
        Christian Wenger (Scottdale, Pennsylvania:
        Herald Press, 1956), pp. 376-383.

[More typical of Anabaptist thought on the relations
between the sexes than Münsterite polygamy is Menno
Simons' discussion of the sinful woman who became a
believer. Certainly less oppressive than John of
Leiden, Menno nevertheless wanted women to remain in
their traditional, inconspicuous place. His most
revolutionary thought in this area seems to have
been the denial of a husband's right to beat his
wife,[3] an opinion expressed, however, in other elements of society as well. Otherwise Menno appears
to confine women in their homes and clothes even
more than sixteenth-century society in general,
giving instructions in modesty followed still by
Mennonite women in our day.

Yet men are no more entitled to luxury and lust than
are women. Menno admonishes men to respect their
Christian sisters, refrain from defiling their bodies,
and marry those whom they "deflower." There is a
certain egalitarianism in Menno's treatment in that
he finds "the whole world filled with sots of both
sexes" and warns both men and women to return to
modesty and purity.

On the other hand, Menno's treatment does not ad-
vance beyond medieval ideas of marriage as a prevention for sins of lust. His concern for proper
regard for the women revolves primarily around the
physical relationship rather than the social bond
of companionship.]

"The Faith of the Woman Who Was a Sinner"

Luke says: One of the Pharisees desired Jesus
that he would eat with him. And he went into the
Pharisee's house and sat down to meat. And, behold,
a woman of the city, which was a sinner, when she
knew that Jesus sat at meat in the Pharisee's house,
brought an alabaster box of ointment and stood at his

feet behind him, weeping, and began to wash his feet
with tears, and did wipe them with the hairs of her
head, and kissed his feet, and anointed them with the
ointment. Luke 7:36-38.

In the case of this woman who was a sinner we
see once more what kind of heart, disposition, fruit,
and life, a sincere, true Christian faith brings with
it. She had been possessed of seven devils (if indeed
she was that woman, or Mary, of whom the evangelists
make mention), and lived, it seems, as she pleased
(for she is called a sinner in the Scriptures) so long
as the Lord had not called her out of darkness into
light, from lies into truth. But as soon as she heard
His Word, she with eagerness received it in a sincere
and renewed heart, by which she, who was such a great
sinner, became a penitent and pious woman. Her un-
righteous, carnal heart was so inspired and touched
that her eyes streamed with tears, so that she wet
the feet of the Savior with them. Her beautiful,
braided hair she used as a towel with which to wipe
His feet. She died to avarice, for she anointed His
head and feet with an ointment so precious that it
might have been sold for three hundred pence. Her
proud heart was humbled, for she did not seek the
highest seat at the table, but sat sorrowfully at the
feet of the Lord and heard His blessed Word.

When the Pharisee saw this, he murmured. And
Christ said to him, Simon, seest thou this woman? I
entered into thine house, thou gavest me no water for
my feet: but she hath washed my feet with tears, and
wiped them with the hairs of her head. Thou gavest
me no kiss: but this woman since the time I came in,
hath not ceased to kiss my feet. My head with oil

thou didst anoint: but this woman hath anointed my
feet with ointment. Wherefore I say unto thee, her
sins, which are many, are forgiven; for she loved
much: for to whom little is forgiven the same loveth
little. And he said unto her, Thy sins are forgiven;
thy faith hath saved thee; go in peace. Luke 7:44-48,
50.

Dear reader, take notice that all the proud,
haughty, avaricious, carnal, and adulterous persons
who call themselves Christians, but are not such (for
they testify by their disposition, heart, mind, and
life that they hate Christ), are thoroughly shamed
and reproved by this regenerate, penitent sinner;
seeing that because she believed, her proud, haughty,
and obdurate heart was changed into a humble, contrite,
and broken one.

They say that they believe, and yet, alas, there
are no limits nor bounds to their accursed haughtiness,
foolish pride and pomp; they parade in silks, velvet,
costly clothes, gold rings, chains, silver belts, pins
and buttons, curiously adorned shirts, shawls, collars,
veils, aprons, velvet shoes, slippers, and such like
foolish finery. They never regard that the exalted
apostles Peter and Paul have in plain and express
words forbidden this all to Christian women. And if
forbidden to women, how much more to men who are the
leaders and heads of their wives! Notwithstanding all
this they still want to be called the Christian Church.

Everyone has as much finery as he can afford and
sometimes more than that. One wants to surpass another in this cursed folly, and they do not reflect
that it is written, Love not the world, neither the

things that are in the world. If any man love the
world, the love of the Father is not in him. For all
that is in the world, the lust of the flesh, and the
lust of the eyes, and the pride of life is not of the
Father, but is of the world. And the world passes
away, and the lust thereof: but he that doeth the will
of God abideth forever. I John 2:15-17.

Once more, this sinful woman became a believer,
and from that moment she was cleansed of her unclean
wicked flesh, for the unclean devil was cast out of it,
as you have heard. But what ugly, shameful unchastity,
adultery, and fornication is practiced among men and
women who boast that they believe, in many cities and
countries, is best known to Him before whose eyes all
things are open, and is alas not wholly concealed before men. It is manifest that the world is full of
harlots, adulterers, fornicators, sexual perverts,
bastards, and illegitimate children, and alas, it has
come to such a pass that they live in freedom and
liberty, notwithstanding that God has commanded through
Moses that both the adulterer and the adulteress should
die (Deut. 22:22), that there were to be neither harlots nor those who patronized them in Israel, and that
the illegitimate children even to the tenth generation
were not to be admitted into the congregation of the
Lord. And further, it was the express command and
ordinance of God that if any one in Israel defiled a
virgin not betrothed or engaged, and it was discovered,
he was compelled to marry her, if her father consented.
And he was not to put her away all his days, because
he had humiliated her. Ex. 22:16.

Ah, reader, reflect upon what the last command

implies. They all boast, however much given to har-
lotry, that they are the spiritual Israel, that they
have the truth, and that they are baptized in the name
of Christ. And yet they are not ashamed to turn their
poor, weak sisters, who are included with them in the
same faith, baptism, holy Supper, and worship, into
poor, disgraced, and degraded strumpets against all
Scripture and Christian love; even though God's own
mouth and the commandment quoted above commands them
that if they be deflowered, then they should take
them to wife and never forsake them. If they would
ponder these things, many a girl would be spared shame
whereas now many an honest man's child is cruelly
wronged, and many a girl is deprived of her honor and
virtue....

I do not mean to say that a person who has in
days gone by ignorantly done this thing must leave
the wife whom he afterwards married and take in her
stead the violated one. Not at all, for I doubt not
but that the merciful Father will graciously overlook
the errors of those who have ignorantly committed
them, and who will now fear and gladly do what is
right. But I write this that everyone should guard
himself against such disgrace, and reflect more pro-
foundly upon the command of the Lord and on love, and
observe how Christ is so wholly despised by the world.
For alas, they are altogether driven by their accursed
lusts, whether they are lords, princes, priests,
monks, noble or ignoble, burghers or peasants, with
few exceptions. They pursue the improper, devilish
shame and accursed adultery with such an avidity as of

a hound after a hare. They are, says Jeremiah (5:8), as fed horses in the morning; every one neighed after his neighbor's wife. There is nothing that can frighten or deter them from this accursed abomination: neither natural reason, nor Moses with all his threatenings, neither the prophets, nor the apostles, nor Christ Jesus Himself; neither heaven nor angels, neither hell nor the devil, neither life nor death. If they can only give free rein to their ugly, unchaste lust, then all is fine as far as they are concerned.

They turn every device to this end. Some they seduce with subtle clever words, others with scoundrel promises and gifts; some by lavish spending, by dress and similar devices; yea, some by their seducing sighings and weepings; just so they can accomplish their ungodly designs and gratify their lusts, then all is fine and dandy. But that they thereby incense Almighty God, transgress His holy Word, disgrace their neighbor, violate love, defile the marriage bed, violate young women, call into being illegitimate children, and condemn their own poor souls forever—about all this they are not worried. They say, This is our portion and our lot, and that is all there is to it....

And even as we find many wicked men who shamefully wrong poor, simple hearts, so on the other hand we find many shameless women and girls who are often the first cause that such disgrace is sought and sometimes practiced upon them. And although many are not guilty of the deed, nevertheless they are not guiltless in that they allow such intimacy with other men and companions, with bold face singing, dancing,

drinking, kissing, flirting, primping and fixing up,
and the like vanity and abominations whereby with some
they kindle the fire of base passions which continue
till consumed, as may be seen....

Now if the afore-mentioned married and unmarried
women were true believers as was this sinful woman,
if they would only fear the Lord, they would abandon
all vanity and ungodly action, and lay snares for none,
nor give any occasion for evil. Yes, they would live
honorably and modestly, avoiding all unnecessary
adornment and pomp and making or desiring no other
clothes than those which are necessary, and which our
daily toil makes right and proper. Then they would
not be seen very often in the idolatrous temple and
idle banquets, for which occasion this pompous show
is generally gotten up.

The sinful woman adorned her soul inwardly and
not her appearance outwardly, for she believed that
these adorn their bodies externally and not their
souls internally, for they believe not.

The sinful woman sighed and wept and feared the
wrath and judgment of the Lord, for she saw that she
had done wrong and sinned. But these people laugh
and dance, sing and waltz about, and do not see their
enormous misdeeds and grievous sins, and therefore do
not fear the coming wrath and judgment of the Lord.

This sinful woman was compassionate and merciful, anointing the head and feet of the Lord, and found
the true worship. But these people are unmerciful
and cruel, and know of no other worship than to go to
the churches, receive holy water, offer tapers and
wax candles to blind blocks and icons; to hear masses

and vespers read, to call upon departed saints for
help, to confess once or twice a year to their idolatrous, drunken, harloting priests; to receive their
abomination-bread and absolution, and the like super-
stitions and deceptions.

The sinful woman sought the company of the righteous, but these people seek the company of the un-
righteous. They come together to deal in all manner
of foolishness, to deprive their neighbors of their
good name, to defame and gossip, to speak disgraceful-
ly of one another, to talk about costly furniture,
houses, goods, and handsome companions, men and fine
clothing. In short, their works openly show that they
have not the faith of the sinful woman and are not in
the congregation of the righteous.

The sinful woman sat at the feet of Jesus and
heard His holy Word, but these people hear teachers
who tickle their ears and preach as they like it. But
why talk at length about it? It is, O God, so corrupted that we find the whole world filled with sots
of both sexes, deaf ears (spiritually, that is), unen-
lightened hearts; the blind are leading the blind in
such a way that they will all together fall into the
pit of eternal death unless they get to see the light
—if we believe it to be true what the mouth of the
Lord has taught us. For it is all false doctrine,
false sacraments, false religion, sheer unbelief, and
vain frivolous life no matter where we turn....

I, therefore, entreat and desire all women
through the mercy of the Lord to take this sorrowful,
sorrowing woman as a pattern and follow her faith.
Humble yourselves before the Lord and reprove your

avarice, pride, impurity, and all manner of evil. Let
all your thoughts be pure; let your words be circumspect and seasoned with salt. And whatsoever you do,
do that in the name and fear of the Lord Jesus. Do
not adorn yourselves with gold, silver, costly pearls
and embroidered hair, and expensive, unusual dress.
Use such clothing as becomes women professing godliness and which is suitable in your occupation. Be
obedient to your husbands in all reasonable things so
that those who do not believe may be gained by your
upright, pious conversation without the Word, as Peter
says.

Remain within your houses and gates unless you
have something of importance to regulate, such as to
make purchases, to provide in temporal needs, to hear
the Word of the Lord, or to receive the holy sacraments, etc. Attend faithfully to your charge, to
your children, house, and family, and to all that is
entrusted to you, and walk in all things as the sinful woman did after her conversion, in order that you
may be true daughters of Sarah, believing women, sisters of Christ, heirs of the lord to come (I Pet. 3:
6), and that you may hear the gracious words, Thy
sins are forgiven. Thy faith hath saved thee; go in
peace.

C.   "How to proceed against Anabaptist women (Würt-
      temberg, 1584)," from *Quellen zur Geschichte der
      Wiedertäufer,* Vol. I. *Herzogtum Württemberg,* ed.
      Gustav Bossert (Leipzig, 1930; reprint New York,
      1971), pp. 577-78.

      [The 1529 Diet of Speyer had decreed the death penalty
      for Anabaptists, but Duke Ulrich of Württemberg, on
      the advice of theologians of the university of Tübingen,

had resorted only to imprisonment or banishment for
the most stubborn and to instruction for the ignorant
heretics. Such a policy, however, forced the officials
to outline procedures for dealing with different situa-
tions arising from the existence of Anabaptists. One
issue, for instance, was the question whether divorce
should be granted to an orthodox believer married to
an Anabaptist. A 1571 procedural statement prescribed
divorce in instances of desertion by the Anabaptist
partners, especially when children were left behind.
Should the abandonment be involuntary, as in the case
of one banished or imprisoned, the abandoned party
should be more patient. Another question, discussed
in a 1584 ordinance supplementing that of 1571, was
how to deal with Anabaptist women whose banishment or
imprisonment might cause hardship to their families.]

For a few years it has often occurred and come to
pass that women whose husbands are not Anabaptists but
of the correct religion are misled and drawn into error by others. They do not let themselves be led
back to proper, circumspect behavior and well-directed
energy by the commissioners and magistrates or by the
chancellery, and they are unaffected by the reminders
and fervent petitions of their husbands. Instead
they persist in their error, and for this reason they
have previously been dealt with by banishment from
the land, as is the case with men by virtue of ordinance. But this has caused many great burdens to
small untrained, even nursing children. For this
reason, and also because of the earnest, plaintive re-
quests of the husbands, such cases have been dealt
with leniently, and such wives have been handed over
to their husbands to be chained in the house. Officials have earnestly been instructed to permit no access to them and to take care that such erring women
not presume to lead their families or others astray.

This procedure should also be followed in the

future in similar cases, and the pastors in such
places should be commanded to go to them—even though
by their conception of the struggle they do not want
to permit this but to turn them away—and deal with
them gently and moderately in order that no possible
opportunity might be lost for our dear God to accomplish something by His grace and Holy Spirit. Previously, however, we have learned that when it was
thought that the women were chained and secured, they
had been freed secretly with the help of their husbands or their servants. And even though sometimes
the deputy commissioners or others came to the place
to inquire, it seems to have occurred that the freed
woman stood on the chain and would not budge until
the visitors had left. Now since they have used de-
ception, the command must be all the more serious
from now on, and a considerable punishment of fine or
imprisonment must be enjoined and inflicted upon the
men given such a serious, high trust. For themselves
there will be no mercy, no release or leniency. And
when punishment is finally imposed on such a one, his
servants or those who at their own instigation, on
their own attempt and will, opened the lock or chain,
the magistrates and their subordinates are commanded
to betake themselves to these same houses unexpected-
ly and without warning in about a month or six weeks.
There they are to gather their own information and
not let themselves be deceived or turned away easily.
For when such erroneous and headstrong women, who
have such ill-timed zeal and now and then could well
scream, are freed, they may sometimes wander secretly
at night to other places and among people, especially

other women, where they may cause harm.

D.   Sebastian Franck, *Sprichwörter; Schöne, Weise*
       Klugreden [*Proverbs, or Clever, Wise Sayings*]
       (Frankfurt am Main, 1548; reprinted by Wis-
       senschaftliche Buchgesellschaft, Darmstadt,
       1972).

       [Perhaps the most negative view of women during this
       period is found in the folk humor where it could be
       expressed without the restraints of moderation, morals,
       or manners. Sebastian Franck (c. 1499-c. 1542), a
       rational spiritualist and writer of chronicles, trans-
       mitted some of this humor in his collection of German
       proverbs. Yet not all the proverbs are critical of
       women; some place a very high value on those women
       possessing the proper virtues. This balance between
       approbation and scorn of women, however, was not recog-
       nized as such by Martin Luther, who was deeply of-
       fended by those proverbs maligning women. In a pref-
       ace to Johann Freder's *Dialogue in Honor of Marriage*
       (1545),[4] Luther launched out against Franck not only
       for his proverbs, which, he said, were typical of
       Franck's inability to say anything good about anyone,
       but also for his lack of belief in anything except
       "Spirit, Spirit, Spirit." Though aware that Franck
       was to some extent merely repeating the trivolous
       sayings of others, Luther felt it served no edifying
       purpose to publish such statements as "When the
       lights are out, women are all alike." Franck, he as-
       serted, should have had more consideration, if not
       for the Virgin and other holy women, at least for
       his own wife and mother. But, we may note, the goals
       of the chronicler are often different from those of
       the moralist.]

"Long skirts, short sense."

A woman is a poor fragile vessel inclined to
anger, small-minded and faint-hearted; she turns from
one thing to the next, as inattentive and talkative
as a child. Therefore St. Peter gives this advice to
men, that they should live with their wives in understanding, aware and tolerant of their weaknesses.

And because this is the way of women, it follows that
they will be fickleness dressed in long skirts, which
is the most honorable adornment for women.

"If you find things going too well, take a wife!"
If you take a wife, you get yourself a devil on
your back. If you take a man, you get good fortune.
St. Jerome uses this proverb and means that
there is no peaceful life except to live alone without a wife. The single state makes for a restful
life. Oh, the weal and woe of many in marriage....
The married life is no breeze. Whoever hopes for
peace and tranquillity here should beware of the ani-
mal wearing braids. If he does this for God's sake,
as do those who make themselves eunuchs for the kingdom of God (Matth. 19), he will have more time, freedom and peace to serve God in conscience (I Cor. 6).

"To strike a woman brings little honor to a man."
A man should not dispute with women, and in case
a woman sets herself up against a man, the man should,
as a reasonable person, give in. When her anger sub-
sides, he should then punish her with words. Otherwise, if he lets himself become indignant and strikes
her with his fists, he brings shame upon himself because he cannot prove his manhood better than on a
poor woman.

"Women have three skins."
Women, it is said, have first of all the skin of
a dog. That is, when one scolds or punishes them,
they howl back like a dog, "Arf! Arf!" The second

skin is that of a sow. To cut through this one needs
a sharp knife; but if the pigskin gets cut she grunts,
"Onk! Onk!" like a pig. The third skin is the human
skin; whoever hits it hears a voice like this: "Oh my
dear man, I will do anything you like." Few men get
to this skin, for the human skin is as thin as a moon-
beam and whoever touches it has won the prize. Otherwise women ordinarily wear the other two skins, and
most of all the dog's skin so they can howl back.

>   "Women carry a sword in their mouths, so they
>   must be struck on the scabbard."

A woman is by nature a prattling, babbling thing.
So some think, as long as they carry their swords in
their mouths, one must knock them on the scabbard,
that is, the mouth. St. Peter speaks of two virtues
which are befitting to women. The first is mild-
temperedness, the second tranquillity, both of these
being virtues of the spirit, for they dress the heart
splendidly before God. The two virtues, however, he
opposes to two vices which are inborn in women. For
wherever there is a woman devoted to honor, who loves
her husband and does not want anything to go wrong,
yet sees things going wrong in the house (the servants
unfaithful, things falling to pieces, harm occurring
here and there), she can't help but scold, curse and
fight it all out with her mouth. She thinks if she
didn't do this, she wouldn't be doing her duty. Now
it is true that a certain sharpness is appropriate in
governing a household. But St. Peter wants Christian
women to be gentle; that is, they should let much pass
before their ears and eyes and through their fingers

without wanting to make everything just right. Otherwise it will be said: she is a cross woman; no one
can please her; nothing one does is worth anything.
And in case the woman of the house does not mean
everything unkindly but just wants to keep the servants working on their toes, still the simple servants
understand only what they see and hear.

>   "A devoted wife is worth more than her weight
>   in gold."

To him whom God has truly blessed He has granted
a devoted wife. There is no greater blessing on
earth than when a man is given a well-bred, obedient,
modest wife. Solomon says, "Parents can bequeath a
child a house, an estate, and great riches, but only
God can provide a reasonable, upright woman." But
since a devoted wife is a great treasure which God
alone gives, this treasure can neither be bought nor
given a price, with either gold or money. For gold
is too small a thing to buy a single gift of God,
even the smallest.

>   "Whoever wants peace at home must do as his
>   wife wishes."

Although this saying refers to all women in general, only the bad and disobedient are meant. For
one finds many devoted, obedient wives who willingly
do whatever they find pleasing to their husbands.
And such a wife is a crown of honor and cannot be
bought with gold.

>   "A devoted wife rules her husband with obedi-
>   ence."

A devoted wife who is obedient to her husband
wins over his heart with love, so that, subjected to
her, he does what she wants and she rules him with
obedience.

E.   Robert Cleaver, *A godly form of householde gov-
     ernment*[5] (London, 1598), pp. 81-84, 88-89, 156-
     161, 168-170, 201-202, 220-221, 225-226, 231-
     235.

   [Although Puritan writers had some earlier precedents
   to guide them, such as Heinrich Bullinger's *Der
   christlich Eestand,* their treatises on "household
   government" are essentially a new genre. Now less
   concerned with fighting Roman Catholic arguments in
   favor of celibacy, they turn their attention to a
   more profound discussion of the marriage relationship. Not only was marriage fully acceptable for
   all Christians, the home itself became the center of
   Christian life and service. This tendency has been
   labelled "the domestication of religion"[6] or, con-
   versely, "the spiritualization of the household."[7]
   Under whichever label, the effect was the same: to
   stress that, in spite of the husband's position of
   authority, Christian love and virtues are to govern
   all family relationships. The husband is under as
   many obligations to love and care for his wife as she
   is to obey him. Women are to be treated with respect
   as reasonable creatures and sharers in eternal life.

   For Robert Cleaver, however, there was, except in
   matters of eternal salvation, no equality between
   husband and wife. Their virtues and duties should
   differ, he being the benevolent provider, she the
   obedient, silent homemaker. In the matter of apparel,
   Cleaver envisions less equality than does Menno
   Simons (see above), allowing men their choice of apparel. Cleaver, on the other hand, finds more reasons
   for women to leave their homes, adding to Menno's
   list the right to perform works of charity and to
   accompany their husbands when needed. For the most
   part, however, women's activities are to be confined
   to the home.

   From the standpoint of the dignity and freedom of
   women, these activities have both favorable and un-

favorable aspects. On the one hand, to be a homemaker is to have a calling; to be diligent in this
calling is no less important for her than for her
husband in his calling. On the other hand, her female physiology determines her destiny, as is evident
in the discussion on breast-feeding: woman is by nature a childbearer and must not seek to deny this
role. In fairness, it should be added, however, that
in the relatively static society of the sixteenth
century, men were accorded only slightly more freedom
of occupational choice than women.]

Now seeing that God hath joined the wife to her
husband, as a helper, she must help him in the provision for her family, so much as lieth in her powers,
and is meet for her to do. And indeed, her industry
and wisdom may do so much herein, that though her husband should be much wanting in his duty, yet she might
hold in the goal. Thus many have done, and so Solomon
saith, the wise woman will do. "A wise woman buildeth
her house" (Pro. 14:1). But it is not every woman's
case, because that all are not wise, as she that Solomon speaketh of. This wise woman is elsewhere called
"a gracious woman" (Pro. 11:16) and "a virtuous woman"
(12:4) because many graces and virtues meet together
in her.

For she is to her

> Husband dutiful, faithful, and loving.
>
> Those of her family, wise and prudent.
>
> In her business, diligent and painful.
>
> To her neighbours, modest, humble, kind
> and quiet.

First, if she be not subject to her husband, to
let him rule all household, especially outward affairs; if she will make head against him, and seek
to have her own ways, there will be doing and undoing.
Things will go backward, the house will come to ruin;

for God will not bless where his ordinance is not
obeyed. This is allowable, that she may in modest
sort shew her mind, and a wise husband will not disdain to hear her advice, and follow it also, if it be
good. But when her way is not liked of, though it be
the best way, she may not thereupon set all at six
and seven, with "What should I labour and travail? I
see my husband taketh such ways, that he will bring
all to nothing." This were nothing else, but when she
seeth the house falling, to help pull it down faster.
Solomon saith: The wise woman buildeth her house much
more than doth she under-prop it, and hold it up,
that by her husband's undiscreet dealing, it be not
pulled down. She must not think herself freed from
duty, because he walketh not in his duty, but hold
her place, and labour for her part, to uphold all,
and so God will either bless the work of her hands,
to the maintenance of the house, or give her husband
more wisdom and care, or else give her a contented
mind with a low estate, which is great riches. One
point of subjection is to be content with such apparel and outward port as her husband's estate can
allow her. They fail in this, who by importunity
and disquietness wring from their husbands more than
he can well cut off his revenues, or gettings.

It is a part of unfaithfulness, secretly to pur-
loin and prowl from him, for to prank up her children, or herself, her house and chambers in bravery;
and besides, it is a close undermining of her house.

Love and peaceableness in the wife towards the
husband is available for the weal of the family, for
where they agree lovingly, there they counting the

good of the one, the benefit of the other, do jointly
watch against all such things in their family, as
might endamage it.

There the servants knowing, that in pleasing one,
they shall please both; and contrariwise, be careful
in all things, to deal well, whereas division in the
governour maketh partaking in the servants, and then
they care not for pleasing, but only that side which
they affect. And such kind of service is but smally
beneficial to thriving.

It can hardly be avoided, but there will be some
squaring and diversity between the man and his wife;
but they must labour to compose such matters privately
and quickly, that they grow not to breaches, for they
be dangerous to thrift.

Let there be therefore reasonings secretly between themselves, of such matters as might breed a
scar; but let them be soon ended, after the occasion
is offered, before the minds be much exasperated. Let
there be no hard words of either side, nor opening of
old matters. Let it be done privately between themselves, and not before children, or servants; for
they will not stick to carry tales, to please the
humors of the party, to whom they are most affected.
Besides, they will spy your infirmities, and grow to
a less regard of you, and they will blaze abroad such
matters, to your discredit.

And though nice dames think it an unseemly thing,
for them to soil their hands about any household matters, and therefore, if they do any thing, it is but
pricking of a clout. Yet the virtuous woman (as Pro.
31:17) "Girdeth her loins with strength, and strength-

eneth her arms." That is, she setteth herself pain-
fully about some work that is profitable, "for she
selleth it afterward" (verse 24). Yea, the particular work is described. "She seeketh wool and flax...
she putteth her hand to the wharve, and her hands
handle the spindle. She maketh carpets." The meaning
is, that she getteth some matter to work on, that she
may exercise herself and her family in, and it is not
some idle toy, to make the world gay withal, but some
matter of good use. "Her family is clothed with
double, and her husband is known in the gate." He is
so comely and trimly appareled, by her diligence at
home, that he is in regard among men, and known where
he goeth."

But what need such as can live by their lands,
to labor with their hands? What need had the woman
that Solomon speaketh of?

The conscience of doing good in the world should
draw them to do that which no need driveth them unto.
Remember that the virtuous woman "stretcheth out her
hands to the poor and needy (Pro. 31:20). She giveth
not of her husband's, she giveth of her own, she
found a way to do good without the hurt of her husband.
S. Paul requireth that women should array themselves
with good works, the comeliest ornament in the world,
if women had spiritual eyes to discern it. Dorcas in
the Acts (9:36) teacheth wives how to get this array,
for she made garments to clothe the naked and the
poor. Thus might women find how to set themselves a
work, though they could live of their own.

But such as have but a mean allowance, God thereby sheweth, that he will have them occupy themselves

in some honest labour, to keep them from idleness and
the evils that issue therefrom. They therefore must
labour, if not to sell cloth, as Solomon's woman did,
not to clothe the poor, as Dorcas did, yet to clothe
her family, that they may not care for the cold.

Let her avoid such occasions as may draw her
from her calling. She must shake off sloth, and love
of ease; she must avoid gossiping, further than the
law of good neighbourhood doth require. S. Paul would
have a woman a good housekeeper. The virtuous woman
is never so well, as when she is in the midst of her
affairs. She that much frequenteth meetings of gossips, seldom cometh better home. Some count it a
disgrace to come much abroad, lest they should be
counted gossips, which name is become odious; but
they must have tatlers come home to them, to bring
them news, and to hold them in a tale, lest they
should be thought to be idle without a cause. They
perceive not how time runneth, nor how untowardly
their business goeth forward, while they sit idle.
They knew not, that great tale-bringers be as great
carriers, and that such make their gain of carrying,
and recarrying. The wise woman will be wary, whom
she admitteth into her house, to sit long there,
knowing that their occupation is but to mark and
carry.

So that a wife is called by God himself, an
helper, and not an impediment, or a necessary evil,
as some unadvisedly do say. And as other some say:
"It is better to bury a wife, than to marry one."

Again, if we could be without women, we should
be without great troubles. These and such like

sayings, tending to the dispraise of women, some ma-
liciously, and undiscreetly, do vomit out, contrary
to the mind of the holy Ghost, who saith, that she
was ordained as a *helper*, and not a hinderer. And
if they be otherwise, it is for the most part,
through the fault, and want of discretion, and lack
of good government in the husband. For married folks,
for two eyes have four and for two hands, as many
more; which being joined together, they may the more
easily dispatch their handy business, and household
affairs. For like as a man having one hand, or one
foot, if by any means he get himself another, may
thereby the more easily lay hold on what he listeth,
or go whither he will; even so, he that hath married
a wife shall more easily enjoy the healthful pleas-
ures, and profitable commodities of this present life.
For in trouble, the one is a comfort to the other; in
adversity, the one a refreshing unto the other; yea,
and in all their life, the one is a help and succour
to the other.

Most true it is, that women are as men are reasonable creatures, and have flexible wits, both to
good and evil, the which with use, discretion, and
good counsel, may be altered and turned. And although there be some evil and lewd women, yet that
doth no more prove the malice of their nature, than
of men, and therefore the more ridiculous and foolish
are they, that have inveighed against the whole sex
for a few evil, and have not with like fury, vituper-
ated and dispraised all mankind, because part of them
are thieves, murderers, and such like wicked livers.

But the marriage and company of the husband and

wife is made amiable, sweet, and comfortable, by
these five means: by godliness, virtue, mutual for-
bearing, mutual love, and by dutifulness performed
busily and godly on both sides....

Now we will (through God his assistance) say
something concerning the three several points contained in this duty....

1. The first whereof is, That the husband must
live with his wife according to knowledge.

This point of doctrine is most plainly proved by
the Apostle Peter, where he saith: "Ye husbands,
dwell with your wives as men of knowledge, giving
honor unto the woman, as unto the weaker vessel, even
as they which are heirs together of the grace of life,
that your prayers be not interrupted." Whereby he
teacheth the husband his duty, to wit, that the more
understanding and wisdom God hath indued him with,
the more wisely and circumspectly he ought to behave
himself, in bearing those discommodities, which
through his wife's weakness, oftentimes cause some
jar and dislike one to the other.

Nevertheless, though she be by nature weaker
than he, yet she is an excellent instrument for him,
made to far most excellent uses; whereupon it followeth, that she is not therefore to be neglected, because she is weak, but on the contrary part, she
ought to be so much the more cared for.

Like as a vessel, the weaker it is, the more it
is to be favoured and spared, if we will have it to
continue; even so a wife, because of her infirmities,
is so much the more to be born withal of her husband
(I Pet. 3:7).

And for so much, as the husband and wife are
equal, in that which is the chiefest, that is to say,
if that gracious and free benefit, whereby they have
everlasting life given them, which otherwise are un-
equal, as touching the governance and conversation at
home, and therefore she is not to be despised, although
she be weak.

And besides, brawlings and chidings must be es-
chewed and cast away, because they hinder prayers, and
the whole service of God, whereunto both the husband
and the wife are equally called.

The best rule that a man may hold and practice
with his wife, to guard and govern her, is to admonish
her often, and to give her good instructions, to repre-
hend her seldom, never to lay violent hands on her;
but if she be good and dutiful, to favour her, to the
end she may continue so, and if she be shrewish and
wayward, mildly to suffer her, to the end that she
wax not worse. But some husbands be of so foul a nature, and so unpleasant in their behavior, that they
can hardly be loved, no not of their wives, their
countenance is so louring, their company so currish,
that they seem angry even when they be best pleased.
They cannot speak fair, scarce will they laugh, when
their wives laugh upon them; a man would say, they
were born in an angry hour.

This is also a duty not to be forgotten, namely,
that husbands be diligent and careful to make provision for their houses, to clothe their wives decent-
ly, to bring up their children virtuously, and to pay
their servants duly: because that in voluntary matters, men may be negligent, but the necessities of

their house, do neither suffer negligence, or forget-
fulness. The duty of the husband is to get goods;
and of the wife, to gather them together, and save
them. The duty of the husband is to travel abroad to
seek living, and the wife's duty is to keep the house.
The duty of the husband is to get money and provision;
and of the wife, not vainly to spend it. The duty of
the husband is to deal with many men; and of the wife,
to talk with few. The duty of the husband is to be
intermeddling; and of the wife, to be solitary and
withdrawn. The duty of the man is to be skillful in
talk; and of the wife, to boast of silence. The duty
of the husband is to be a giver; and of the wife, to
be a saver. The duty of the man is to apparel himself as he may; and of the woman, as it becometh her.
The duty of the husband is to be Lord of all; and of
the wife, to give account of all. The duty of the
husband is to dispatch all things without door;* and
of the wife, to oversee and give order for all things
within the house. How where the husband and wife
performeth these duties in their house, we may call
it a college of quietness; the house wherein these
are neglected, we may term it a hell.

It is to be noted, and noted again, that as the
provision of household dependeth only on the husband,
even so the honour of all dependeth only on the woman;
in such sort, that there is no honour within the
house, longer than a man's wife is honourable. And
therefore the Apostle calleth the woman, "The glory
of the man." But here it must be noted and remembered,

---

*Without door = outside the home.

that we do not intitle honourable to such, as be only beautiful, comely of face, of gentility, of comely personage, and a good housewife, but only, of her that is virtuous, honest of life, temperate and advised in her speech.

A wise husband, and one that seeketh to live in quiet with his wife, must observe these three rules: often to admonish; seldom to reprove; and never to smite her. Let the husband also remember, that the infirmities of his wife must be either taken away, or born withal. So that he that can take them quite away, maketh his wife far more commodious and fit for his purpose; and he that can bear with them, maketh himself better, and more virtuous.

The husband is also to understand, that as God created the woman, not of the head, and so equal in authority with her husband: so also he created her not of Adam's foot, that she should be trodden down and despised, but he took her out of the rib, that she might walk jointly with him, under the conduct and government of her head.

And in that respect, the husband is not to command his wife in manner, as the Master his servant, but as the soul doth the body, as being conjoined in like affection and good will. For as the soul in governing the body, tendeth to the benefit and commodity of the same: so ought the dominion and commandment of the husband over his wife, to tend to rejoice and content her.

* * *

So much is the wife's will subject to her husband: yet it is not meant, that the wife should not employ her knowledge and discretion, which God hath given her, in the help, and for the good of her husband. But always it must be with condition to submit herself unto him, acknowledging him to be her head, that finally they may so agree in one, as the conjunction of marriage doth require. Yet as when in a lute, or other musical instrument, two strings concurring in one tune, the sound nevertheless is imputed to the strongest and highest: so in a well ordered household, there must be a communication, and consent of counsel and will, between the husband and the wife: yet such, as the counsel and commandment may rest in the husband.

True it is, that some women are wiser and more discreet, than their husbands. As Abigail the wife of Nabal, and others. Whereupon Solomon saith: "A wise woman buildeth up the house, and blessed is the man, that hath a discreet wife." Yet still a great part of the discretion of such women, shall rest in acknowledging their husbands to be their heads, and so using the graces that they have received of the Lord, that their husbands may be honoured, not contemned, neither of them, nor of others, which falleth out contrary, when the wife will seem wiser than her husband.

Moreover, a modest and chaste woman that loveth her husband, must also love her house, as remembering, that the husband that loveth his wife, cannot so well like of the sight of any tapestry, as to see his wife in his house. For the woman that gaddeth from house to house, to prate, confoundeth her self, her husband,

and her family (Tit. 2:5). But there are four reasons, why the woman is to go abroad. First, to come
to holy meetings, according to the duty of godliness.
The second, to visit such as stand in need, as the
duty of love and charity do require. The third, for
employment and provision in household affairs committed to her charge. And lastly, with her husband,
when he shall require her (Genes. 20:1.etc.)

The evil and unquiet life, that some women have,
and pass with their husbands, is not so much for that
they commit with, and in their persons, as it is for
that they speak with their tongues. If the wife
would keep silence, when her husband beginneth to
chide, he should not have so unquiet dinners, neither
she the worse supper: which surely is not so, for at
the same time, that the husband beginneth to utter
his grief, the wife then beginneth to scold and chafe.
Whereof doth follow, that now and then most unnatural-
ly they come to handy grips, more beastlike than
christianlike, which their so doing, is both a great
shame, and a foul discredit to them both.

The best means therefore, that a wife can use to
obtain and maintain the love and good liking of her
husband, is to be silent, obedient, peaceable, patient, studious to appease his choler, if he be angry,
painful and diligent in looking to her business, to be
solitary and honest. The chief and special cause,
why most women do fail, in not performing this duty
to their husbands, is, because they be ignorant of
the word of God, which teacheth the same, and all
other duties; and therefore their souls and consciences, not being brought into subjection to God
and his word, they can never until then, yield and

perform true subjection and obedience to their husbands, and behave themselves so every way, as christian wives are in duty bound to do.

Amongst the particular duties, that a christian
wife ought to perform in her family, this is one:
namely, that it belongeth to her, to nurse her own
children, which to omit, and to put them forth to
nursing, is both against the law of nature, and also
against the will of God. Besides, it is hurtful both
for the child's body, and also for his wit; and lastly, it is hurtful to the mother herself, and is an
occasion, that she fall into much sickness thereby.

First, nature giveth milk to the woman, for none
other end, but that she should bestow it upon her
child. We see by experience, that every beast, and
every fowl, is nourished and bred of the same, that
did bear it; only some women love to be mothers, but
not nurses. And as every tree doth cherish and nourish, that which it bringeth forth: even so also, it
becometh natural mothers, to nourish their children
with their own milk.

2. Secondly, the examples of the scriptures are
many, that prove this. As Sarah, who nursed Isaac,
though she were a Princess, and therefore able enough
to have had others to have taken that pains: as also
having been a beautiful woman, even in old age, being of great years, yet she herself nurseth and giveth suck to her son.

Also Anna, whom the holy Ghost hath left it recorded, as a commendation unto her, for that she
nursed her own son Samuel. So when God chose a nurse
for Moses, he led the hand-maid of Pharoah's daughter

to his mother, as though God would have none to nurse
him, but his mother. Likewise after, when the Son of
God was born, his father thought none fit to be his
nurse, but the virgin his mother. It is a commendation of a good woman, and set down in the first place,
as a principal good work in a widow, that is well reported of, if she have nursed her children.

And therefore such as refuse thus to do, may
well and fitly be called nice and unnatural mothers;
yea, in so doing they make themselves but half-mothers,
and so break the holy bond of nature, in locking up
her breast from her child, and delivering it forth
like the cuckoo, to be hatched in the sparrow's nest.

3. Again, the children's bodies be commonly so
affected, as the milk is, which they receive. Now,
if the nurse be of an evil complexion, and as she is
affected in her body, or in her mind, or have some
hid disease, the child sucking of her breast, must
need take part with her. And if that be true, which
the learned do say, that the temperature of the mind,
follows the constitution of the body, needs must it
be, that if the nurse be of a naughty nature, the
child must take thereafter. Yet if it be, that the
nurse be of a good complexion, of an honest behavior:
(whereas contrariwise, maidens that have made a scape,*
are commonly called to be nurses) yet can it not be,
but that the mother's milk should be much more natural for the child, than the milk of a stranger.

As by experience, let a man be long accustomed
to one kind of drink, if the same man change his air,

---

*Scape = a breach of morals.

and his drink, he is like to mislike it. As the eggs
of a hen are altered under a hawk. Nevertheless,
such women, as be oppressed with infirmities, diseases,
want of milk, or other just and lawful causes, are to
be dispensed withal, but whose breasts have this perpetual drought; forsooth it is like the gout, no beg-
gars may have it, but citizens or gentlewomen.   In the
9. of Hosea. verse 14. dry breasts are named for a
curse. What a lamentable hap have gentlewomen, to
light upon this curse, more than other? Sure if their
breasts be dry (as they say) they should fast and pray
together, that this curse might be removed from them.

     4. And lastly, that it is hurtful to the mothers
themselves, both physicians can tell, and some women
full oft have felt, how they have been troubled with
sore breasts, besides other diseases, that happen to
them, through plenty of milk.

     The wife is further to remember, that God hath
given her two breasts, not that she should employ and
use them for a shew, or of ostentation, but in the
service of God, and to be a help to her husband, in
suckling the child common to them both. Experience
teacheth, that God converteth her blood into the milk,
wherewith the child is nursed in the mother's womb.
he bringeth it into the breasts, furnished with nip-
ples, convenient to minister the warm milk unto the
child, whom he indueth with industry, to draw out the
milk for his own sustenance.

     The woman therefore, that can suckle her child,
and doth it not, but refuseth this office and duty of
a mother, declareth herself to be very unthankful to
God, and (as it were) forsaketh and contemneth the

fruit of her womb. And therefore the brute breasts
lying upon the ground, and granting not one nipple or
two, but six or seven, to their young ones, shall rise
in judgment against these dainty half-mothers, who for
fear of wrinkling of their faces, or to avoid some
small labor, do refuse this so necessary a duty of a
mother due to their children.

F.　William Gouge, *Of Domesticall Duties,* Eight
Treatises (London, 1622), pp. 4-7, 26-7, 128,
211, 219, 256-260, 268-273, 299, 336, 390,
396-399.

[William Gouge (1578-1653) followed in the same general
tradition as Robert Cleaver. For such writers the subjection of women was simply one aspect of scriptural
obedience. The text on which Gouge's commentary is
based, Ephesians 5:21-25, could hardly be more forth-
right in its command of wifely submission. Yet in his
exegesis, Gouge, utilizing his early proficiency in
dialectic, managed to soften the harshness of the in-
junction by distinguishing various forms of submission
and treating them as different types of Christian love.
His positions on adultery and common duties indicate a
desire to bestow on women a certain measure of equality.
Nevertheless, he aroused the opposition of some women
in his congregation by his refusal to allow women joint
property rights with their husbands. In this he was no
less conservative than his time and in fact appealed
primarily to the law of the land as the support for
his position. Yet to demonstrate that he was not "an
hater of women," he emphasized in this introduction to
his book that the restrictions on a wife's property
rights were not to apply "to the proper goods of a
wife no nor overstrictly to such goods as are set
apart for the use of the family, nor to extraordinary
cases, nor always to an express consent, nor to the
consent of such husbands as are impotent or far and
long absent."[8] Later in the century Richard Baxter
(see below) came out more directly in favor of considering the wife a joint proprietor with the husband.
This right, he felt, was already given in the words of
the marriage ceremony, "with all my worldly goods I
thee endow."[9]]

It is a general mutual duty appertaining to all
Christians, to submit themselves one to another. For
this precept is as general as any of the former, belonging to all sorts and degrees whatsoever; and so
much doth this word "one another" imply: in which extent the Apostle in another place exhorteth to "serve
one another": and again, "every man to seek another's
wealth."

Concerning *inferiours,* it is without question
clear, that they ought to submit themselves to their
superiours; yea, concerning *equals* no great question
can be made, but they in giving honour must go one
before another, and so submit themselves. But concerning *superiours,* just question may be made, whether
it be a duty required of them to submit themselves to
their inferiours.

To resolve this doubt, we must first distinguish
betwixt subjection of *reverence,* and subjection of
service.

Subjection of reverence is that whereby one tes-
tifieth an eminency and superiority in them whom he
reverenceth, and that in speech, by giving them
titles of honour; or in gesture, by some kind of
obeisance; or in action, by a ready obeying of their
commandment. This is proper to inferiours.

Subjection of service is that whereby one in his
place is ready to do what good he can to another.
This is common to all Christians: a duty which even
superiours owe to inferiours, according to the forenamed extent of this word "one another": in which respect even the highest governour on earth is called
a minister, for the good of such as are under him.

Secondly, we must put difference betwixt the
work itself and the *manner* of doing it. That work
which in itself is a work of superiority and authority, in the manner of doing it may be a work of submission, viz. if it be done in humility and meekness
of mind. The magistrate by ruling with meekness and
humility, submitteth himself to his subject. In this
respect the Apostle exhorteth that "nothing" (no not
the highest and greatest works that can be) "be done
in vain-glory, but in meekness"....

Be not high-minded, nor swell against another,
though in outward estate some may be higher than
other, yet "in Christ all are one whether bond or
free": all "members of one and the same body." Now
consider the mutual affection (as I may so speak) of
the members of a natural body one towards another:
not any one of them will puff itself up, and rise
against the other: the head which is the highest and
of greatest honour will submit itself to the feet in
performing the duty of an head, as well as the feet
to the head in performing their duty; so all other
parts. Neither is it hereby implied that they which
are in place of dignity and authority should forget
or relinquish their place, dignity, or authority, and
become as inferiours under authority, no more than the
head doth: for the head in submitting itself doth
not go upon the ground and bear the body, as the feet;
but it submitteth itself by directing and governing
the other parts, and that with all the humility,
meekness, and gentleness that it can. So must all
superiours: much more must equals and inferiours
learn with humility, and meekness, without scorn or

disdain, to perform their duty.... We know that it is
unnatural, and unbeseeming the head to scorn the feet,
and to swell against them, but more than monstrous
for one hand to scorn another. What shall we then
say if the feet swell against the head?...

Ephes. 5:22: "Wives submit yourselves unto
your own husbands, as unto the Lord."

The word by which the Apostle hath noted out the
duties of wives, is of the middle voice, and may be
translated passively as many have done, or actively
as our English doth ("submit yourselves") and that
most fitly: for there is a double subjection.

1. A *necessary* subjection: which is the subjection of *order*.

2. A *voluntary* subjection: which is the subjection of *duty*.

The necessary subjection is that degree of in-
feriority, wherein God hath placed all inferiours,
and whereby he hath subjected them to their superiours,
that is, set them in a lower rank. By virtue thereof,
though inferiours seek to exalt themselves above their
superiours, yet are they subject unto them, their ambition doth not take away that order which God hath
established. A wife is in an inferiour degree, though
she domineer never so much over her husband.

The *voluntary* subjection is that dutiful respect which inferiours carry towards those whom God
hath set over them: whereby they manifest a willing-
ness to yield to that order which God hath established.
Because God hath placed them under their superiours,
they will in all duty manifest that subjection which
their place requireth.

Because it is a duty which is here required, the
voluntary subjection must needs be here meant; and to
express so much, it is thus set down, "submit yourselves."

Though the same word be here used that was in
the former verse, yet it is restrained to a narrower
compass, namely to *subjection of reverence*.

Here learn that to necessary subjection, must
voluntary subjection be added: that is, duty must be
performed according to that order and degree wherein
God hath set us. This is to make a virtue of necessity.

Ephes. 5:33: "Nevertheless, let every one of
you in particular so love his wife, even as himself:
and the wife see that she reverence her husband."

The Apostle having made a large digression about
the mutual relation betwixt Christ and the Church,
whom he propounded as patterns to husbands and wives,
he now returneth to the main post intended, namely to
the duties of husbands and wives; and so much doth
the first particle imply ("nevertheless") as if he had
thus said, "Though I have a little digressed into
the mystery of the union of Christ and the Church,
yet nevertheless do ye, o husbands and wives, call to
mind that which I principally aimed at, even your
duties."

This verse then containeth a conclusion of the
Apostle's discourse, concerning the duties of husbands and wives.

Two points are especially noted therein.

1. A declaration of their several and distinct
duties.

2. A direction to apply their own proper duties
each of them to themselves.

Their distinct duties are noted in two words,

Love.
Fear.

These two, as they are distinct duties in themselves, so are they also common conditions which must
be annexed to all other duties. *Love* as sugar to
sweeten the duties of authority which appertain to an
husband. *Fear* as salt to season all the duties of
subjection which appertain to a wife. The Apostle
therefore hath set them down as two marks for husbands and wives to aim at in every thing wherein they
have to deal one with the other.

Let now the admirers and praisers of a single
estate bring forth all their reasons, and put them
in the other school against marriage. If these two
be duly poised, and rightly weighed, we shall find
single life too light to be compared with honest marriage. All that can be said for the single estate,
is grounded upon accidental occasions. Saint Paul,
who of all the pen-men of holy Scripture hath spoken
most for it, draweth all his commendations to the
head of expediency, and restraineth all unto present
necessity.

Object. He useth these words "good," and "better."

Answ. Those words have relation not to virtue,
but to expediency; neither are they spoken in opposition to vice and sin, for then would it follow,
that to marry (which is God's ordinance, and honourable in all) were evil and sinful: which is to re-

vive that ancient heresy, that marriage is of the
devil. Of old they who have called lawful marriage
a defilement, have been said to have the apostate
dragon dwelling in them. But the Apostle styleth that
good, which is commodious, and that *better* which is
more expedient: and yet not simply more expedient,
but to some persons at some times. For if any have
not the gift of continency, it is not only commodious
or more expedient that they marry, but also absolute-
ly necessary. They are commanded so to do (I Cor.
7:9). Yet on the other side, if any have the gift of
continency, they are not simply bound from marriage;
there be other occasions, beside avoiding fornication,
to move them to marry. It is therefore truly said
that "Virginity is not commanded, but advised unto.
We have no precept for it, but leave it to the power
of them that have that power." So far forth as men
and women see just occasion of abstaining from marriage (being at least able so to do) they are by the
Apostle persuaded to use their liberty and keep themselves free. But all the occasions which move them
to remain single arise from the weakness and wickedness of men. Their wickedness who raise troubles
against others, their weakness who suffer themselves
to be disquieted and too much distracted with affairs
of the family, care for wife, children, and the like.
Were it not for the wickedness of some, and weakness
of others, to please an husband or a wife would be
no hindrance to pleasing of the Lord. If therefore
man had stood in his entire and innocent estate, no
such wickedness or weakness had seized upon him; and
then in no respect could the single estate have been

preferred before the married. But since the fall,
virginity (where it is given) may be of good use; and
therefore the Church doth give due honour both to virginity and marriage.

   Quest. Is the bond of marriage as much violated
on the man's part when he committeth adultery as on
the woman's when she doth so?

   Answ. Though the ancient Romans and Canonists
have aggravated the woman's fault in this kind far
above the man's, and given the man more privileges
than the woman, yet I see not how that difference in
the sin can stand with the tenour of God's word. I
deny not but that more inconveniences may follow upon
the woman's default than upon the man's: as, greater
infamy before men, worse disturbance of the family,
more mistaking of legitimate, or illegitimate children, with the like. The man cannot so well know
which be his own children, as the woman; he may take
base children to be his own, and so cast the inheri-
tance upon them; and suspect his own to be basely
born, and so deprive them of their patrimony. But
the woman is freed from all such mistakings. Yet in
regard of the breach of wedlock, and transgression
against God, the sin of either party is alike. God's
word maketh no disparity betwixt them. At the beginning God said of them both, "they two shall be one
flesh": not the woman only with the man, but the man
also with the woman is made "one flesh." Their power
also over one another in this respect is alike. If
on just occasion they abstain, it must be with mutual
consent. If the husband leave his wife, she is as
free, as he should be, if she left him. Accordingly

the punishment which by God's law was to be inflicted
on adulterers is the same, whether the man or the woman be the delinquent (Deut. 22:22). If difference
be made, it is meet that adulterous husbands be so
much the more severely punished, by how much the more
it appertaineth to them to excel in virtue, and to
govern their wives by example.

Hitherto I have delivered such common duties as
mutual respect the husband and wife, and are to be
performed of each to other. There are other common
duties which they are both jointly bound to perform
to other persons: and those either *members* of the
family, or *strangers* coming to the family.

Concerning the *members* of the family, though
there be some peculiar duties belonging to the master,
and some to the mistress, some to the father, and
some to the mother, of which we shall speak in their
due place; yet in general the government of the family, and the several members thereof belongeth to the
husband and wife both (if at least they have a family)
and a joint common duty it is to be helpful one to
another therein....

Object. "A woman is not to teach, nor to usurp
authority over the man."

Answ. 1. That branch of teaching hath respect
to public assemblies, and Churches, in which she may
not teach: but not to private families, in which she
may, and ought to teach: for Bathshebah taught Solomon. When Apollos was brought to the house of Aquila,
Priscilla the wife of Aquila did help to expound to
Apollos the way of God more perfectly.

2. The other branch concerning authority,

hath not reference to the inferiour members in the
family, over which the wife of an household governour
hath authority, but only to the husband, over whom if
she take any authority, she usurpeth it. Therefore
neither this place of Scripture, nor any other doth
exclude the wife, being jointly considered with the
husband, to rule and govern those in the family which
are under them both.

    2. Object. This joint government of the wife
doth much impair the dignity and authority of the
husband.

    Answ. Nothing less: for she is subordinate
to her husband, and must so rule others as she be
subject to her husband, and not command any thing
against his command (provided that his command be not
against the Lord, and his word.) We see that in all
estates the king or highest governour hath other
magistrates under him, who have a command over the
subjects, and yet thereby the king's supreme authority is no whit impaired, but rather the better established, and he the more honoured. So it is in a
family.... Besides there are many things in well governing a family more fit for one to meddle withal
than for the other: as for the husband to meddle with
the great and weighty affairs of the family (as performing God's worship, appointing and settling good
orders, providing convenient house-room, and other
necessaries for the family; keeping children when
they grow great, or wax stubborn, in awe; ruling men
servants, with the like). And for the wife to meddle
with some less, but very needful matters, as nourish-
ing and instructing children when they are young,

adorning the house, ordering the provision brought into the house, ruling maid servants, with the like. Yea further, as the man especially is to perform the very actions of prayer, reading the word, catechizing, and other like duties in the family, so the wife may be a great help in putting her husband in mind both of the duty itself, and of the time of performing it, and encouraging him to do it, in gathering the family together, and exhorting them to be forward, in making herself an example to the rest by her diligent and reverend attention, in oft urging and pressing to her children and servants such points of instruction as her husband hath taught; yea, in praying, reading, teaching, and performing like exercises herself, so far as she is able, when her husband is absent, or negligent and careless, and will not himself do them; or it may be, is not able to do them; or if she perform them not herself, in getting some other to perform them....

The first point to be handled in the treatise of wives' particular duties is the general matter of all (*subjection*) under which all other particulars are comprised, for it hath as large an extent as that honour which is required in the first commandment, being applied to wives. When first the Lord declared unto woman her duty, he set it down under this phrase, "Thy desire shall be subject to thine husband" (Gen. 3:16).

Object. That was a punishment inflicted on her for her transgression?

Answ. And a law too, for trial of her obedience, which if it be not observed, her nature will be more

depraved, and her fault more increased. Besides, we
cannot but think that the woman was made before the
fall, that the man might rule over her. Upon this
ground the Prophets and Apostles have oft urged the
same. Sarah is commended for this, that she was *subject* to her husband (I Pet. 3:6). Hereby the holy
Ghost would teach wives, that *subjection* ought to be
as salt to season every duty which they perform to
their husband. Their very opinion, affection, speech,
action, and all that concerneth the husband, must
savour of *subjection*. Contrary is the disposition of
many wives, whom ambition hath tainted and corrupted
within and without: they cannot endure to hear of
subjection: they imagine that they are made slaves
thereby. But I hope partly by that which hath been
before delivered concerning those common duties which
man and wife do mutually owe each to other, and partly
by the particulars which under this general are comprised, but most especially by the duties which the
husband in particular oweth to his wife, it will evi-
dently appear, that this *subjection* is no servitude.
But were it more than it is, seeing God requireth subjection of a wife to her husband, the wife is bound to
yield it. And good reason it is that she who first
drew man into sin, should be now subject to him, lest
by the like womanish weakness she fall again....

Contrary to the forenamed subjection is the
opinion of many wives, who think themselves every way
as good as their husbands, and no way inferiour to
them.

The reason whereof seemeth to be that small in-
equality which is betwixt the husband and the wife:

for of all degrees wherein there is any difference betwixt person and person, there is the least disparity
betwixt man and wife. Though the man be as the head,
yet is the woman as the heart, which is the most excellent part of the body next the head, far more excellent than any other member under the head, and almost equal to the head in many respects, and as necessary as the head. As an evidence, that a wife is to
man as the heart to the head, she was at her first
creation taken out of the side of man where his heart
lieth; and though the woman was at first "of the man"
created out of his side, yet "is the man also by the
woman." Ever since the first creation man hath been
born and brought forth out of the woman's womb: so as
"neither the man is without the woman, nor the woman
without the man": yea, "as the wife hath not power of
her own body, but the husband, so the husband hath not
power of his own body, but the wife." They are also
"heirs together of the grace of life." Besides, wives
are mothers of the same children, whereof their husbands are fathers (for God said to both, "multiply
and increase") and mistresses of the same servants
whereof they are masters (for Sarah is called mistress) and in many other respects there is a common
equity betwixt husbands and wives; whence many wives
gather that in all things there ought to be a mutual
equality.... Though there seem to be never so little
disparity, yet God having so expressly appointed subjection, it ought to be acknowledged; and though husband and wife may mutually serve one another through
love: yet the Apostle suffereth not a woman to rule
over the man.

....The truth and life of that general acknowl-
edgement of husband's honour, consisteth in the particular application thereof unto their *own* proper husbands.

The next duty therefore is, that wives acknowledge their *own* husbands, even those to whom by God's
providence they are joined in marriage, to be worthy
of an husband's honour, and to be their superiour;
thus much the Apostle intendeth by that particle of
restraint (*own*) which he useth very often. So likewise doth S. Peter, exhorting wives to be in subjection to their *own* husbands; and hereunto restraining
the commendation of the ancient good wives, that they
were in subjection to their *own* husbands.

Object. What if a man of mean place be married
to a woman of eminent place, or a servant be married
to his mistress, or an aged woman to a youth, must
such a wife acknowledge such an husband her superiour?

Answ. Yea verily: for in giving herself to be
his wife, and taking him to be her husband, she ad-
vanceth him above herself, and subjecteth herself
unto him. It booteth nothing what either of them
were before marriage: by virtue of the matrimonial
bond the husband is made the head of his wife, though
the husband were before marriage a very beggar, and
of mean parentage, and the wife very wealthy and of
a noble stock; or though he were her prentice, or
bondslave; which also holdeth in the case betwixt an
aged woman and a youth: for the Scripture hath made
no exception in any of those cases.

2. Object. But what if a man of lewd and
beastly conditions, as a drunkard, a glutton, a pro-

fane swaggerer, an impious swearer, and blasphemer,
be married to a wise, sober, religious matron, must
she account him her superiour, and worthy of an husband's honour?

    <u>Answ</u>. Surely she must. For the evil quality
and disposition of his heart and life, doth not deprive a man of that civil honour which God hath given
unto him. Though a husband in regard of evil qualities may carry the image of the devil, yet in regard
of his place and office he beareth the image of
God....

    *Of the reasons against a wife's property in the
common goods of the family.*
    2. <u>Answ</u>. It may be safely denied that a wife
hath a property in the common goods of the family
whereof she is no heir, for property in goods is a
civil matter, and to be limited according to the law
of man under which we live. Where the law, or custom of the place, make all the children coheirs, all
have an equal right to their several parts; where
the eldest only is made heir, he hath a right to all;
but neither the law of nations, nor of the land where
we live give the wife a property. By the common law
marriage is a gift of all the goods and chattels personal of the wife to her husband, so that no kind of
property in the same remaineth in her. And all personal goods and chattels during marriage given to the
wife are presently *ipso facto* transferred (as to the
property of them) to the husband. So that by our law
she is so far from gaining any property by her marriage in her husband's goods, as she loseth all the
property she formerly had in her own goods. Yea her

necessary apparel is not hers in property. While she
remaineth a wife she is (to use the law-phrase) *under
covert baron*. She can neither let, sell, alien, give,
nor otherwise of right make any thing away, no nor
yet make a will so to dispose any goods while her husband liveth without his consent: which yet an husband
may while his wife liveth, and that without or against
her consent.

   Object. The law states a wife in great part of
the husband's goods, providing for her jointer or
thirds which the husband cannot make away without her
consent.

   Answ. This provision is only for the time of
her widowhood in case she overlive him; but for the
time that she remaineth his wife he may make away all,
and she can recover none, till he be dead.

   Object. This restraint of wives is only in the
court of men.

   Answ. Seeing it is not against the law of God,
it must hold good in the court of conscience. Nay it
is agreeable to the law of God and grounded thereupon.

   For (to omit the proofs before alleged) what
might be the reason that the daughters of Zelophehad,
who were heirs to their father, were forbidden to
marry out of their father's tribe, and that a law
was made that no daughters that possessed any inheri-
tance should marry out of their father's tribe, but
because all that a woman had before marriage, passed
upon the husband and became his by virtue of marriage?
This also for that purpose is by some not unfitly,
nor without probability noted, that it is the common
phrase of Scripture to term husbands (but not wives)

rich, implying thereby that riches by a property appertain to husbands: yea usually in Scripture goods and lands are said to be the husband's.

Of the extent of a wife's obedience.

The extent of a wife's subjection (which remaineth now to be handled) is set down under these general terms (in *every* thing) which are not so generally to be taken as if they admitted no restraint or limitation, for then would they contradict such cautions as these, "in the fear of the Lord," "as to the Lord," "in the Lord." For man is so corrupt by nature, and of so perverse a disposition, that oft he willeth and commandeth that which is contrary to God's will and commandment: which when he doth, that Christian principle laid down as a ruled case by the Apostle must take place, "we ought rather to obey God than men."

Quest. Why then is this extent laid down in such general terms?

Answ. 1. To teach wives that it is not sufficient for them to obey their husbands in some things, as they themselves think meet, but in all things whatsoever they be wherein the husband by virtue of his superiority and authority hath power to command his wife. Thus this general extent excludeth not God's will, but the wife's will. She may do nothing against God's will; but many things must she do against her own will if her husband require her.

2. To shew that the husband's authority and power is very large: it hath no restraint but God's contrary command, whereof if a wife be not assured, she must yield to her husband's will.

Of husbands beating their wives.

<u>Quest</u>. May not then an husband beat his wife?

<u>Answ</u>. With submission to better judgments, I
think he may not: my reasons are these:

  1. There is no warrant throughout the
whole Scripture by precept, or example for it: which
argument though it be negative, yet for the point in
hand is a forceable argument in two respects. 1. Because the Scripture hath so plentifully and particularly declared the several duties of husbands and
wives: and yet hath delivered nothing concerning an
husband's striking and beating his wife. 2. Because
it hath also plentifully and particularly spoken of
all such as are to correct, and of their manner of
correcting, and of their bearing correction who are
to be corrected, and of the use they are to make
thereof; and yet not any thing at all concerning an
husband punishing, or a wife's bearing in this kind.
The Scripture being so silent in this point, we may
well infer that God hath not ranked wives among those
in the family who are to be corrected.

  2. That small disparity which (as I have
shewed) is betwixt man and wife, permitteth not so
high a power in an husband, and so low a servitude in
a wife, as for him to beat her. Can it be thought
reasonable that she who is the man's perpetual bed-
fellow, who hath power over his body, who is a joint
parent of the children, a joint governour of the family, should be beaten by his hands? (As they must
needs: for how can such a thing be done in the house
and they of the house know it not?) Can they respect
her as a mother, or a mistress who is under correction

as well as they?

      3. The near conjunction, and very union
that is betwixt man and wife suffereth not such dealing to pass betwixt them. The wife is as a man self,
"They two are one flesh." No man but a frantic, furious, desperate wretch will beat himself. Two sorts
of men are in Scripture noted to cut and lanch their
own flesh: idolaters, and the Baalites, and daemoniacs,
as he that was possessed with a legion of devils.
Such are they who beat their wives, either blinded in
their understanding, or possessed with a devil.

    Of an husband's provident care for his wife.

    In this provident care which an husband ought to
have of his wife, he will consider the $\left\{\begin{matrix}\text{Extent}\\\text{Continuance}\end{matrix}\right\}$
thereof.

    It ought to extend both to *herself,* and to
others.

    In regard of herself, to her $\left\{\begin{matrix}\text{Soul.}\\\text{Body.}\end{matrix}\right\}$

    For her *Soul,* means of spiritual edification
must be provided, and those both private and public.
Private means, are holy and religious exercises in
the house, as reading the word, prayer, catechising,
and such like; which being the spiritual food of the
soul are to be every day, as our bodily food, provided and used. An husband as a master of a family
must provide these for the good of his whole house;
but as an husband, in special for the good of his
wife: for to his wife, as well as to the whole house
he is a King, a Priest, and a Prophet....

    To the body also must an husband's provident
care of his wife extend: and that both in health and

sickness. In health by providing such things as are
needful to preserve health, as competent food, raiment,
and the like necessaries. Where the Prophet to aggra-
vate the misery of the people saith, "Seven women
shall take hold of one man," saying, "We will eat our
own bread, and wear our own apparel, only let us be
called by thy name," intimateth, that it was an husband's duty to provide bread and apparel, that is, all
necessaries for his wife. Which the law also implieth,
where it enjoineth him that taketh one wife upon another, not to diminish the food and raiment of the
former. In sickness such things are to be provided as
are needful either to recover her health, or to comfort, cherish and refresh her in her sickness.

G.   John Milton, *The Doctrine and Discipline of*
      Divorce Restor'd to the good of both Sexes
      (London, 1644), 7-9, 60-61.

      [Milton's treatise on divorce, perhaps the best known
      of this group of selections, is nevertheless one of the
      most difficult to evaluate. Widely regarded by both
      contemporaries and by later generations as revolution-
      ary, the work can also be viewed as no more than the
      logical development of previous Protestant and humanist
      discussions. One scholar has remarked, "...the truth
      is that it does not contain a single point which was
      not either previously advocated or actually in practice,
      although certain principles are emphasized more than
      they had been before."[10] Milton in fact stressed his
      lack of originality in an attempt to lend respectability
      to his ideas. Erasmus and Bucer, he noted, had already
      offered England the same ideas on divorce.[11] Indeed,
      Erasmus, presaging Milton's arguments, had included in-
      compatibility among the many impediments to marriage.
      Although sixteenth-century Protestants had not explicit-
      ly included this among the grounds for divorce, there
      was considerable emphasis on the social aspects of the
      marriage relationship. Calvin, for instance, in dis-
      cussing the Genesis passage which Milton here quotes,

had written against those who considered procreation
the sole purpose of marriage, calling Eve "the inseparable associate of [Adam's] life."[12] From this it
was only a short—though admittedly significant—step
to Milton's argument that, if marriage consists of companionship, there is no marriage where there is no companionship.

As far as women were concerned, however, Milton seems
to have been less positively inclined than some of his
predecessors. Although his subtitle indicates he was
writing for the "good of both sexes," his treatise,
written while soured by a bad marriage, seems to have
served in part as a male counter-offensive against
those who considered divorce mainly a protection for
women.]

For all sense and equity reclaims* that any Law
or Covenant how solemn or strait soever, either between God and man, or man and man, though of God's
joining, should bind against a prime and principal
scope of its own institution, and of both or either
party covenanting: neither can it be of force to engage a blameless creature to his own perpetual sorrow,
mistaken for his expected solace, without suffering
charity to step in and do a confessed good work of
parting those whom nothing holds together, but this
of God's joining, falsely supposed against the express end of his own ordinance. And what his chief
end was of creating woman to be joined with man, his
own instituting words declare, and are infallible to
inform us what is marriage, and what is no marriage,
unless we can think them set there to no purpose:
"It is not good," saith he, "that man should be
alone; I will make him a help meet for him." From
which words so plain, less cannot be concluded, nor

---

*Reclaims = cries out in protest, denies.

is by any learned interpreter, than that in God's intention a meet and happy conversation is the chiefest
and noblest end of marriage: for we find here no expression so necessarily implying carnal knowledge, as
this prevention of loneliness to the mind and spirit
of man. To this Fagius, Calvin, Pareus, Rivetus,[13]
as willingly and largely assent as can be wished.
And indeed it is a greater blessing from God, more
worthy so excellent a creature as man is, and a higher end to honour and sanctify the league or marriage,
whenas the solace and satisfaction of the mind is regarded as provided for before the sensitive pleasing
of the body. And with all generous persons married
thus it is, that where the mind and person pleases
aptly, there some unaccomplishment of the body's delight may be better born with, than when the mind
hangs off in an unclosing disproportion, though the
body be as it ought; for there all corporal delight
will soon become unsavoury and contemptible. And the
solitariness of man, which God had namely and principally ordered to prevent by marriage, hath no remedy, but lies under a worse condition than the lone-
liest single life; for in single life the absence
and remoteness of a helper might inure him to expect
his own comforts out of himself or to seek with hope;
but here the continual sight of his deluded thoughts
without cure, must needs be to him, if especially
his complexion incline him to melancholy, a daily
trouble and pain of loss in some degree like that
which reprobates feel. Lest therefore so noble a
creature as man should be shut up incurably under a
worse evil by an easy mistake in that ordinance which

God gave him to remedy a less evil, reaping to himself sorrow while he went to rid away solitariness,
it cannot avoid to be concluded, that if the woman be
naturally so of disposition, as will not help to re-
move, but help to increase that same God-forbidden
loneliness which will in time draw on with a general
discomfort and dejection of mind, not beseeming either
Christian profession or moral conversation, unprofitable and dangerous to the Commonwealth, when the household estate, out of which must flourish forth the
vigor and spirit of all public enterprizes, is so ill
contended and procured at home, and cannot be supported; such a marriage can be no marriage whereto the
most honest end is wanting: and the aggrieved person
shall do more manly, to be extraordinary and singular
in claiming the due right whereof he is frustrated,
than to piece up his lost contentment by visiting the
stews, or stepping to his neighbour's bed, which is
the common shift in this misfortune; or else by suffering his useful life to waste away, and be lost
under a secret affliction of an unconscionable size
to human strength. Against all which evil the mercy
of this Mosaic Law was graciously exhibited.

      Lastly, if divorce were granted, as Beza[14] and
others say, not for men, but to release afflicted
wives; certainly it is not only a dispensation, but
a most merciful Law: and why it should not yet be in
force, being wholly as needful, I know not what can
be in cause but senseless cruelty. But yet to say,
divorce was granted for relief of wives, rather than
husbands, is but weakly conjectured, and is manifest
the extreme shift of a huddled exposition. Whenas it

could not be found how hardness of heart should be
lessened by liberty of divorce, a fancy was devised
to hide the flaw by commenting that divorce was permitted only for the help of wives. Palpably uxorious!
Who can be ignorant that woman was created for man,
and not man for woman; and that a husband may be injured as insufferably in marriage as a wife. What an
injury is it after wedlock not to be beloved, what to
be slighted, what to be contended with in point of
houserule who shall be the head, not for any parity
of wisdom, for that were something reasonable, but
out of a female pride. "I suffer not" saith Paul,
"the woman to usurp authority over the man." If the
Apostle could not suffer it, into what mould is he
mortified that can? Solomon saith that "a bad wife
is to her husband, as rottenness to his bones, a continual dropping: better dwell in a corner of the
house top, or in the wilderness" than with such a
one (Prov. 12:4; 19:13; 21:9, 19). "Who so hideth her
hideth the wind, and one of the four mischiefs that
the earth cannot bear" (Prov. 27:16; 30:21-23). If
the Spirit of God wrote such aggravations as these,
and as may be guessed by these similitudes, counsels
the man rather to divorce than to live with such a
colleague, and yet on the other side expresses nothing
of the wife's suffering with a bad husband; is it not
most likely that God in his Law had more pity towards
man thus wedlocked, than towards the woman that was
created for another? The same Spirit relates to us
the course which the Medes and Persians took by occasion of Vashti, whose mere denial to come at her
husband's sending lost her the being Queen any longer,

and set up a wholesome Law, "that every man should
bear rule in his own house" (Esther 1:22). And the
divine relater shews us not the least sign of dis-
liking what was done; how should he if Moses long before was nothing less mindful of the honour and pre-
eminence due to man? So that to say divorce was
granted for woman rather than man, was but fondly in-
vented. Esteeming therefore to have asserted thus an
injured law of Moses from the unwarranted and guilty
name of a dispensation, to be again a most equal and
requisite law, we have the word of Christ himself,
that he came not to alter the least tittle of it; and
signifies no small displeasure against him that shall
teach to do so. On which relying, I shall not much
waver to affirm, that those words which are made to
intimate, as if they forbad all divorce but for adultery (though Moses have constituted otherwise) those
words taken circumscriptly, without regard to any
precedent law of Moses or attestation of Christ himself, or without care to preserve those his fundamental and superior laws of nature and charity, to
which all other ordinances give up their seals, are
as much against plain equity, and the mercy of religion, as those words of "Take, eat, this is my
body," elementally understood, are against nature
and sense.

And surely the restoring of this degraded law,
hath well recompensed the diligence was used, by en-
lightening us further to find out wherefore Christ
took off the Pharisees from alleging the law, and
referred them to the first institution, not condemning, altering, or abolishing this precept of divorce,

which is plainly moral, for that were against his
truth, his promise, and his prophetic office; but
knowing how fallaciously they had cited, and concealed
the particular and natural reason of the Law, that
they might justify any froward reason of their own,
he lets go that sophistry unconvinced, for that had
been to teach them else, which his purpose was not.
And since they had taken a liberty which the law
gave not, he amuses and repels their tempting pride
with a perfection of Paradise, which the law required
not; not thereby to oblige our performance to that
whereto the law never enjoined the fallen estate of
man; for if the first institution must make wedlock,
what ever happen, inseparable to us, it must make it
also as perfect, as meetly helpful, and as comfortable, as God promised it should be, at least in some
degree; otherwise it is not equal or proportionable
to the strength of man, that he should be reduced into such indissoluble bonds to his assured misery, if
all the other conditions of that covenant be manifest-
ly altered.

H.   Richard Baxter, *A Christian Directory: Or, A
      Summ of Practical Theologie, and Cases of
      Conscience* (London, 1673), pp. 480-482, 531,
      532.

      [Richard Baxter (1615-1691), one of the greatest
      Puritan ministers and theologians, wrote his im-
      mense volume entitled *A Christian Directory* after
      the 1662 Act of Uniformity forced him into the role
      of writer rather than preacher. The work was di-
      vided into four main parts: "Christian Ethicks, or
      private duties; Christian Oeconomicks, or Family
      Duties; Christian Ecclesiasticks, or Church Duties;
      Christian Politicks, or Duties to our Rulers and
      Neighbors." Written with a candor and realism

seldom found in such works, its purpose was "the resolving of practical cases of conscience and the re-
ducing of theoretical knowledge into serious Christian
practice."[15] In thus applying theory to practice,
Baxter combined the cynicism of folk wisdom with the
seriousness of Puritan ethics to produce a more re-
luctant endorsement of married life than those of his
Puritan colleagues. Advocacy of celibacy for religious
reasons seems not too distant for him, though the primary reason would not be the inherent sinfulness of
sexual activity but rather the distractions from prayer
and study.

The following selection begins in the middle of his
discussion of the drawbacks to marriage. In his own
life, however, Baxter seemed to find the advantages of
marriage weightier than the disadvantages. Though he
married late (age 46), he outlived his wife and, upon
her death, made very positive judgments about the marriage: "She near nineteen years lived with me, cheer-
ful wise and a very useful life, in constant love and
peace and concord, except for differing opinions about
trivial occurrences"; "We lived in inviolated love and
mutual complacency, sensible of the benefit of mutual
help."[16] One of these "differing opinions about trivial occurrences" concerned his wife's method of house-
keeping. Baxter felt her too intent upon cleanliness
and thought the servants could have spent some of their
time more profitably in reading, a feeling also expressed
in the latter part of this selection.]

And it is no small patience which the natural
imbecility of the female sex requireth you to prepare.
Except it be very few that are patient and manlike,
women are commonly of potent fantasies, and tender
passionate impatient spirits, easily cast into anger,
or jealousy, or discontent: and of weak understandings,
and therefore unable to reform themselves. They are
betwixt a man and a child. Some few have more of the
man, and many have more of the child; but most are
but in a middle state. Weakness naturally inclineth
persons to be froward and hard to please; as we see

in children, old people, and sick persons. They are
like a sore distempered body. You can scarce touch
them but you hurt them. With too many you can scarce
tell how to speak or look but you displease them.   If
you should be very well versed in the art of pleasing,
and set yourselves to it with all your care, as if
you made it your very business and had little else to
do, yet it would put you hard to it, to please some
weak impatient person, if not quite surpass your abil-
ity and skill. And the more you love them the more
grievous it will be, to see them still in discontents,
aweary of their condition, and to hear the clamorous
expressions of their disquiet minds. Nay the very
multitude of words that very many are addicted to,
doth make some men's lives a continual burden to them.
Mark what the Scripture saith, Prov. 21:9: "It is better to dwell in a corner of the house top, than with
a brawling woman in a wide house." Vers. 19: "It is
better to dwell in the wilderness, than with a contentious and an angry woman." So 25, vers. 24. And
Prov. 27:15: "A continual dropping in a very rainy
day, and a contentious woman are alike." Eccles.
7:28: "One man among a thousand have I found; but a
woman among all those have I not found."

     And there is such a meeting of faults and imper-
fections on both sides, that maketh it much the harder
to bear the infirmities of others aright. If one
party only were froward and impatient, the steadfast-
ness of the other might make it the more tolerable.
But we are all sick in some measure of the same disease. And when weakness meeteth with weakness, and
with pride, and passion with passion, it exasperateth

the disease and doubleth the suffering. And our corruption is such, that though our intent be to help one
another in our duties, yet we are apter far to stir up
one another's distempers.

The business, care, and trouble of a married life,
is a great temptation to call down our thoughts from
God, and to divert them from the "one thing necessary"
(Luk. 10:42), and to distract the mind, and make it
indisposed to holy duty, and to serve God with a di-
vided heart as if we served him not. How hard it is
to pray, or meditate with any serious fervency, when
you come out of a crowd of cares and businesses....

The business of a married state doth commonly de-
vour almost all your time, so that little is left for
holy contemplations, or serious thoughts of the life
to come. All God's service is contracted and thrust
into a corner, and done as it were on the by. The
world will scarce allow you time to meditate, or pray,
or read the Scripture. You think yourselves (as Martha) under a greater necessity of dispatching your
business, than of sitting at Christ's feet to hear
his Word. O that single persons knew (for the most
part), the preciousness of their leisure, and how free
they are to attend the service of God, and learn his
Word, in comparison of the married!

There is so great a diversity of temperaments
and degrees of understanding, that there are scarce
any two persons in the world, but there is some un-
suitableness between them. Like stones that have
some unevenness, that maketh them lie crooked in the
building: some crossness there will be of opinion, or
disposition, or interest, or will, by nature, or by

custom and education, which will stir up frequent discontents.

There is a great deal of duty which husband and
wife do owe to one another: as to instruct, admonish,
pray, watch over one another, and to be continual
helpers to each other in order to their everlasting
happiness; and patiently to bear with the infirmities
of each other. And to the weak and backward heart of
man, the addition of so much duty doth add to the
weariness, how good soever the work be in itself.
And men should feel their strength, before they undertake more work.

And the more they love each other, the more they
participate in each other's griefs. And one or other
will be frequently under some sort of suffering. If
one be sick, or lame, or pained, or defamed, or
wronged, or disquieted in mind, or by temptation fall
into any wounding sin, the other beareth part of the
distress. Therefore before you undertake to bear all
the burdens of another, and suffer in all another's
hurts, it concerneth you to observe your strength,
how much more you have than your own burdens do require.

And if you should marry one that proveth ungodly, how exceeding great would the affliction be? If
you loved them, your souls would be in continual danger by them. They would be the powerfullest instruments in the world to pervert your judgements, to
deaden your hearts, to take you off from a holy life,
to kill your prayers, to corrupt your lives, and to
damn your souls. And if you should have the grace to
scape the snare, and save yourselves it would be by

so much the greater difficulty and suffering, as the
temptation is the greater. And what a heart-breaking
would it be to converse so nearly with a child of the
Devil, that is like to lie for ever in Hell? The
daily thoughts of it would be a daily death to you.

Women especially must expect so much suffering
in a married life, that if God had not put into them
a natural inclination to it, and so strong a love to
their children, as maketh them patient under the most
annoying troubles, the world ere this would have been
at an end, through their refusal of so calamitous a
life. Their sickness in breeding, their pain in
bringing forth, with the danger of their lives, the
tedious trouble night and day which they have with
their children in their nursing and their childhood;
besides their subjection to their husbands, and continual care of family affairs: being forced to con-
sume their lives in a multitude of low and troublesome businesses. All this and much more would have
utterly deterred that sex from marriage, if Nature
itself had not inclined them to it.

And O what abundance of duty is incumbent upon
both the parents towards every child for the saving
of their souls? What uncessant labour is necessary
in teaching them the doctrine of salvation? Which
made God twice over charge them to "teach" his word
"diligently" (or "sharpen" them) "unto their children,
and to talk of them when they sit in their houses,
and when they walk by the way, and when they lie down,
and when they rise up" (Deut. 6:6, 7. & 11:19). What
abundance of obstinate rooted corruptions are in the
hearts of children which parents must by all pos-

sible diligence root up? O how great and hard a work
is it, to speak to them of their sins and Saviour, of
their God, their souls, and the life to come, with
that reverence, gravity, seriousness, and unwearied
constancy as the weight of the matter doth require?
And to suit all their actions and carriage to the
same ends! Little do most that have children know,
what abundance of care and labour God will require of
them, for the sanctifying and saving of their children's souls! Consider your fitness for so great a
work before you undertake it.

It is abundance of affliction that is ordinarily
to be expected, in the miscarriages of children, when
you have done your best, much more if you neglect
your duty, as even godly parents too often do. After
all your pains, and care, and labour, you must look
that the foolishness of some, and the obstinacy of
others, and the unthankfulness of those that you have
loved best, should even pierce your hearts. You must
look that many vices should spring up and trouble you;
and be the more grievous by how much your children
are the more dear. And O what a grief it is to breed
up a child to be a servant of the Devil, and an enemy
of God and godliness, and a persecutor of the Church
of God! And to think of his lying in Hell for ever?
And alas how great is the number of such?

And it is not a little care and trouble that
servants will put you to. So difficult is it to get
those that are good, much more to make them good; so
great is your duty in teaching them, and minding
them of the matters of their salvation; so frequent
will be the displeasures about your work and worldly

business, and every one of those displeasures will
hinder them for receiving your instructions; that
most families are houses of correction or affliction.

And these marriage crosses are not for a year,
but during life. They deprive you of all hope of relief while you live together. There is no room for
repentance, nor casting about for a way to escape
them. Death only must be your relief. And therefore
such a change of your condition should be seriously
fore-thought on, and all the troubles be foreseen and
pondered.

And if love make you dear to one another, your
parting at death will be the more grievous. And when
you first come together, you know that such a parting
you must have. Through all the course of your lives
you may foresee it. One of you must see the body of
your beloved, turned into a cold and ghastly clod.
You must follow it weeping to the grave, and leave it
there in dust and darkness. There it must lie rot-
ting as a loathsome lump, whose sight or smell you
cannot endure; till you shortly follow it, and lie
down yourself in the same condition. All these are
the ordinary concomitants and consequents of marriage: easily and quickly spoken, but long and hard
to be endured! No fictions, but realities, and less
than most have reason to expect. And should such a
life be rashly ventured on in a pang of lust or such
a burden be undertaken without forethought?

The wife that expecteth comfort in a husband,
must make conscience of all her own duty to her husband. For though it be his duty to be kind and
faithful to her though she prove unkind and froward,

yet 1. Men are frail and apt to fail in such difficult duties as well as women; 2. And it is so ordered
by God, that comfort and duty shall go together, and
you shall miss of comfort, if you cast off duty.

Be specially loving to your husbands. Your natures give you the advantage of this; and love feed-
eth love. This is your special requital for all the
troubles that your infirmities put them to.

Live in a voluntary subjection and obedience to
them. If their softness or yieldingness cause them
to relinquish their authority; and for peace they are
fain to let you have your wills; yet remember that
it is God that hath appointed them to be your heads
and governours. If they are so silly as to be unable,
you should not have chosen such to rule you as are
unfit; but having chosen them, you must assist them
with your better understanding in a submissive and
not a ruling masterly way. A servant that hath a
foolish master may help him without becoming master.
And do not deceive yourselves by giving the bare
titles of government to your husbands, when yet you
must needs in all things have your own wills. For
this is but mockery, and not obedience. To be subject and obedient is to take the understanding and
will of another to govern you before (though not
without) your own; and to make your understandings
and wills to follow the conduct of his that governeth
you. Self-willedness is contrary to subjection and
obedience.

Affect not a childish gaudiness of apparel, nor
a vain or costly or troublesome curiosity, in any
thing about you. Uncleanness and nastiness is a

fault, but very small in comparison of this pride and
curiosity. It dishonoureth your sex and selves to be
childish as to overmind such toyish things. If you
will needs be proud, be proud of somewhat that is of
worth and proper to a man. To be proud of reason or
wisdom or learning or goodness, is bad enough; but
this is to be proud of something. But to be proud of
fashions and fine clothes, of spots and nakedness, or
sumptuous entertainments, and neat rooms, is to be
proud of your *shame* and not your *virtue;* and of that
which you are not so much as commendable for. And
the cost, the time (O precious time) which themselves
and their servants must lay out, upon their dressings,
entertainments and other curiosities will be the
shame and sorrow of their souls, whenever God shall
open their eyes, and make them know what time was
worth, and what greater matters they had to mind. If
vain and empty persons like yourselves, commend you
for your bravery or curiosity, so will not any judi-
cious sober person, whose commendation is much worth.
And yet I must here with grief take notice, that when
some few that in other matters seem wise and religious,
are themselves a little tainted with this childish
curiosity and pride, and let fall words of disparage-
ment against those whose dress and dwellings and entertainments are not so curious as their own, this
proves the greatest maintainer of this sin, and the
most notable service to the devil. For then abundance will plead this for this sinful curiosity and
pride; and say, "I shall else be accounted base or
sordid: even such and such will speak against me."
Take heed, if you will needs be such yourselves, that

you prate not against others that are not as vain and
curious as you. For the nature of man is more prone
to pride and vanity, than to humility, and the im-
provement of their time and cost in greater matters;
and while you think that you speak but against inde-
cency, you become the Devil's preachers, and do him
more service than you consider of. You may as wisely
speak against people for using to eat or drink too
little, when there is not one of a multitude that
liveth not ordinarily in excess; and so excess will
get advantage by it.

*Be specially careful in the government of your
tongues; and let your words be few, and well considered before you speak them.* A double diligence is
needful in this, because it is the most common miscarriage of your sex. A laxative running tongue is
so great a dishonour to you, that I never knew a woman very full of words, but she was the pity of her
friends, and the contempt of others, who behind her
back will make a scorn of her, and talk of her as
some crackt-brained or half-witted person; yea though
your talk be good, it will be tedious and contemptible, if it be thus poured out, and be too cheap.
Prov. 10:19: "In the multitude of words there want-
eth not sin, but he that refraineth his lips is wise."
You must answer in judgement for your "idle words,"
Matth. 12:36. You will take it ill to be accounted
fools, and made the derision of those that talk of
you. Judge by the Scripture what occasion you give
them. Eccles. 5:3, 7: "A dream cometh by the multitude of business, and a fool's voice is known by the
multitude of words." "In the multitude of dreams

and many words, there are divers vanities." Eccles.
10:12, 13, 14. "The words of a wise man's mouth are
gracious, but the lips of a fool will swallow up himself. The beginning of the words of his mouth is
foolishness, and the end of his talk is mischievous
madness. A fool also is full of words." Whereas a
woman that is cautelous and sparing of her words, is
commonly reverenced and supposed to be wise. So that
if you had no higher design in it, but merely to be
well thought of and honoured by men, you can scarcely
take a surer way, than to let your words be few and
weighty: though the avoiding of sin, and unquietness,
should prevail with you much more.

CHAPTER THREE

WOMEN AND LEARNING

In the area of female education, the age of
the Renaissance and the Reformation brought significant improvements. The same could be said, to be
sure, of male education in this period. Renaissance
humanism, after all, was at core a reform of education, and the Reformation, in maintaining the centrality of Scripture, relied strongly on literacy.
Yet the printing press would almost inevitably have
advanced the cause of learning, even if the intellectual movements of the time had not so eagerly exploited this invention. Thus we must agree with
Vern Bullough in recognizing that changes in the importance of female education "were not so much the
result of any change in attitude toward women as a
change in the concepts of education."[1] Similarly,
wide variations in the educational opportunities
open to particular women were less a reflection of
religious differences than of social status or re-
gional policy.

Women's education during the era of Renaissance
and Reformation faced two different problems, the
first affecting well-to-do women, the second, women
of all classes: (1) Should women receive the same

intellectual training as men, in particular, instruction in classical languages and literature? (2)
Should all girls, as well as boys, receive basic instruction in reading and writing? The first question
provoked fervid debates in learned circles. The second engendered little controversy, for, so far as I
am aware, no one seriously opposed teaching girls to
read, but neither was it taken for granted that provision should be made for this.

The controversy on the first question took
place primarily in the humanistic courts of the aristocracy. Girls of this class customarily were provided a certain degree of education through tutors or
convent schools. As humanism aroused enthusiasm for
more serious intellectual enterprise among the males
of the aristocracy, so, too, many aristocratic women
took an interest in reading the classics. Christine
de Pisan (c. 1363-c. 1431) was one of the first to
defend explicitly the right of women to equal education. The issue was later debated among the court
men and ladies of Urbino as depicted in Baldassare
Castiglione's *The Courtier* (1528), where one partici-
pant dared to suggest women might be fit, as in Plato's *Republic,* to govern cities and command armies.
Opponents of advanced learning for women were satir-
ized by Erasmus in his colloquy "The Abbot and the
Learned Woman." The anti-intellectual abbot expresses the customary objections: women's brains are too
fragile, they have no use for Latin in their household duties, and learning undermines their moral in-
nocence.

Such Christian humanists as Erasmus, Thomas

More, and Juan Luis Vives countered such charges by
asserting that women were mentally capable of higher
education and that knowledge of good books made them
more dutiful wives and prevented a lapse into idleness, from which immorality might result. Yet their
arguments did not silence the opposition, for in the
following century the suspicion persisted tenaciously
that too much learning would drive a woman to insanity
(see selection D). Furthermore, the humanists themselves were often somewhat patronizing in their visions of girls' education. Morality, of course, was
always a major goal of humanistic education, but in
Vives' *Instruction of a Christian Woman*, for example,
moral education far outweighs intellectual training
in importance. Girls are less advised than boys to
read the pagan classics; they are, after all, being
trained as virtuous wives and mothers, not as scholars.
Erasmus did suggest that women might take over as di-
vinity professors,[2] but this is more a threat to
arouse monks from their sloth than a serious proposal.

Only such a non-conformist as Agrippa of Nettesheim was bold enough at this point to upend tradition and argue for female superiority. Pointing to
past accomplishments of women in such areas as religion, philosophy, magic, oratory, and poetry, Agrippa
ventures the belief that "except it had been forbidden
women to learn letters in these days, even now, as yet
might be had women of most famous learning, more excellent in wit than men."[3] Agrippa's volume was soon
translated into French, German, English, and Italian,
but Italy—probably the least pious country at the
time—seems to have been the most receptive. In 1549

Lodovico Domenichi, in the manner of Castiglione,
put forth Agrippa's ideas in the context of a debate.[4]
At the end of the century Lucretia Marinella presented
a much more extensive defense of women's superiority
and accomplishments as well as men's weaknesses.[5]

Yet the idea of women's superiority, if it was
to be defended theologically, depended on such an
imaginative reinterpretation of biblical passages
that it ran counter not only to Christian tradition
but also to biblical literalism. Thus it found vir-
tually no support among mainstream religious reformers or so-called "radical" reformers who clung to the
literal text of the Bible. Even equality of the
sexes is not easily supported by Scripture in any
other than a spiritual sense. The women we encounter
among the religious groups under consideration here
did not attempt to use their education in order to
become leaders in society. The Puritan concept of
the role of the wife allowed no room to pursue a career outside the home. Even highly educated single
women, such as Anna Maria van Schurman and Magdalena
Marschalck von Pappenheim, remained within socially
accepted patterns of living, supported by their families or religious institutions. Women were sometimes employed as schoolteachers, but as teachers of
girls they did not qualify as intellectual leaders.
And those, such as Anne Bradstreet, who made a name
for themselves as poets nevertheless earned their
livelihood through their domestic duties rather than
their poetry. The Reformation, then, radical groups
included, was not a leading force in support of higher education for women. In those cases where Protes-

tant women attained high levels of learning, they
were generally the beneficiaries of Renaissance humanism rather than Protestant theology.

On the lower levels of schooling Protestants
did make some significant contributions. Even on
this level, however, Protestant efforts are somewhat
eclipsed by pre-Reformation accomplishments. In the
later Middle Ages, the Netherlands and Bohemia had
established schools for both sexes at an elementary
level. In the former this was done by the city gov-
ernments, in the latter by the Bohemian Brethren.
This strong Bohemian interest in widespread education
perhaps explains why the Hutterites, of the various
Anabaptist groups, accomplished most toward educating
girls (or boys, for that matter). The Mennonites in
Holland, on the other hand, were concerned to keep
the schools under secular control in order to prevent
a Calvinist indoctrination of their children. In
such countries as Germany and Switzerland, fear of
increased persecution probably prevented Anabaptists
from organizing schools. The precarious existence of
Anabaptists, then, must be considered a major reason
for lack of a systematic educational program for
either boys or girls. But perhaps just as important
was a basic anti-intellectualism typical of the movement. Even the Hutterites saw higher education as
conflicting with the fear of God, and, accordingly,
limited educational opportunity to the elementary
grades.

Such an attitude was in marked contrast to the
view of Luther, who, after all, was a university professor. Of the major reform groups in the sixteenth

century, the Lutherans contributed most toward elementary education for girls as well as education in
general. Whereas Calvin exhibited little interest
in instruction for girls beyond the catechism, Luther
urged that all girls be sent to schools (not merely
taught in the home) and instructed in religion, languages, and history. At the urging of Philip Melanchthon and Johannes Bugenhagen, city councils in
many German towns made provisions for public schools,
including a fair number for girls. To be sure, even
these scattered schools offered a limited fare, the
curriculum consisting primarily of Bible reading and
lessons in the articles of faith. Yet the very existence of public schools for girls in the 1520s
placed Germany far ahead of England, where humanists
had done so much for women of the upper classes.

Although English girls whose parents could afford tutors often received a very strong education,
there was as yet no public provision for girls' education. The dissolution of the monasteries in 1537
removed one source of schooling, a fact regretted
even by the Protestant Reformer Thomas Becon. The
most outspoken English advocate of girls' schools in
the mid-sixteenth century, Becon urged "that by public authority schools for women-children be erected
and set up in every Christian commonweal, and honest,
sage, wise, discreet, sober, grave, and learned ma-
trons made rulers and mistresses of the same."[6] His
appeal was to little avail, however; those girls'
schools which emerged in England in the sixteenth
and seventeenth centuries were organized not by public authorities but by charitable foundations,

wealthy individuals or religious refugees.

Because of the disparate opportunities available for different social classes and in different
regions, it is difficult to determine whether or not
radical Protestants in England gave their daughters
a better education than did others. It has been
said that girls in "puritan-oriented families" had
the brightest prospects in seventeenth-century England,[7] but convincing evidence is yet to be forth-
coming. Quakers are often given most credit for
their educational provisions for girls, and it is indeed noteworthy that George Fox early turned his attention to the founding of boarding schools for girls
as well as boys. Of the fifteen schools operated by
Friends in 1671, two were for girls alone, two others
for girls and boys.[8] The significance of such figures is unclear, however, without comparable statis-
tics for other religious groups.

Evidence of the situation in colonial America
is similarly inconclusive. Both Massachusetts and
Virginia made heads of households legally responsible
for the education of all youth under their charge.
Thus, as in England, much instruction continued to be
carried on at home. But most towns in New England
also provided a public school. Girls were specifically admitted to some of these, but specifically excluded from others. In the majority of cases, the
extent of girls' attendance is unknown.[9] Consequently, it would be difficult to credit New England Puritans with any unusual concern for educating their
daughters. On the other hand, it would be just as
difficult to prove W. H. Kilpatrick's contention that

the English-speaking colonies practiced a discrimina-
tion against girls which was absent in the Dutch colonies.[10]

In summary, at our present stage of scholarship,
there is little reason to believe that the radical
Protestant groups under study here differed significantly from society at large in their ideas and practices affecting the education of women. The main im-
pulse for education had come from humanism and had
lost its driving force by the seventeenth century.
Protestantism's major contribution was the insistence
that girls as well as boys learn to read the Bible.
Bohemian Brethren, Hutterites, and Quakers stand out
among other radical Protestants, perhaps also among
Protestants in general. Of Protestant countries, the
Netherlands probably offered most for girls.

Yet the exceptional persons who appear among
the following selections reflect their religious af-
filiations only to a limited extent. To a greater extent they are the products of their own intellect and
aspirations. Significantly, both Lucy Hutchinson and
Anna Maria van Schurman experienced an inner conflict
between learning and faith as their beliefs became
more radical. Humanistic education may have been appropriate for a moderate Puritan or Dutch Calvinist
but was troublesome to a Baptist sympathizer or a
Labadist.

A. Report of Stephan Gerlach on his Visit to the
    Hutterites, September 22-23, 1578, from *Quellen zur*
    Geschichte der Wiedertäufer, Vol. I: *Herzogtum*
    Württemberg, ed. Gustav Bossert (Leipzig, 1930;
    reprint New York, 1971), 1106-1107.

[In its first few years the Anabaptist movement was centered in Switzerland, South Germany, and Tyrol. Widespread persecution in these regions, however, led many to migrate to more peaceful Moravia, where the Hussites of the previous century had paved the way for religious toleration. Here Anabaptists could work out a communal form of life to an extent not possible in less tolerant lands. Known as Hutterites or Hutterian Brethren because of Jacob Hutter's leadership, they established nearly ninety Bruderhofs in Moravia during the century after their arrival in 1529. One characteristic of these collectivist settlements was communal residence for the children along with some education for all. Yet in no way did this entail complete equality of the sexes.

Stephan Gerlach, writer of this account and later professor in Tübingen, was the son and brother of Anabaptists but not himself a sympathizer.]

Here [in Stiegnitz] I found my other sister Sara,who is married to a vine-dresser and keeps the children clean in their Anabaptist school. For all Anabaptist settlements have a school in which they place children above two years (up to this point they remain with their mothers) in order to learn to pray and read; other than this they do not study. The daughters commonly learn only prayer, not much writing; the boys, however, learn to read and write until they are a little older when they are allowed to learn a handicraft or some other work.

The children go a few times every day into the field or the neighbouring woods in order that they not be constantly on top of one another but also get some fresh air.

They are also provided with certain women who do nothing else than watch over the children, wash them, wait on them, and keep their beds and clothes

clean and neat. After they are older they sleep together by twos.

Every morning and evening they hold their
prayers, asking God to let them be brought up in
fear of Him, grant them good people, keep them in
knowledge of Him and also protect their brothers and
sisters in the country against all misfortune. Following this prayer, which they say kneeling, they
repeat the Lord's Prayer.

My sister Sara was not eager to take her husband, but could say nothing against it. For they
proceed in the following way in their marriages: on
a certain Sunday the leaders call together into one
house the young men and women who are marriageable.
They put them opposite each other and ask the girls
which of two or three partners they would like.
They must then take one; to be sure, they are not
coerced, but they may not do anything against the
leaders.

B.   J. A. Comenius, *The Great Didactic,* from *Opera*
        Didactica Omnia (Amsterdam, 1657, reprint
        Prague, 1957), pp. 44-45.

   [In the century following the founding of Hutterite
   communities in Moravia, the same land produced an
   even more outspoken advocate of universal education.
   For Jan Amos Comenius (1592-1670), leader of the
   Moravian Brethren in their time of expulsion during
   the Thirty Years' War, universal education was the
   means to a religious goal, unity of mankind in the
   worship of the one God. This goal was an outgrowth
   of his overriding concern to re-establish Protestantism in his native land. The apparent hopelessness
   of the Brethren's situation drew him to faith in
   eschatological prophecies, according to which the
   efforts of educated Protestants of all Europe would
   help to liberate his country from the Antichrist as

manifested in the Pope, the Jesuits, and the Haps-
burgs. But just as this hope failed to be realized,
so his religious and educational ideas were not as
widely accepted as he would have hoped. Some of
his ideas influenced the Pietists Spener and Francke,
but not until the nineteenth century did his writings
on universal education receive widespread attention
among educational theorists.]

"All Youth of both Sexes to be sent to School."

That not only the children of the wealthy or
noble, but all equally, noble and ignoble, rich and
poor, boys and girls, in all cities and towns, vil-
lages and farms are to be sent to school, is proved
by the following reasons.

First, all men are born to the same principal
end, that they may be men, which is to say, a rational creature, lord of creatures, the express image of
their creator. And so all are to be promoted toward
this end, so that, instructed skillfully in letters,
virtues, and religion, they may be able to pass
through the present life in a useful way, and moreover, to be prepared worthily for the future life.
In the sight of God there is no respect of persons,
as He Himself so often bears witness. If therefore
we admit only certain ones to the cultivation of the
mind, with others excluded, we are unjust not only
towards brethren of the same nature, but towards God
Himself, who wishes to be known, loved, and praised
by all in whom He implanted His image. And certainly
this will become the more fervent the more the greater light of knowledge is kindled. For we love to the
extent that we know....

Nor is it possible to give a sufficient reason
why the inferior sex (that I may give some advice

concerning this in particular) should be entirely
excluded from studies of wisdom (whether in Latin
or translated into the native tongue). For they are
equally the image of God and share equally in grace
and in the kingdom of the future age. They are
equal in mental agility and capable (often far beyond our sex) of being instructed in wisdom; access
to high places is equally open to them, for often
they have been called by God Himself to the ruling
of peoples, to giving useful advice to kings and
princes, to the science of medicine or other things
salutary for the human race, even the office of prophecy, and chiding priests and bishops. Why therefore should we indeed admit them to the alphabet but
afterward drive them away from books? Do we fear
their rashness? But the more we occupy our minds,
the less room will be found for rashness, which usually arises in emptiness of mind.

Let this be done, however, in such a way that
no mere mixture of books be accessible to them, or
to the other sex as well—it is to be deplored that
not more care has been taken up to this point—but
instead books from which they may be able to draw
continuously with the true knowledge of God and His
works, true virtues and true piety.

Let no one therefore hold before me the words
of the Apostle, "I do not permit a woman to teach"
(I Tim. 2:12), or the saying of Juvenal from *Satire
6:*

> . . . don't let the wife of your bosom
> ever acquire the style of an orator, whirling the sentences
> Heaving the enthymeme, or the undisturbed middle

Don't let her know too much about historical matters.[1]

Or that which Hippolytus says in Euripides:

> But the keen-witted hate I: in mine house
> Ne'er dwell one subtler than is woman's due;
> For Cypris better brings to birth her mischief
> In clever women.[2]

These things, I say, do not in any way oppose
our advice, since we urge women to be instructed not
toward inquisitiveness but toward honor and blessed-
ness. These are the matters which are most fitting
for them to know, both for managing the affairs of
the family in a worthy manner and for advancing their
own welfare and that of their husbands, children, and
families.

It might be asked, "What will happen if workers,
farmhands, day-laborers and even girls are made lit-
erate?" I reply, it will happen that when this universal education of youth is arranged by lawful
means, good material for thinking, choosing, striving,
and even working will thereafter be lacking to no one.
And all may know what is the aim of all actions and
desires of life, through what bounds one should proceed, and how each person should regard his station.
Afterwards all will take pleasure, even amidst their
labors, in meditation on the words and works of
God. They will avoid leisure dangerous for flesh
and blood by frequent reading of the Bible and other
good books (whither these better allurements draw
those already enticed). And finally, they will
learn to see God everywhere, to praise Him everywhere, to embrace Him everywhere; and for the same
reason to pass through this toilsome life more

pleasantly and to look forward to eternal life with
greater desire and hope. Should not indeed such a
state of the Church represent as much of Paradise as
is possible for us to have under the sky?

C.   Letter of Caspar Schwenckfeld to Magdalena
      Marschalck von Pappenheim, September 25,
      1542, *Corpus Schwenckfeldianorum* (Leipzig,
      1927), VIII, 281-285.

> [Magdalena Marschalck von Pappenheim, a noblewoman
> and Benedictine nun in a Swabian convent, had at
> one time been attracted to the teachings of
> Schwenckfeld. Before Schwenckfeld was able to
> instruct her in his form of theology, however, she
> came under the influence of the Anabaptist Pilgram
> Marpeck, who tried to dissuade her from Schwenck-
> feld's ideas. Nevertheless, she and Schwenckfeld
> exchanged letters for a time and she thereby served
> as the instigator and intermediary for the important
> theological encounter between the two men. Helena
> Streicher, a close friend of both Magdalena and
> Schwenckfeld, also figured prominently in the ex-
> change as a transmitter of the correspondence. The
> debate brought out all the significant differences
> between Anabaptism and Spiritualism, focusing on the
> questions of the relationship between inner and
> outer man, Word and Spirit, and Old and New Testa-
> ments. Yet Schwenckfeld has been thought by some,
> including Marpeck, to have been more concerned about
> the support of the women involved than about the
> theological issues.[3] For this reason, George
> Williams has described the debate "with some exag-
> geration" as "the war of the radical ladies."[4]]

The grace of our Lord Jesus Christ and my willing service first of all. Most virtuous dear lady,
I have received your answer to my letter and am
grateful to you that you point me to the Scriptures
and admonish me to read the New Testament more to
see what it teaches me. This I will do as diligently as possible with the help of Christ. And I will

not only see what the Scriptures teach me but also
what the Master of all Scripture—the One who in-
scribes the New Testament into all believing hearts
—namely, what the Holy Spirit teaches. He alone
leads us correctly in all truth and teaches us perfectly in Christ. May the Lord grant me thereto
ears which hear and an understanding heart. Amen.

    Among other things you write regarding Pilgram
that my scolding and praising of him is difficult
for you to judge. That is, I accuse him of imperfect
doctrine and error, but yet allow him to be an honorable, god-fearing man. It is not difficult, dear
lady, because there are without doubt many Papists,
monks and others (I will not now speak of other peoples) who may be honorable, god-fearing people and
yet not all know the true savior Christ or hold Him
in their hearts. Paul called the Jews god-fearing
when he preached the word of salvation to them (Acts
13[:16, 25]); yet they had not accepted it but instead had reviled Christ. And Luke writes of a god-
fearing soldier (Acts 10[:7]).

    I am pleased that you have defended Pilgram's
stance. You should know that as yet I know nothing
else of him than what I write you, nor even whether
it is true. It would make me truly sorry indeed if
I should inflict not only Pilgram but even the least
of persons with untruth and thus make someone suspect without cause. But I have sufficient cause
from him, especially in the fact that he wilfully opposes the resurrected glory of our reigning Lord and
king Christ, which God the Father graciously has revealed to us. Pilgram warns against our doctrine

and faith, calling our Christ an arrogant, proud
Christ. This is shown sufficiently in his letter
written under your name. Thus to you I must give
honor to our living, exalted and glorified Christ;
in sincere warning against Pilgram's teaching I
will show you what kind of Christ he expounds. Previously he recognized His holy humanity and gave hon-
or to Him in his heart. But what he has now added
beyond that you will be able to see from the enclosed
copy of a document which was recently sent to me from
Ulm together with Pilgram's letters. I send it to
you only that you may be instructed of the truth if
Pilgram should accuse me in your presence as elsewhere of inflicting untruths upon him....

* * *

This I have wanted to show you, dear lady, in
response to your letter in behalf of Pilgram, with
the request that, if he comes to you, you might present it to him and admonish him to give an account
of his faith. Also, that you would keep your heart
open in an unpartisan way to the truth and the saving
knowledge of Christ and in this spirit pray diligently. Thus you may yet learn many things which can
serve the true furtherance of your knowledge in
Christ. For I hope to God the time may not be long
wherein the Lord will reveal His living Word, purify
all kinds of doctrines, yea uncover all sorts of errors and let Himself be better known to eager hearts
with peace, joy and comfort in His kingdom. May He
graciously allow you and us to experience this to
the praise of His glory. Amen.

D.   *Winthrop's Journal, "History of New England,"*
       1630-1649, ed. James Kendall Hosmer (New
       York, 1908), II, 225.

       [Not all men were as eager to encourage female learn-
       ing as Schwenckfeld. Probably more common was the
       opinion that too much attention to learning was psych-
       ologically dangerous for a woman, her mental capacity
       being much more limited than that of a man. Such was
       the view of John Winthrop (1588-1649), devout Puritan
       and first governor of the Massachusetts Bay Colony.
       This is by no means to imply any form of misogyny on
       Winthrop's part. Married four times, his letters to
       his third wife Margaret are well known for his expres-
       sions of love and respect for her. She was well
       enough educated to write her replies, but also modest
       enough to know her limits.]

     April 13 (1645): Mr. Hopkins, the governor of
Hartford upon Connecticut, came to Boston, and brought
his wife with him (a godly young woman, and of special
parts), who was fallen into a sad infirmity, the loss
of her understanding and reason, which had been grow-
ing upon her divers years, by occasion of her giving
herself wholly to reading and writing, and had written many books. Her husband, being very loving and
tender of her, was loath to grieve her, but he saw
his error, when it was too late. For if she had at-
tended her household affairs, and such things as belong to women, and not gone out of her way and calling
to meddle in such things as are proper for men, whose
minds are stronger, etc., she had kept her wits, and
and might have improved them usefully and honorably
in the place God had set her. He brought her to Boston, and left her with her brother, one Mr. Yale,[5]   a
merchant, to try what means might be had here for her.
But no help could be had.

E.   Cotton Mather, *Magnalia Christi Americana:
        or, The Ecclesiastical History of New-England*
        (Hartford, 1852), I, 134f.

[It was possible, in spite of opinions such as that
expressed in the previous selection, for a woman to
achieve great respect, even among men, for her intellectual accomplishments. Perhaps the most successful
such woman in America was Anne Bradstreet (1612/13-
1672), one of the first resident colonial poets. *The
Tenth Muse,* her collection of early poems, was brought
to publication in 1650 by her brother-in-law, the
Reverend John Woodbridge, without her knowledge.
Prefatory material was written by nine men to introduce the poetess to her English readers and convince
them of the work's value. Many of these poetic testi-
monials confront directly the question whether a woman's poetry can compare with that of men. While
their answers today might be considered patronizing,
the men, professing great personal humility, commend
this one woman as having surpassed, or at least
equalled, the poetry of men. Yet part of the praise
she merited was not for her poetry but, in the words
of John Woodbridge, "for her gracious demeanour, her
eminent parts, her pious conversation, her courteous
disposition, her exact diligence in her place, and
discreet managing of her family occasions."[6] Anne
Bradstreet, in fact, was a dedicated wife and mother
of eight, whose poems, far from being her main occupation, were "the fruit but of some few hours, cur-
tailed from her sleep, and other refreshments."[7]
Many of her later poems dealt with such family matters as the birth of a child or the departure of her
husband to England as well as with spiritual subjects.]

But when I mention the poetry of this gentleman

[Thomas Dudley] as one of his accomplishments, I must

not leave unmentioned the fame with which the poems

of one descended from him have been celebrated in

both Englands. If the rare learning of a daughter

was not the least of those bright things that adorned

no less a Judge of England than Sir Thomas More; it

must now be said, that a Judge of New-England, namely

Thomas Dudley, Esq., had a daughter (besides other

children) to be a crown unto him. Reader, America
justly admires the learned women of the other hemis-
phere. She has heard of those that were tutoresses
to the old professors of all philosophy; she hath
heard of Hippatia, who formerly taught the liberal
arts; and of Sarocchia, who more lately was very often
the moderatrix in the disputations of the learned
men of Rome: she has been told of the three Corinnaes,
which equalled, if not excelled, the most celebrated
poets of their time: she has been told of the Empress
Endocia, who composed poetical paraphrases on divers
parts of the Bible; and of Rosuida, who wrote the
lives of holy men; and of Pamphilia, who wrote other
histories unto the life: the writings of the most re-
nowned Anna Maria Schurman have come over unto her.
But she now prays, that into such catalogues of au-
thoresses as Beverovicius, Hottinger, and Voetius[8]
have given unto the world, there may be a room now
given unto Madam *Ann Bradstreet,* the daughter of our
Governour Dudley, and the consort of our Governour
Bradstreet, whose poems, divers times printed, have
afforded a grateful entertainment unto the ingenious,
and a monument for her memory beyond the stateliest
marbles. It was upon these poems that an ingenious
person bestowed this epigram:

> Now I believe tradition, which doth call
> The Muses, Virtues, Graces, females all.
> Only they are not nine, eleven or three;
> Our auth'ress proves them but an unity.
> Mankind, take up some blushes on the score;
> Monopolize perfection hence no more.
>
> In your own arts confess your selves outdone;
> The moon hath totally eclipsed the sun:
> Not with her sable mantle muffling him,

> But her bright silver makes his gold look dim;
> Just as his beams force our pale lamps to wink,
> And earthly fires within their ashes shrink.

F.   Lucy Hutchinson, *Memoirs of the Life of
      Colonel Hutchinson,* ed. Harold Child (Lon-
      don, 1904), pp. 32-34.

[Sixteenth-century England was replete with examples
of learned ladies.[9] Thomas More's daughters, Queen
Mary, Lady Jane Grey, and Queen Elizabeth were but a
few of the English women with impressive educational
credentials. Juan Luis Vives and Roger Ascham promoted the cause not only by tutoring some of the
ladies but also by writing on the theory and method
of education. By the seventeenth century, education
in the liberal arts was fashionable for middle-class
girls as well as the nobility. Thus Lucy Hutchinson
(b. 1620), daughter of Sir Allen Apsley, was exceptional more for her intellectual capacity and moti-
vation than for the manner and extent of her training.

With the increased piety of her adulthood, she came
to regret some of her intellectual pursuits, particularly her translation of "this crabbed poet"
Lucretius, whose discoveries, she avowed, "are so
silly, foolish and false, that nothing but his
lunacy can extenuate the crime of his arrogant ignorance."[10] She also came under Baptist influence
and refused in 1647 to have her infant baptized.

The following excerpt is from an autobiographical
fragment published in 1806 together with her well-
known memoirs of her husband's life, significant for
their portrayal of a Puritan family during the English civil war.]

The privilege of being born of and educated by
such excellent parents, I have often revolved with
great thankfulness for the mercy, and humiliation
that I did no more improve* it. After my mother had
had 3 sons she was very desirous of a daughter, and

---

*Improve = turn to profit, avail oneself of.

when the women at my birth told her I was one, she
received me with a great deal of joy; and the nurse's
fancying, because I had more complexion and favour
than is usual in so young children, that I should not
live, my mother became fonder of me, and more endea-
voured to nurse me. As soon as I was weaned a French
woman was taken to be my dry nurse, and I was taught
to speak French and English together. My mother,
while she was with child of me, dreamt that she was
walking in the garden with my father, and that a
star came down into her hand, with other circumstances,
which, though I have often heard, I minded not enough
to remember perfectly; only my father told her, her
dream signified she should have a daughter of some
extraordinary eminency; which thing, like such vain
prophecies, wrought as far as it could its own accomplishment: for my father and mother fancying me
then beautiful, and more than ordinarily apprehensive,
applied all their cares, and spared no cost to improve me in my education, which procured me the ad-
miration of those that flattered my parents. By that
time I was four years old I read English perfectly,
and having a great memory, I was carried to sermons,
and while I was very young could remember and repeat
them so exactly, as being caressed, the love of
praise tickled me, and made me attend more heedfully.
When I was about 7 years of age, I remember I had at
one time 8 tutors in several qualities, languages,
music, dancing, writing, and needlework, but my gen-
ius was quite averse from all but my book, and that
I was so eager of, that my mother thinking it preju-
diced my health, would moderate me in it; yet this

rather animated me than kept me back, and every moment I could steal from my play I would employ in
any book I could find, when my own were locked up
from me. After dinner and supper I still had an hour
allowed me to play, and then I would steal into some
hole or other to read. My father would have me learn
Latin, and I was so apt that I outstript my brothers
who were at school, although my father's chaplain
that was my tutor was a pitiful dull fellow. My
brothers who had a great deal of wit, had some emu-
lation at the progress I made in my learning, which
very well pleased my father, tho' my mother would
have been contented, I had not so wholly addicted myself to that as to neglect my other qualities: as for
music and dancing I profited very little in them and
would never practise my lute or harpsicords but when
my masters were with me; and for my needle I absolute-
ly hated it; play among other children I despised,
and when I was forced to entertain such as came to
visit me, I tired them with more grave instructions
than their mothers, and pluckt all their babies to
pieces, and kept the children in such awe, that they
were glad when I entertained myself with elder company; to whom I was very acceptable, and living in
the house with many persons that had a great deal of
wit; and very profitable serious discourses being
frequent at my father's table and in my mother's
drawing room, I was very attentive to all, and gathered up things that I would utter again to great ad-
miration of many that took my memory and imitation
for wit. It pleased God that thro' the good instructions of my mother, and the sermons she carried to me,

I was convinced that the knowledge of God was the
most excellent study, and accordingly applied myself
to it, and to practise as I was taught: I used to exhort my mother's maids much, and to turn their idle
discourses to good subjects; but I thought, when I
had done this on the Lord's day, and every day performed my due tasks of reading and praying, that then
I was free to any thing that was not sin, for I was
not at that time convinced of the vanity of conversation which was not scandalously wicked, I thought it
no sin to learn or hear witty songs and amorous son-
nets or poems, and twenty things of that kind, wherein I was so apt that I became the confident in all
the loves that were managed among my mother's young
women, and there was none of them but had many lovers
and some particular friends beloved above the rest.

G.   Pierre Yvon, "Abrégé sincere de la vie et
        de la Conduite et des vrais sentimens de
        feu Mr. De Labadie, [On the Life, Conduct,
        and Faith of Mr. De Labadie]," from *Gottfrid
        Arnolds Unparteyische Kirchen- und Ketzer-
        historie* (Frankfurt am Main, 1715) II, 1261-
        1270.

        [Considered the most learned woman of her age, Anna
        Maria van Schurman (1607-1678) was cited by writers
        favorable to the advancement of women as the proof
        of women's intellectual capacities. Samuel Torshell,
        in *The Womans Glorie*,[11] for example, quoted extensive-
        ly from her letters supporting scholarship among wo-
        men. Jan van Beverwyck (see above p. 5) dedicated
        his book *On the Excellence of the Female Sex* to her.
        Nevertheless, while she believed women should be
        benefitted by education she felt their learning should
        enrich their leisure time rather than make them lead-
        ers in society.[12] Aware of male resistance, she
        chose to advance the feminist cause as inconspicuous-
        ly as possible and, accordingly, urged Beverwyck to

refrain from writing his dedication:

> Do not think I am altogether of your opinion,
> especially, having raised up so many examples
> of illustrious women to so high renown, that
> your discourse seemeth to procure them more
> envy than admiration. Wherefore, I do heartily
> intreat you, yea by our inviolable friendship
> I beseech you, that you would not (as according
> to your accustomed favour toward me, you seem
> to intend) dedicate this book to me. For you
> are not ignorant, with what evil eyes the great-
> est part of men (I mean not so much men of the
> meanest rank, whom it is easy to condemn, as
> men of great esteem) do behold what tendeth to
> our praise. So that, they think we are well
> dealt with, if we obtain pardon for aspiring
> to these higher studies, so far are they from
> being pleased, if they should suspect me to
> have given the least occasion of sounding forth
> our praises after that manner.[13]

Yet she also, like Lucy Hutchinson, later came to
the point in life when she regretted her previous
absorption in learning. She came under influence
of Jean de Labadie (1610-1674), early pietistic
preacher, and became one of the leaders of the Labadist fellowship. The following treatment of her
life was included by Pierre Yvon (1646-1707), another leading Labadist, as part of a biography of
Labadie.]

Because she was born in Cologne her father and
mother felt particularly inclined to consecrate her
to God, promising Him to raise her by His grace in
the knowledge, fear, and love of Him. Both of them
actively took it upon themselves to do this throughout their whole lives, thus giving her an example of
that which they were trying constantly to engrave upon her soul. In this way God rendered her suscept-
ible at an early age to good and holy impressions.

She herself told in her *Eucleria*[14] how she
felt touched at the age of four by the words of the

catechism which said at the beginning that *a Christian does not live to himself, but to Jesus Christ
his faithful Savior*. And she said this feeling never
passed from her heart, remaining quite strong yet in
the last year of her life....

She was quite well instructed in the truth when
she was only seven or eight years old. Her father
and mother lived in Utrecht when the Remonstrants had
seized the public churches there. Once when she was
sent to the sermon she could scarcely remain until
the end, feeling such repugnance toward all she had
heard preached against the truths of predestination
and grace. There was no way to make her go again, although her parents, who did not attend, had believed
she was not capable of deciding what evils or errors
were being preached.

At the age of eleven while reading the *History
of Martyrs* she felt such an ardent desire to suffer
for Jesus Christ that, when subsequently she had been
pledged to Him and was finally to sacrifice all to
Him to be faithful to that which she felt above her
of His holy will, she did so joyously; she felt in
her heart the renewal of that feeling she had when
she adjudged she would be infinitely happy if one
day she could suffer something for His name.

Having thus since tenderest childhood felt in
her heart living sparks of love for God and our Savior Jesus Christ, she found herself by slow degrees
engaged by her father in studies. He had noted the facil-
ity with which she understood what she heard. When
she found herself present at the instruction of her
brothers, she took away without any difficulty, as in

passing, all that they were taught. As she loved and respected her father tenderly, and he himself wanted to take care to school her in languages and sciences, she rendered obedience to his desire. She gave herself then by inclination to the cultivation of that which had cost her little to acquire and in which she made prodigious progress.

As she had received from God a hand as skillful and as fortunate as her mind, she succeeded admirably in designing, painting, sculpting, engraving, and writing in all sorts of languages, surpassing the best masters and the most delicate workmen. At the age of 10 she took away after three hours' time the art of embroidery; and at the age of eight she was able after a few weeks to sketch flowers in a surprising manner.

From her youth she learned, in addition to arithmetic, geography, astronomy, and vocal and instrumental music, also the Latin, Greek, and Hebrew languages. And she knew them so perfectly that when she wanted to apply herself with some care, she expressed herself either in speech or in writing, and all this in such a manner as to surprise and delight the most learned and best trained in writing or speaking the languages. She also acquired a good deal of knowledge of all the Oriental languages which had some bearing on or relation to Hebrew, such as Syriac, Chaldean, Arabic, and Ethiopian. As for living languages, in addition to Flemish, she understood German, English, French, and Italian and was able to make use of them all without trouble or difficulty.

As for the human sciences, she recognized more

and more how little of substance they contained, feeling how little they sufficed to satisfy a spirit and
heart made for God Himself, the supreme Being, the
infinite Good, the necessary and eternal Truth; yet
there was nothing of them which she had not considered
fairly closely and of which she did not possess a good
deal of knowledge and discernment.

Theology, scripture, and the truths of faith and
piety were constantly her greatest and liveliest inclination. Since childhood she had turned her heart
toward God and our Savior Jesus Christ; she had also
searched until she had fully and perfectly found Him,
and she rejoiced by His grace in blissful eternity.

Although her knowledge surpassed that ordinarily
reached by persons of her sex, it left her as humble
and small in her own eyes as any could be who only
occupied herself with ordinary matters and was considered lowly. Even with regard to these ordinary
matters she was so uncommonly well instructed that
one would often be surprised when upon occasion she
would speak in her humble, modest way of what she
knew. But this was only when the occasion engaged
her or demanded. For beyond those occasions you
would have said that she hadn't the slightest knowledge, and it would have been the same regarding all
the other matters she had mastered and of which she
had such rare and special knowledge.

When the twentieth year of the century had
passed she began to become known at the age of 13 or
14 years through the verses of the Pensionary of Holland, M. Cats,[15] who subsequently would have wished
for her to become engaged to marry him. She often

blessed God for having preserved her from marriage in
order that she could follow Him with little hesita-
tion and with holy liberty.

The 21st year of the century she heard M.
Rivet[16] preach and was very touched by one of his
sermons. She began from that time to bear him a re-
spectful love which she retained her whole life. Her
father was to die two years later at Franeker...but
this was not until he had given her very holy and
wise lessons, strongly exhorting his dear daughter
to flee the world and secular dealings and to beware
above all of entering readily into the estate of marriage, which, undertaken as it ordinarily is, binds
more to society and the world than to God and our
Savior Jesus Christ.

Her father died, then, when she was 18 years
old, but she pursued her studies and remained on the
general course which her father had had her take.
Her mother retired with her family to Utrecht, where
one of her [Anna Maria's] paternal uncles, who came
with his wife to stay with her mother, served in
place of her father. Ultimately, God took to Himself
her dear mother, who had sought Him from her youth
and who went to Him with the feeling of glorious and
ineffable joy.

Because her daughter was so far from wanting to
produce anything herself or have anyone know or esteem what she knew, the public would have known little of her had not the three persons whom she es-
teemed highly for their piety as well as their knowledge drawn her with a certain force from her private
life. One of them was M. Rivet, whom she had re-

spected as her father; the second M. Voetius,[17] and
the third M. Spanheim the elder.[18] The latter would
subsequently, in spite of all her objections, be the
promoter of the publication of her works, where one
finds panegyrics accorded her lavishly on all sides,
as to a marvel or a prodigy of her century.

In the United Provinces three other persons besides M. Cats also contributed especially to making
her known. One was M. Saumaise,[19] who considered
himself quite honored by her correspondence; the second M. Beverwyk, and the third M. Huygens.[20] All
three of them carried on correspondence with her for
a long time. The Princess Palatine Elizabeth,
daughter of the king of Bohemia, had a fondness for
her from her youth. She loved and revered her to the
end of her life, having wished to imitate her from
the beginning of her studies.

Of the French, it is known that M. Balzac[21]
placed her among the great minds. M. Conrart[22] above
all, who had written her a large number of letters,
developed a very special regard for her. As far as
the learned are concerned, the philosopher Gassendi,[23]
as well as Father Mersenne,[24] and above all M.
Bochart[25] were delighted to be able to correspond
with her, as they did quite often. And among great
men, Cardinal Richelieu was extremely pleased to see
some products of her pen and her hand; he himself
sent, in the hands of M. Noyers, who didn't like him,
a sign of his esteem for her to keep.

When M. Descartes was in Holland before passing
on to Sweden, he came to see her in Utrecht. There
occurred something extraordinary in their conversation,

of which Mlle de Schurman wanted to leave some record.
I believe I shall be able to reproduce it here ac-
curately.

There was at that time on the table a Hebrew
Bible from which she usually read, and M. Descartes
asked her what it was. Hearing that it was the Holy
Scripture in Hebrew and that she applied herself to
the study of the language, he registered astonishment
that a person with a mind such as that of Mlle de
Schurman should spend her time, which was, he said,
so valuable, at a thing of so little importance. She
explained to him that it seemed to her this language
was well worth the trouble and that after all there
was always a notable difference between being able to
read an author in his own language and being able to
read only a translation. It was rare, even with regard to a secular author, for a translator, no matter
how capable, to be able to hit upon all the meanings
of what he was translating and not to lose anything
in the change of language. And how much more rare
with respect to the sacred writers, of whom one could
only have true understanding by being enlightened by
the Spirit which had made them write, which was not
the spirit of man, but the Spirit of God Himself. He
responded that at one time he had had the same thought
and that to this end he had learned the language
called sacred. He had then sat down to read the first
chapter of Genesis which speaks of the creation of the
world. But as much as he thought about it, he still
could conceive nothing clear and distinct. He didn't
understand what Moses was trying to say, and because
he saw that instead of shedding light on everything he

said, it served only to becloud it the more, he ceased
his attempt there. This answer surprised Mlle de
Schurman very much and, deeply offending her, gave her
such a repulsion toward this philosopher, that she
took care never again to have anything to do with him.
In a memoir in which she mentions him, she wrote these
words under the title of "Blessings of the Lord": "God
has turned my heart away from profane men, and he has
used it as a goad to excite me to piety and to make
me more fully devoted." The Lord, in fact, gave her
this heart. When she noticed this impious spirit in
any one of those with whom she could have had some
conversation or correspondence, she immediately broke
off all ties with him, and refused him all access to
her....

For a long time she had great difficulty in
consenting to have her works published separately, because she believed rightly that in doing so she would
cause people to think ill of her and to suspect her of
being desirous of vainglory. So they published some
of her works along with those of other writers. Thus
in 1639, M. Beverwyk published her Latin letter *On the
End of Life*[26] in a collection containing writings of
several famous men on the same subject. He included
two others among those which he brought to light some
time later under the name of *Epistolicae Quaestiones*.[27]
Others did the same in the collections of letters
which they published. In 1641, they went further by
publishing separately her *Dissertation* and some letters written on the same subject between M. Rivet and
herself.[28] Finally in 1646, M. Rivet and M. Spanheim
the elder so entreated her that she agreed to permit

the publication of a collection of her separate works.[29]

But if the products of her mind won her renown,
they also kept her busy. Her visits and correspond-
ences multiplied despite the difficulty she had with
them. Still she approached it with great discernment.
For in order to speak with all those desirous of seeing her, she could scarcely have done anything else;
and also, to answer all those who wrote to her, she
would have to spend all her time writing. This obliged
her to grant neither easily, and to do it only by specific appointment.... She believed that her position
and her modesty excused her sufficiently, and safe-
guarded her from the reproach which might have been
levelled at her, that she rendered herself inaccessi-
ble because of the great esteem in which she held herself....

Yet there was no nobleman or person of quality
who passed through Holland without seeking the opportunity of conversing with her for a mere quarter of an
hour. To have been in Utrecht without having seen
Mlle de Schurman was like having been in Paris without having seen the king. Several princes paid her a
visit and admired the greatness of her mind and her
extraordinary qualities. The Queen of Poland, Marie
Louise de Gonzague, during the trip which she made in
1645 to join her husband, King Vladislas IV, passed
through that city and also wanted to see her. She
went to her residence followed by the Bishop of Orange,
her chief physician, and three or four other persons,
of whom one was Sr. le Laboureur, who wrote the history of her trip.[30] This queen looked with admira-
tion on the works of her hands but was more astonished

on hearing her speak so many languages and with such
great learning. Afterwards, when the account of the
queen's trip had been published, Mlle de Schurman,
trying to defend herself from the glory which sur-
rounded and followed her, made herself much less accessible than before, as is evidenced by the small
number of papers she kept after having burned most of
them five or six years before her death....

It was, in fact, her humility that caused her
to act forcibly, and which was equally visible, both
in the access she granted to some and the refusal she
gave to others' visits.... It is a rare thing to find
this virtue even in idiots; it is still rarer to meet
it in the learned, especially if they excel above
others; but to find it in such sincerity and constancy in a person of her sex, of her learning, of her
self-sufficiency and reputation, in the midst of the
universal praise of all the learned, is a very extraordinary thing; and it can indeed be said that, if
she has not been alone in that, she has had very little company. Also this has been what most impressed
those who knew how to assess things, and form a solid
judgment. They admire the capacity of her mind, and
the skill of her hands; but there is nothing which
delights them more than her extreme modesty. It was
so natural to her that nothing passed from her which
did not have that character. It crept even into her
verses, where ordinarily it is least likely to be
found. M. de Balzac, having seen some of her Epi-
grams, speaks of this strength in one of his letters:
"It must be admitted that Mlle de Schurman is a marvelous young woman, and that her verses are not the

least of her marvels. I do not think that Sulpitia,
whom Martial praised so highly, composed any more
beautiful, nor more Latin: but what modesty and
honesty there is among the graces and beauties of
her verses! How agreeably the virtue of her soul
blends with the products of her mind!"

CHAPTER FOUR

WOMEN IN THE CHURCH

In Christ there may be neither male nor female
(Galatians 3:28), but in the Church there have always
been distinctions based on sex. St. Paul's dictum
against women speaking in church, until explained
away as intended for the specific problems of the Co-
rinthian church or as a reflection of St. Paul's social milieu, closed most church offices to women. Yet
women sometimes achieved prominence in the apostolic
church (most notably Priscilla) and had two possibilities for attaining official status. Mention is made
in the New Testament of deaconesses ministering to
the needy (Romans 16:1; I Timothy 3:11). Widows also
formed a special class, supported by the Church and
in return offering up constant prayer (I Timothy 5:3-
12). These functions have had a spotty record in
Christian history: at times they have been ecclesiasti-
cally insignificant; at other times they evolved into
positions of considerable influence.

Hardly anything is heard about deaconesses from
New Testament times until the third century, when the
Apostolic Didascalia recommends a female diaconate as
if it were an innovation. The women were to be as-
sistants to the bishops, particularly in ministering
to other women. The office of widow remained distinct

from that of deaconess and consisted still in the service of prayer. At the end of the fourth century the
status of deaconess underwent a metamorphosis: whereas
previously it was not of clerical stature, deaconesses
were now ordained, receiving the imposition of hands.[1]
The office was now limited to virgins or first-time
widows, and the duties were directed more exclusively
toward other women.

In the East the office continued in this form
through the twelfth century, but in the West it gradually merged into that of the abbess or consecrated
nun (as distinct from that of ordinary professed nuns).
Such women could say the daily offices and in some
orders hear confessions. Furthermore, the abbesses,
as heads of ecclesiastical units, sometimes had considerable jurisdictional power over both spiritual
and temporal matters affecting the convent and its
lands.[2] In the early Middle Ages some also presided
over double monasteries, in which both sexes of religious lived. In the later Middle Ages, however, the
situation was reversed: the large increase in women
entering a religious calling, combined with the tight-
ened organizational efforts of Popes Gregory VII and
Innocent III, brought an increase in male influence
over women in orders. Abbesses lost whatever rights
of spiritual leadership over men they had previously
exercised. Nevertheless, within the convent there was
considerable opportunity for leadership in important
charitable and educational efforts.

When sixteenth-century reformers aroused opposition to monastic establishments, they were not thinking in terms of closing women's primary outlets for

leadership. If pressed, they would no doubt have replied that governance of a household under the domination of a husband was a greater privilege than governance of a convent under the domination of a Pope. But
what role did that leave women in the Church?

Luther, of course, defended the priesthood of
all believers. He recognized that, logically, this
could be applied to women. Yet for women to preach
would go contrary to Paul's advice that women should
not teach men. In the improbable case where no men
were present to preach, it would, he allowed, "be
necessary for the women to preach."[3] His reasons for
limiting female preaching to such occasions were not
solely biblical: the preacher needs "a good voice,
good eloquence, a good memory and other natural
gifts."[4] The implication is that any man, excepting
the dumb, incompetent, or handicapped, has more of
these qualities than any woman.

On the other hand, women in Lutheranism were allowed an ecclesiastical function which they were denied in Calvinism. Because of the importance attached
to baptism as a prerequisite to salvation, Lutherans
continued the Roman Catholic custom of allowing a mid-
wife, in emergency cases, to baptize an infant in
mortal danger. Lutheran church orders made special
provision for midwives to be instructed in baptismal
procedure.[5] Calvin's reasons for condemning this
practice hinged partially on his confidence that un-
baptized infants were not necessarily prevented from
salvation. But just as important was his conviction
that in the early church "a woman was not allowed to
speak in the church, and also not to teach, to baptize,

or to offer."[6]

    This became a controverted issue between Anglicans, who continued to allow lay baptism in emergencies, and Puritans, who, with Calvin, insisted that only an ordained minister could baptize (ipso facto excluding women).[7] On another disputed issue, it is difficult to determine which side should be considered more pro-feminist. Puritans rejected the ancient custom of churching women after childbirth, labelling the practice a "Jewish purification." Anglicans responded that it was not intended to imply a need for cleansing on the part of the mother; rather, it was an occasion for rejoicing and was properly called "the thanksgiving of women after childbirth."[8]

    More significant, perhaps, was the conflict over reviving the office of widow. Some Mennonite congregations in the Netherlands and North Germany already had deaconesses performing charitable work.[9] Puritans, intent upon being faithful to New Testament practices, advocated the restoration of this function (although in common with their own and later times, they merged the offices of widow and deaconess into one). Richard Hooker countered that, as widows could not receive ordination, "to make them ecclesiastical persons were absurd."[10] The Separatists of Amsterdam, influenced by the Mennonites and in a position to put such beliefs into practice, did indeed rank the widow or deaconess (minimum age sixty) among the church officers[11] and had at least one deaconess in the congregation.

    Because this office was open to such a small percentage of women, however, the best means of under-

standing the status of women in the various churches
is a comparison of opinions on the voting rights of
women on congregational issues. So long as churches
were governed by bishops, ministers and/or elders, the
question did not arise. Anabaptists were no exception
here. But when some Puritans began to claim the entire congregation was the seat of ecclesiastical authority, the question had to be faced. Here we see a
clear distinction between Separating and Non-Separating Congregationalists. The Puritans of New England,
wishing to retain their ties with the Church of England, did not wish to offend their Presbyterian colleagues by making unnecessary claims for women. There
was, after all, strong biblical precedent for re-
stricting women's activities. The Amsterdam Separatists, however, who in most respects were at least
equally biblicistic, developed in this case a less
literalistic interpretation of the Pauline texts.
True, women were not ordinarily to maintain positions
of authority, but in view of biblical references to
women prophesying, such a possibility could not be
categorically excluded. A similar qualified approval
of women's participation was advanced during the English Civil War period by John Rogers. Yet women sometimes took more liberties than even their most supportive male theorists would approve, as we will observe in the next chapter.

  Only in the group which is sometimes considered
the logical final development of Puritanism,[12] the
Society of Friends, was the theory of women's equality
developed with conviction (though even here women were
at best "separate but equal"). Margaret Fell Fox and

George Fox managed to reconcile the passages of Joel 2 and Acts 2, according to which women may prophesy, with the Pauline subordinationist passages. The latter, they said, belong to the time of the law, the former to the time of the gospel. Whatever the organic relationship between Quakers and moderate Puritans, the Quaker belief that the redeemed were already living in the age of the Spirit clearly separated them from those who considered biblical law still binding. Only because of this important theological difference could the Friends attempt in the visible Church the equality of the sexes which other Christians could envision only in the Heavenly Kingdom.

A.   John Robinson, *A justification of Separation from the Church of England* (n. pl., 1610), pp. 150, 206, 236-37.

[The branch of Puritans known as Separatists, contending that the established church could not be purified, severed all ties with the Church of England. Having taken this step, they were not motivated, as were the Non-Separating Congregationalists, to please the conservative parties in the church by reasserting the traditional, silent role of women. Within the confines of biblical authority, therefore, the Separatists recognized certain legitimate occasions for women to speak in church.

John Robinson (c. 1575-1625) represents here the cause of Separatism, though it should be noted that he was at times willing to maintain fellowship with those outside his congregation. He joined the Separatist group in Scrooby after his refusal to conform to the anti-Puritan canons caused his suspension from the office of preaching elder at St. Andrew's Church, Norwich. In 1608 he fled with other Separatists to Holland, settling eventually in Leiden. As a student of theology at the University of Leiden, Robinson received certain legal immunities which allowed him and his followers to practice and publish their beliefs.

It was this congregation which, a few years later,
emigrated to America and became known as "Pilgrim
Fathers." Robinson, however, lived out his life in
Leiden.]

And hereupon also it followeth necessarily, that
one faithful man, yea or woman either, may as truly,
and effectually loose, and bind, both in heaven, and
earth, as all the ministers in the world....

I do therefore answer in few words: it is not necessary that every one of the people should speak to the
offender, no nor of the officers neither. If but one
officer do sufficiently evince, and reprove the party,
what needs more speak? The rest, both officers and
people, may manifest their consent either by voice,
sign, or silence, yet so as liberty be preserved for
any in place, and order, to speak, either by way of
addition, limitation, or dissent. And for women, they
are debarred by their sex, as from ordinary prophe-
cying, so from any other dealing wherein they take authority over the man. I Cor. 14:34-35. I Tim. 2:11-
12. Yet not simply from speaking: they may make profession of faith or confession of sin, say Amen to the
Church's prayer, sing Psalms vocally, accuse a brother
of sin, witness an accusation, or defend themselves
being accused, yea in a case extraordinary, namely
where no man will, I see not but a woman may reprove
the Church, rather than suffer it to go on in apparent
wickedness and communicate with it therein. Now for
children, and such as are not of years of discretion,
God and nature dispenseth with them, as for not com-
municating in the Lord's supper now, so under the law
for not offering sacrifices, from which none of years
were exempted: neither is there respect of persons with

God in the common duties of Christianity.

    And for that so oft reinforced objection of au-
thority given to two or three, and therefore not to all,
I have answered and do, that to two, or three, and yet
to all when there are but two or three in all, as usually comes to pass in the raising, and dispersing of
Churches....

    But now lest any should object "may women also
prophesy?", the Apostle prevents that objection, and it
may be reproves that disorder amongst the Corinthians,
ver. 34. by a flat inhibition, enjoining them expressly
to keep silence in the Church, in the presence of men
to whom they ought to be subject, and to learn at home
of their husbands, v. 35. and not by teaching the men,
to usurp authority over them, I Tim. 2: 11-12, which
the men in prophesying do lawfully use. Now this restraint of women from prophesying, or other speaking
with authority in the Church, both in this place to
the Corinthians, and in the other to Tim. doth clear
the former objections. In that Paul forbids women, he
gives liberty to all men gifted accordingly, opposing
women to men, sex to sex, and not women to officers,
which were frivolous. And again in restraining women,
he shews his meaning to be of ordinary not extraordinary prophesying, for women immediately, and extraordi-
narily, and miraculously inspired, might speak without
restraint. Exo. 15:20; Judg. 4:4; Luk. 2:36; Act.
21:17-18.

B.-F.   [Richard Mather (1596-1669) and John Cotton (1585-1652)
        had both been English Puritans whose conflicts with Eng-
        lish ecclesiastical authorities led them to emigrate to
        America, where they became leading Congregationalist
        ministers in the Massachusetts Bay Colony. They never-
        theless wished to maintain ties with the Church of Eng-
        land and sought to sway their mother church in the
        direction of Congregationalism.

        Mather's statement denying female participation in church
        government is part of a treatise designed to inform the
        English, during the deliberations of the Westminister As-
        sembly, of the working and successes of the congregation-
        al system in New England. Toward the same end, John
        Cotton's treatise, *The Keys of the Kingdom of Heaven,* was
        provided with an introduction by Thomas Goodwin and
        Philip Nye, two of the very few spokesmen for Independen-
        cy or Congregationalism at the Assembly.

        Two Presbyterians in attendance at the Assembly responded
        to the New Englanders with considerable skepticism.
        Daniel Cawdrey (1588-1664) found it inconsistent that
        Congregationalists should want to give governing rights
        to all male church members yet deny them to women and
        children. That in congregational polity such rights
        would inevitably be extended to women was the accusation
        of Robert Baillie (1599-1662), a learned Scottish Presby-
        terian. By implication Baillie contended that to approve
        of the Independent way would open the door to such mis-
        guided women as Anne Hutchinson (see Chapter five) and
        the female preachers in London. Not even the marriage
        bond would be holy.

        Cotton, however, remained convinced that the Bible pro-
        vided a safeguard against the extension of speaking or
        voting rights to women. His *The Way of Congregational
        Churches Cleared,* a counter-attack against both Cawdrey
        and Baillie, reaffirmed the Congregational adherence to
        biblical injunctions against women speaking in the church.
        His efforts were to no avail, however, for the West-
        minster Assembly, having been dominated by Presbyterians,
        refused the New England Way. The colony, nevertheless,
        persisted in its congregational polity while at the same
        time adopting the doctrinal statement of the Assembly.
        Congregationalism was made official polity for Massachu-
        setts Bay in the Cambridge Platform of 1648, formulated
        largely by Mather.]

B.   Richard Mather, *Church Government and Church
        Covenant discussed* (London, 1643), p. 60.

Question 16: Whether do you not permit women
to vote in Church matters?

The rule is express and plain that women ought
not to speak in the Church, but to be in silence. I
Cor. 14:34. I Tim. 2:11-12. And therefore they ought
not to vote in Church matters, besides voting imports
some kind of government, and authority and power: now
it is not government and authority, but subjection and
obedience which belongs unto women, by the rule, and
so is the practice of women amongst us.

C.   Thomas Goodwin and Philip Nye, preface to John
        Cotton, *The Keyes of the Kingdom of Heaven*
        (London, 1644), p. A3.

As he [the author] supposeth, each Congregation,
such, as to have the privilege of enjoying a Presbytery,
or company of more or less elders, proper unto itself;
so being thus presbyterated, he asserteth this incor-
porate body of society to be the first and primary
subject of a complete and entire power within itself
over its own members; yea, and the sole native subject
of the power of ordination and excommunication which
is the highest censure. And whereas this corporation
consisteth both of elders and brethren (for as for
women and children, there is a special exception by a
statute-law of Christ against their enjoyment of any
part of this public power), his scope is to demonstrate
a distinct and several share and interest of power, in
matters of common concernment, vouchsafed to each of
these, and dispersed among both, by charter from the
Lord.

D.   Daniel Cawdrey, *Vindiciae Clavium* [*Judgment
          of the Keys*] (London, 1645), pp. 9-10.

          Again, if the keys were given to Peter as a be-
liever, I see no reason but women and children may
come in and challenge a power in the keys. It suffices
not to say (as the Epistolers say, pag. 3) "Women and
children are excepted by a statute law of Christ,
against their enjoyment of any part of this public
power." For though they be forbidden to speak in the
congregation or might by impotence (as some say) be excepted in some particulars; yet there seems no reason
why they should be exempted from that power here given
to the fraternity, which concerns them as well as men,
and they are as well able to exercise it as men; viz.
to give a (passive) consent, or to withdraw from the
party excommunicated; which they may and must do as
well as men. For as women may be offended, so they
should in reason have satisfaction, by consenting to
the sentence. And as women may offend, in keeping
company with a brother or sister excommunicated, so
they ought to withdraw from them; and then if this be
any exercise of the power of the keys, you may hear
them gingle at the womens girdles; which is an extreme
beyond the Brownists,[1] even downright Anabaptistical.
But you give the fraternity more power than this here-
after, there we shall consider it. Hitherto you have
given them nothing, but what is common to them with
women.

E.   R. Baillie, *A dissuasive from the errours
          of the time* (London, 1645), pp. 110-111,
          115-116.

          It is true, the Synod of New England maketh not

only the fraternity, but as they speak, the sorority
also to be subject of the private power of the keys of
the Kingdom of heaven; also we have shown how they have
permitted women to be leaders to their whole Churches,
and chief pastors in Church actions of the highest nature: we have good witness that a woman was the founder
of Mr. Simpson's Church at Rotterdam; that a woman, and
that none of the best led away Mr. Cotton, and with him
great numbers of the best note in New England, towards
the vilest errours, and to the brink of a new separation from all the Churches there. Notwithstanding all
this, none of the Independents either in New England or
Holland, neither the Brownists of Amsterdam, did ever
give unto any women any public ecclesiastic power. In
this, our London Independents exceed all their brethren,
who of late begin to give unto women power of debating
in the face of the Congregation, and of determining ecclesiastic causes by their suffrages, if Doctor Bast-
wick be rightly informed.

Concerning the power of the sacraments, Mistress
Chidley is permitted to print in defence of the Independent cause,[2] without the reproof of any of that
party, so far as I have heard, that not only pastors
but private men out of all office, may lawfully cele-
brate both the sacraments....

First, for the marriage blessing, they applaud
the Brownists' Doctrine, they send it from the Church
to the town-house, making its solemnization the duty of
the magistrate; this is the constant practice of all in
New-England: the prime of the Independent Ministers now
at London, have been married by the magistrate, and all
that can be obtained of any of them is to be content

that a minister in the name of the magistrate and as
his commissioner may solemnize that holy band.

Concerning divorces, some of them go far beyond
any of the Brownists, not to speak of Mr. Milton, who
in a large treatise[3] hath pleaded for a full liberty
for any man to put away his wife, when ever he pleaseth,
without any fault in her at all, but for any dislike,
or dyspathy of humour; for I do not certainly know
whether this man professeth Independency (albeit all
the heretics here, whereof ever I heard, avow themselves Independents). What ever therefore may be said
of Mr. Milton, yet Mr. Gorting and his Company were
men of renown among the New-English Independents, before Mistress Hutchinson's disgrace; and all of them
do maintain, that it is lawful for every woman to de-
sert her husband, when he is not willing to follow her
in the Church way, and to take herself for a widow,
loosed from the bond of obedience to him, only because
he lives without that Church whereof she is become a
member.

F.   John Cotton, *The way of congregational churches
        cleared* (London, 1648), Book 2, p. 19.

But (saith Vindex)[4] if place, or order in the
Church, do give the people out of office, any power in
the keys; that is, in the Ordinances, then may women
and children claim an interest in those keys, for they
have a place and order in the Church as well as men.

Answer: It is not every place or order in the
Church, that giveth power to receive the ordinance ad-
ministered by others, much less power, themselves to
dispense ordinances. Children have not power to receive

the Lord's Supper, much less to administer it.   And
for women, God hath expressly forbidden them all place
of speech and power in the Church   (I Cor. 14:34; I
Tim. 2:11,12) unless it be to join with the rest of
the Church, in singing forth the public praise of the
Lord.   Let every soul enjoy such privileges and liberties, as the Lord hath given him in his place and order: and neither affect nor attempt more.   The female
sex, and nonage, fall short of some powers, which
Christ hath given to the brotherhood.

G.   John Rogers, *Ohel or Beth-shemesh* (London,
          1653), pp. 463-464, 469-477.

     [The execution of King Charles I in 1649 released a
     wave of religious millenarianism which interpreted
     the execution as the defeat of Antichrist and the
     beginning of Christ's Kingdom on earth. According
     to this view none but Christ was entitled to the
     throne. To instate Christ's rule, however, it was
     necessary not only that Charles be ousted but also
     that the clergy be purged and the national church
     destroyed. The leaders of the new society would be
     the elect saints, who would impose a godly rule on
     the ungodly.

     As is usually the case in millenarian movements,[5]
     the Fifth Monarchists, as John Rogers' group was
     called, were drawn largely from the lower economic
     levels of society and included a high percentage
     of women.[6] In the projected upheaval of society
     toward egalitarianism, women and the poor had, of
     course, the most to gain. Likewise, within the
     church the movement brought a struggle for women's
     equality. Several women claimed to have received
     divine prophetic inspiration. Yet while women
     achieved greater status among the Fifth Monarch-
     ists than among the more moderate religious groups
     of the day, the rights of women to teach and preach
     were still questioned.[7] Equality in the church
     meant just that——the right to be equal but not
     superior.]

>   That in the Church all the members, even
>   sisters as well as brothers, have a right
>   to all Church-affairs; and may not only
>   implicitly but explicitly vote and offer
>   or object, etc.

The furies and harpies are flown up very high
upon this point, and most men do arrogate a sovereign-
ty to themselves which I see no warrant for. The difference that is to be made is already proved to be between the precious, and the vile, the clean and unclean; and not to be a difference of sexes, ages, or
relations. Now because there be too bitter conten-
tions about this...we shall prove their liberty, and
leave others to practise accordingly. Proofs for this
may be taken from prophecy, precept, and practise, and
which we shall ratify by firm reasons out of the Word
of God, and answering objections, shall leave all to
stand or fall according to their foundation and bottom....

But we come now to the reasons and arguments
which confirm this practise and confute the contrary.
And,

I. Is taken (*a toto ad partes*). Thus, that
which concerns the whole, is (by all the rule of reason) to be done by the whole; or that which concerns
all (brothers and sisters), reason requires should be
done (or ordered) by all (brothers and sisters); but
to choose this or that officer, to vote this or that
thing, to cast out this or that offender, to take in
this or that member, concerns all (sisters as well as
brothers)....

2. (*A fortiore.*) If it be lawful for women to
have any office in the Church (which implies a power

and authority) then it is (much more) lawful for women to vote, wish, or offer any thing to the Church
(which implies subjection and obedience): but it is
lawful for women to have office in the Church. See
I Tim. 5:9. There were women that were chosen to
look after the poor, sick, lame, strangers, etc. and
so Phoebe a deaconess, Rom. 16:1; and so Phil. 4:3,
some women that laboured with *Paul* in the Gospel, and
Philip's four daughters were prophetesses. Now doubt-
less, and by an undeniable consequence, it follows,
that women must have the common liberty of members to
vote or the like in the Church.

    3. (*Ab aequali libertate omnium in uno.*) Sev-
eral arguments run from the equal liberty of all members purchased by Christ. And to follow Melanchthon
de libertate christiana in his *Common Places,* I could
argue thus, *Quos filius liberavit, vere liberi sunt,
sed etc.* "Those whom the Son hath made free, are
free indeed," Joh. 8:36; but all the Saints of Christ
(without difference of sexes; sisters as well as
brothers) are made free by Christ, Gal. 3:28. "There
is neither Jew nor Greek, bond nor free, male nor female, for ye all are one in Christ." I pray mark,
the Apostle puts you in mind of their equal liberty
in Christ, and therefore, that they should not con-
tend or differ, in saying this is a Jew or Gentile,
this is a servant or a woman, why ye are all one body,
have all one head, and are all one (without any such
difference) in Christ; in Christ there is no such
thing as subjection one to another.... All sorts of
believers are under a civil or spiritual rule. In
the civil there are such differences of fathers,

children, masters, servants, magistrates, subjects,
men and women; but in the spiritual rule, and government of Christ in his Church and Saints all are one,
without respect of persons; no difference should arise
amongst them.   There is no such thing as Jew, i.e. as
opposed to Gentile: nor as Presbyterian, i.e. as opposed to Independent: nor Independent, i.e. as opposed
to Anabaptist: nor as a servant, i.e. as opposed to
the free: nor as rich, i.e. as opposed to poor: nor as
the learned, i.e. as opposed to the unlearned in
tongues and arts: nor as a man or brother, i.e. as opposed to a woman or sister; for they are all one in
Christ's account, in Christ's Kingdom, without any
such respect of persons, opinions, sexes, or ages;
and have all one and the same liberty in and by Christ.
Thus *Gualther*[8] gives out, and bitterly complains of
such as are enemies to Christ and his Church, that
make differences about persons, opinions, sexes, or
the like, and that would rob any one of their liberty
bought them by Christ.   Now Christian liberty hath
these two parts, viz. deliverance from, and freedom
to; deliverance from the curse, power and punishment
of the Law, and from the observations of traditions,
Col. 2:20, which women have equal benefit of, with
men.   And so in freedom to the worship and service of
God, the ordinances of Christ, the kingdom of Christ,
grace and glory; which also appertains to women as
well as men, being restored by Christ to that equal
liberty (in the things of God, and in the Church of
Christ) with men, which they lost by the fall; and
they are now again to become meet and mutual helps:
for all are one in Christ, says the text.   Now though

there is a civil subjection to men in their economical
relations as we said before, that there is not any
servile subjection due to them, whereby poor souls
are enslaved and kept under in bondage from doing
their duty to God, or taking their Christian liberty
in the things of God. Bernard in *lib. de gratia &
lib. arbit.* tells us of a threefold liberty, i.e. of
nature, grace and glory, and every woman (as well as
man) is made happy by it, ever since Christ turned
Eva to Ave, they have been restored into spiritual
liberty and Christian equality in the Church: and the
Apostle, Jam. 2:1, in his "Catholic Epistle" (so
called) says it agrees not with the profession to
make difference of persons in the Church of Christ,
therefore my brethren have not the faith of our Lord
Jesus with respect of persons: not only in not pre-
ferring the rich before the poor, but not the strong
before the weak, (nor the men before the women) and
"is not this partiality so to do?" (says he) vers. 4.
Or have ye not made a difference, where Christ hath
made none? Now the force of the argument is full for
us. For where there ought to be no respect of persons, there ought to be no difference betwixt men and
women, (for the general includes the particular) but
in the Church of Christ there ought to be no respect
of persons. *Ergo,* women (as members) must have equal
liberty with men....

        7. Reason runs from their excellencies and
abilities of some women surpassing men for piety and
judgement; and therefore ought to have equal liberty
with them in Church-affairs. The argument is free,

the proof's clear, for prudent Abigail excelled her
husband; for knowledge, Priscilla Apollos (though a
preacher). For faith, the Canaanitess, of whom Christ
said, "I have not seen so great faith no not in Israel." For affection and zeal, the Queen of the South
shall rise up against the men of this generation, Luk.
11:31. And Mary Magdalene, for piety and spirit, out-
ran, and outreached all the twelve disciples in her
diligence to seek out Christ: to whom Christ first
discovered himself after his resurrection, and bid
her declare it to his disciples; she was the first
preacher of Christ's resurrection. So we read how
Jael excelled in courage, Deborah in thankfulness,
Lois and Eunice in faith and obedience; Lydia in en-
tertaining the Word, Act. 16:14. The Shunamite in
faith and zeal, and understanding, excelled her husband, 2 King. 4:8, 9; 22:30. So the Samaritaness the
rest of the citizens, Joh. 4:4. And we read of some
women exhorted to win in their husbands to the truth,
I Pet. 3:2. Yea and Manoah's wife, Judg. 13:22, 23.
you shall find of a sounder judgement and faith than
her husband. So that all these examples prove the
reason which requires their just liberty in the Church
of Christ. I remember I have read in Jerome's day of
many holy women that exceeded others in learning and
abilities, and in the studying of the Scriptures, and
they had their commentaries upon them of their own
making. Furthermore, the Kingdom of heaven is compared to a woman, and Christ's Church is called his
wife and spouse, Rev. 19, Cant. 2. And as Mary said
it, in the behalf of other good women, "He that is
mighty hath magnified me," and therefore they are not

to be so rejected of men who are so highly received
and honoured of God. But to the

8. Reason, which is taken from their strong affection to the truth, when once they be in the way of
Christ; and for the most part they are exceeding men
therein. Hence it is that Satan so often makes the
first trial of women for his turn and service, seeing
where they take, their affections are strongest (for
the most part) and he sped so well at first, that he
can't forget it; so he found out a Dalilah for Samson,
a Jezebel for Ahab, Pharaoh's daughter for Solomon, etc.
For where they are bad, they are extreme bad; but
where they are good, they are exceeding good, and most
fondly affected with the things of God.... For as the
gold which is of the purest substance soonest receives
the form, and much sooner than the sturdy steel, or
hard iron which is of a gross and massy metal (says
Cawdrey); so are women more readily wrought upon, and
sooner persuaded and formed into the truth than men,
who are for the most part like sturdy steel and iron,
hard to work upon. And as gold (so women) many times
take the surest stamp and fullest impression: but I
pass by this; yet before I conclude, I must speak a
word or two both to men and women. Let not men despise them then in the Church of Christ (as the weak-
est vessels) nor wrong them of their liberty of voting
or speaking in common affairs, (yet with subjection,
civility, and in order) to prevent disorders and rude-
ness; we were wont in Dublin to call over their names
one by one, as well as men's: I know the ordinary objection is objected out of I Cor. 14:34, 35. "Let

your women keep silence in the Church, for it is not
permitted unto them to speak." So I Tim. 2:12.

Ans. 1. Grant it in that sense the Apostle
spake it, which he declares all along the chapter,
both before in vers. 1, 2, 3, 22, 24, 31, 32. and
after in vers. 37, 39. which is, that they keep from
public preaching, or prophesying, or teaching as officers or ministers do; or the like, etc. which all
expositors grant that I have met with. Now we plead
not for this; but for the common ordinary liberty due
to them as members of the Church, viz. to speak, object, offer, or vote with the rest, which this Scripture (nor no other as I know of) doth in the least
hinder, but rather help, being rightly considered.
For,

2. He saith it is not permitted...by reason of
the disorders and differences that then were in the
Church, it was thought inconvenient to allow women's
liberty to preach publicly, whereby they brought but
confusion into the Church, as appears in the ante-
cedent and subsequent words, vers. 33. and vers. 40,
so that the ill consequence was the cause of this
rule of prudence, not any positive command of God's,
but he spake as in I Cor. 7:6. So that from this
very Scripture (besides a hundred others) I do verily
believe that handmaids shall prophecy, and have more
public liberty than now they have; but however this
does nothing at all disallow or deny them their common, private, proper liberty as members of Christ's
body; equally with men; I say as members (though not
as officers) and so subjective to the whole.

2. To women, I wish ye be not too forward, and
yet not too backward, but hold fast your liberty, in
Gal. 5:1, which the Apostle speaks as well to the
sisters as the brethren; Christ hath made ye free,
male and female, ye are all one in Christ; and ought
to be so in the Church; wherefore, stand fast, (says
he) that is, keep your ground which Christ hath won
and got for you; maintain your right, defend your
liberty, even to the life, lose it not, but be coura-
geous and keep us. And yet be cautious too, (*festina
lente*) not too fast, but first, be swift to hear, slow
to speak, Jam. 1:19. unless occasion requires you;
your silence may sometimes be the best advocate of
your orderly liberty, and the sweetest evidence of
your prudence and modesty...and yet ye ought not by
your silence to betray your liberty, trouble your
consciences, lose your privileges and rights; or see
the truth taken away or suffer before your eyes; but
I say, be not too hasty nor too high; for as the note
that comes too nigh the margin is in danger to run
into the text the next impression, so spirits that
run too high at first, may soon fall into disorder,
and irregularity. It is said, when Cyrus was young,
his grandfather made Sacas his overseer, to order him
both in his diet, time, and recreations; but when he
came to riper years, he became a Sacas to himself,
and took not so much liberty as he had leave to do,
and as was allowed him by his governour Sacas. And
so indeed that may be lawful to you, that is not (as
yet) expedient for you; and rather than run into disorder and confusion, hold your liberty a little in

suspense, and wave it on some occasions wherein you
lawfully may, but lose it not for all the world which
Christ paid so great a price for, and prepare for
fairer gales. As the miller does, for though he cannot command the wind, yet he will spread his sails
out, and open them in a readiness, when he is in hopes
of its coming; and so do you, and when the wind blows
(which begins) your liberty with full sails, shall
bring forth abundantly to serve all the country round.
In the meantime, make much of the ordinances, prize
your (hitherto) liberty, and practise accordingly.

And in a word, I say to all, "Those whom God
hath joined together, let no man put asunder."

H.   Margaret Asket Fell, *Womens Speaking Justified,*
       Proved and Allowed of by the Scriptures (London,
       1667), pp. 3-4, 6-10.

> [Of the free church groups begun in the sixteenth
> and seventeenth centuries, none were more open to,
> or indebted to, the participation of women than the
> Society of Friends. In the same decade (1640s)
> which saw the rise of many other radical sects,
> George Fox, still searching for the Light, made the
> acquaintance of Elizabeth Hooton, who was to become
> the first female Quaker preacher. But the woman
> who was to exert the greatest influence on the So-
> ciety was Margaret Fell (1614-1702), wife of Justice
> Thomas Fell (1598?-1658), Vice-Chancellor of the
> Duchy of Lancaster. When, in 1652, Fox included
> their home, Swarthmoor Hall, in his preaching tour,
> Margaret Fell was readily convinced of the "Lord's
> truth."[9] From that time Swarthmoor Hall became
> the virtual headquarters of the Quaker movement;
> in spite of the fact that Justice Fell never became
> an avowed member, he did not discourage the meetings
> of Friends in his home or his wife's active support
> of the persecuted sect. In the decade following
> his death she was imprisoned for four years in
> Lancaster Castle on the charge of holding unlawful

meetings. During that time she wrote several
short books, one of which was a bold reinterpretation of the biblical position on women in
spiritual life.]

Whereas it hath been an objection in the minds
of many, and several times hath been objected by the
clergy, or ministers, and others, against women's
speaking in the Church; and so consequently may be
taken, that they are condemned for meddling in the
things of God; the ground of which objection, is taken
from the Apostle's words, which he writ in his first
Epistle to the Corinthians, chap. 14. vers. 34, 35.
And also what he writ to Timothy in the first Epistle,
chap. 2, vers. 11, 12. But how far they wrong the
Apostle's intentions in these Scriptures, we shall
shew clearly when we come to them in their course and
order. But first let me lay down how God himself
hath manifested his Will and Mind concerning women,
and unto women.

And first, when "God created Man in his own
image; in the image of God created he them, male and
female: and God blessed them, and God said unto them,
Be fruitful, and multiply: And God said, Behold, I
have given you of every herb, etc.," Gen. 1. Here
God joins them together in his own image, and makes
no such distinctions and differences as men do; for
though they be weak, he is strong; and as he said to
the Apostle, "His grace is sufficient," and his
"strength is made manifest in weakness," 2 Cor. 12:9.
And such hath the Lord chosen, even "the weak things
of the world, to confound the things which are mighty;
and things which are despised, hath God chosen, to
bring to nought things that are," I Cor. 1. And God

hath put no such difference between the male and female as men would make.

It is true, "The serpent that was more subtle
than any" other "beast of the field," came unto the
woman, with his temptations, and with a lie; his sub-
tilty discerning her to be more inclinable to hearken
to him; when he said, "If ye eat, your eyes shall be
opened": and the woman saw that "the fruit was good
to make one wise," there the temptation got into her,
and "she did eat, and gave to her husband, and he did
eat" also, and so they were both tempted into the
transgression and disobedience; and therefore God said
unto Adam, when that he hid himself when he heard his
voice, "Hast thou eaten of the tree which I commanded
thee that thou shouldest not eat?" And Adam said,
"The woman which thou gavest me, she gave me of the
tree, and I did eat." And the Lord said unto the woman, "What is this that thou hast done?" and the woman
said, "The serpent beguiled me, and I did eat." Here
the woman spoke the truth unto the Lord. See what
the Lord saith, vers. 15, after he had pronounced
sentence on the serpent: "I will put enmity between
thee and the woman, and between thy seed and her seed;
it shall bruise thy head, and thou shalt bruise his
heel," Gen. 3.

Let this word of the Lord, which was from the
beginning, stop the mouths of all that oppose women's
speaking in the power of the Lord; for he hath put
enmity between the woman and the serpent; and if the
seed of the woman speak not, the seed of the serpent
speaks; for God hath put enmity between the two seeds,
and it is manifest, that those that speak against the

woman and her seed's speaking, speak out of the enmity
of the old serpent's seed; and God hath fulfilled his
word and his promise, "When the fulness of time was
come, he hath sent forth his Son, made of a woman,
made under the Law, that we might receive the adoption
of sons," Gal. 4:4, 5....

Thus we see that Jesus owned the love and grace
that appeared in women, and did not despise it, and by
what is recorded in the Scriptures, he received as
much love, kindness, compassion, and tender dealing
towards him from women, as he did from any others,
both in his life time, and also after they had exercised their cruelty upon him, for Mary Magdalene, and
Mary the Mother of Joses, beheld where he was laid:
"And when the Sabbath was past, Mary Magdalene, and
Mary the Mother of James, and Salome, had brought
sweet spices that they might anoint him. And very
early in the morning, the first day of the week, they
came unto the sepulchre at the rising of the sun, And
they said among themselves, Who shall roll us away the
stone from the door of the sepulchre? And when they
looked, the stone was rolled away for it was very
great," Mark 16:1, 2, 3, 4. Luke 24:1, 2. "and they
went down into the sepulchre," and as Matthew saith,
"The angel rolled away the stone, and he said unto
the women, Fear not, I know whom ye seek, Jesus which
was crucified: he is not here, he is risen," Mat. 28.
Now Luke saith thus, That there stood two men by them
in shining apparel, and as they were perplexed and
afraid, the men said unto them, he is not here; remember how he said unto you when he was in Galilee,
that the Son of Man must be delivered into the hands

of sinful men, and be crucified, and the third day
rise again, and they remembered his words, and returned from the sepulchre, and told all these things
to the eleven, and to all the rest."

It was Mary Magdalene, and Joanna, and Mary the
Mother of James, and the other women that were with
them, which told these things to the Apostles, "And
their words seemed unto them as idle tales, and they
believed them not." Mark this, ye despisers of the
weakness of women, and look upon your selves to be so
wise: but Christ Jesus doth not so, for he makes use
of the weak: for when he met the women after he was
risen, he said unto them, "All hail," and they came
and held him by the feet, and worshipped him, then
said Jesus unto them, "Be not afraid, go tell my
brethren that they go into Galilee, and there they
shall see me," Mat. 28:10; Mark 16:9. And John saith,
when Mary was weeping at the sepulchre, that Jesus
said unto her, "Woman, why weepest thou? what seekest
thou? And when she supposed him to be the Gardener,
Jesus saith unto her, Mary; she turned herself, and
saith unto him, Rabboni, which is to say master;
Jesus saith unto her, Touch me not, for I am not yet
ascended to my Father, but go to my brethren, and say
unto them I ascend unto my Father, and to my God, and
your God," John 20:16, 17.

Mark this, you that despise and oppose the message of the Lord God that he sends by women, what had
become of the redemption of the whole body of mankind,
if they had not believed the message that the Lord
Jesus sent by these women, of and concerning his resurrection? And if these women had not thus, out of

their tenderness and bowels of love, who had received
mercy, and grace, and forgiveness of sins, and virtue,
and healing from him, which many men also had received
the like, if their hearts had not been so united, and
knit unto him in love, that they could not depart as
the men did, but sat watching, and waiting, and weeping about the sepulchre until the time of his resurrection, and so were ready to carry his message, as
is manifested, else how should his Disciples have
known, who were not there?

Oh! blessed and glorified be the glorious Lord,
for this may all the whole body of mankind say, though
the wisdom of man, that never knew God, is always
ready to except against the weak; but the weakness of
God is stronger than men, and the foolishness of God
is wiser than men.

And in Act. 18 you may read how Aquila and Priscilla took unto them Apollos, and expounded unto him
the way of God more perfectly; who was an eloquent
man, and mighty in the Scriptures: yet we do not read
that he despised what Priscilla said, because she was
a woman, as many now do.

And now to the Apostle's words, which is the
ground of the great objection against women's speaking. And first, I Cor. 14. let the reader seriously
read that chapter, and see the end and drift of the
Apostle in speaking these words: for the Apostle is
there exhorting the Corinthians unto charity, and to
desire spiritual gifts, and not to speak in an unknown
tongue, and not to be children in understanding, but
to be children in malice, but in understanding to be
men; and that the spirits of the prophets should be

subject to the prophets, for God is not the author of
confusion, but of peace: And then he saith, "Let your
women keep silence in the Church," etc.

Where it doth plainly appear that the women, as
well as others, that were among them, were in confusion, for he saith, "How is it brethren? when ye come
together, every one of you hath a psalm, hath a doctrine, hath a tongue, hath a revelation, hath an interpretation? let all things be done to edifying."
Here was no edifying, but all was in confusion speaking together. Therefore he saith, "If any man speak
in an unknown tongue, let it be by two, or at most by
three, and that by course, and let one interpret, but
if there be no interpreter, let him keep silence in
the Church." Here the man is commanded to keep silence as well as the woman, when they are in confusion and out of order.

But the Apostle saith further, "They are commanded to be in obedience," as also saith the Law;
and "if they will learn any thing, let them ask their
husbands at home, for it is a shame for a woman to
speak in the Church."

Here the Apostle clearly manifests his intent;
for he speaks of women that were under the Law, and
in that transgression as Eve was, and such as were
to learn, and not to speak publicly, but they must
first ask their husbands at home, and it was a shame
for such to speak in the Church. And it appears
clearly, that such women were speaking among the
Corinthians, by the Apostles exhorting them from malice and strife, and confusion, and he preacheth the
Law unto them, and he saith, in the Law it is written,

"With men of other tongues, and other lips, will I
speak unto this people," vers. 2:[21].

And what is all this to women speaking? that
have the everlasting Gospel to preach, and upon whom
the promise of the Lord is fulfilled, and his Spirit
poured upon them according to his word, Acts 2:16, 17,
18. And if the Apostle would have stopped such as had
the Spirit of the Lord poured upon them, why did he
say just before, "If any thing be revealed to another
that sitteth by, let the first hold his peace?" and
"you may all prophesy one by one." Here he did not
say that such women should not prophesy as had the
revelation and Spirit of God poured upon them, but
their women that were under the Law, and in the transgression, and were in strife, confusion and malice in
their speaking, for if he had stopped women's praying
or prophesying, why doth he say: "Every man praying
or prophesying having his head covered, dishonoureth
his head; but every woman that prayeth or prophesieth
with her head uncovered, dishonoureth her head? Judge
in yourselves, Is it comely that a woman pray or
prophesy uncovered? For the woman is not without the
man, neither is the man without the woman, in the
Lord," I Cor. 11:3, 4, 13.

Also that other Scripture, in I Tim. 2, where
he is exhorting that prayer and supplication be made
everywhere, lifting up holy hands without wrath and
doubting; he saith in the like manner also, that "Women must adorn themselves in modest apparel, with
shamefastness and sobriety, not with broidered hair,
or gold, or pearl, or costly array." He saith, "Let
women learn in silence with all subjection, but I

suffer not a woman to teach, nor to usurp authority
over the man, but to be in silence; for Adam was first
formed, then Eve; and Adam was not deceived, but the
woman being deceived was in the transgression."

Here the Apostle speaks particularly to a woman
in relation to her husband, to be in subjection to
him, and not to teach, nor usurp authority over him,
and therefore he mentions Adam and Eve. But let it
be strained to the utmost, as the opposers of women's
speaking would have it, that is, that they should not
preach nor speak in the Church, of which there is
nothing here. Yet the Apostle is speaking to such as
he is teaching to wear their apparel, what to wear,
and what not to wear; such as were not come to wear
modest apparel, and such as were not come to shamefastness and sobriety, but he was exhorting them from
broidered hair, gold, and pearls, and costly array;
and such are not to usurp authority over the man, but
to learn in silence with all subjection, as it becometh women professing godliness with good works.

And what is all this to such as have the power
and spirit of the Lord Jesus poured upon them, and
have the message of the Lord Jesus given unto them?
must not they speak the Word of the Lord because of
these undecent and unreverent women that the Apostle
speaks of, and to, in these two Scriptures? And how
are the men of this generation blinded, that bring
these Scriptures, and pervert the Apostle's words,
and corrupt his intent in speaking of them? and by
these Scriptures, endeavour to stop the message and
Word of the Lord God in women, by contemning and de-
spising of them. If the Apostle would have had

women's speaking stopped, and did not allow of them,
why did he entreat his true yoke-fellow to help those
women who laboured with him in the Gospel? Phil. 4:3.
And why did the Apostles join together in prayer and
supplication with the women, and Mary the mother of
Jesus, and with his brethren, Acts 1:14, if they had
not allowed, and had union and fellowship with the
Spirit of God, wherever it was revealed in women as
well as others? But all this opposing and gain-saying
of women's speaking, hath risen out of the bottomless
pit, and spirit of darkness that hath spoken for these
many hundred years together in this night of apostacy,
since the revelations have ceased and been hid, and so
that spirit hath limited and bound all up within its
bond and compass, and so would suffer none to speak,
but such as that spirit of darkness, approved of, man
or woman.

I.   George Fox, "An encouragement to all the faith-
        ful women's meetings" (Letter CCCXX), *The Works
        of George Fox,* Vol. VIII (Philadelphia, 1831),
        pp. 92-97.

        [George Fox (1624-1691), who, after many years of
        working closely with Margaret Fell, married her in
        1669, had long been a supporter of women's right to
        speak in religious assemblies. Early in his ministry
        he engaged in a dispute over a priest's rebuke of a
        woman who had raised a question at a church meeting.[10]
        Later, as his movement took organized form with
        monthly, quarterly and yearly meetings, Fox encour-
        aged the formation, in 1671, of Women's Meetings on
        the same regular basis as those of men. While the
        women's tasks were still those which might be con-
        sidered typically feminine (helping the poor, needy,
        and suffering and overseeing education and marriages),
        nevertheless the mere existence of such separate
        meetings for women aroused opposition, even within
        the ranks of the Quakers.[11]]

An encouragement to all the faithful women's meetings in the world, who assemble together in the fear of God, for the service of the truth. Wherein they may see how the holy men encouraged the holy women, both in the time of the law, and in the time of the gospel; though selfish and unholy men may seek to discourage them. But go on in the name and power of Christ, and prosper. (Marshgrainge, September 16, 1676).

Friends,—You may read in the old world, how one family after another, till Noah's time, served the Lord God. And then from Noah, Abraham, Isaac, and Jacob, and their wives, and after Moses and Aaron had brought the children of Israel out of Egypt, and that they were come to be a great people, Moses said, "I would all the Lord's people were prophets." Numb. 11:29. And when a young man said unto Moses, "Eldad and Medad do prophesy in the camp"; and he would have had Moses to forbid them: but Moses answered and said unto him again, "Would to God all the Lord's people were prophets, and that the Lord would put his spirit upon them."

So Moses here (who was captain, governor, and judge over Israel), was far from restraining any from prophesying in the camp, but reproved his envy that would have had him forbid them; and did moreover encourage them, by saying, "I would to God all the Lord's people were prophets": and surely all the Lord's people are made up of both men and women.

And the Lord having given his law to the children of Israel, which was holy, just and good, the Lord, said, "I have poured out my spirit upon the

house of Israel: so that by this spirit, they might
understand his law, which was spiritual." Ezek. 39:29.

Now in the time of the law, there were the assemblies of the women; for all the women that were
wise of heart, did work with their hands those holy
things which God had commanded.

And all the women whose hearts stirred them up
in wisdom, these women wrought about those holy things
that belonged to the tabernacle and sanctuary; as you
may see in Exod. 35.

And likewise the assemblies of the women, in
the 38th chapter, and of the women's assembling at
the door of the tabernacle of the congregation; and
in the margin it is said, they assembled by troops.

Now, here you may see, that the women were in
the work and service of God, as well as the men; and
they had their assemblies. For God had poured out
his spirit upon the house of Israel, to give them an
understanding, both men and women, to do that, and
make those things which God had commanded, which were
called holy things; which were but figures and shadows
of the substance, Christ Jesus, the holy one.

Now Moses and Aaron, and the seventy elders,
did not say to those assemblies of the women, we can
do our work ourselves, and you are more fit to be at
home to wash the dishes; or such-like expressions;
but they did encourage them in the work and service
of God, in those things which God had commanded them
in the time of the law.

For God having poured his spirit on the house
of Israel, to give them an understanding, to do those
things which God had commanded them; by which spirit

their hearts were stirred up to do God's work, both
males and females.

And in the time of the law, the women were to
offer up sacrifices and offerings, as well as the men,
upon God's altar; as you may see, Hannah when she
brought Samuel, and offered him up to the Lord, she
brought him to the house of the Lord in Shiloh, and
when she brought him, she took up with her three bul-
locks, besides flour and wine: so see how she paid
her vows to the Lord, and offered up her sacrifices
upon God's altar. And other places might be shown of
the women's offerings and sacrifices.

And you may see Hannah's fervent zeal to God,
and what a large speech she made in magnifying and
exalting the Lord, in I Sam. 1st and 2nd chapters.

And so you may see, the offerings and sacrifices
of the women were accepted upon God's altar, as well
as the men's.

But the hire of a whore was not to be brought
into the house of God for any vow, for it was an abomination to the Lord. Deut. 23:10.

Now Hannah's husband, and the other women's husbands, that offered up their offerings upon God's altar, were not offended at them, nor did they say,
their offerings were enough for them both; but every
one was to offer up their peace-offerings and thanks-
giving-offerings themselves, and other offerings.

So here you may see the service and work of the
women, and how serviceable the women were in their
assemblies in the time of the law, about the tabernacle and holy things, and how the women offered upon
God's altar, as well as the men; they had their

liberty. But the hire of the whore was to be kept
out of God's house, and not to be offered up upon
God's altar.

So you may see man and woman were meet-helps
in paradise, before the fall; and death reigned from
Adam till Moses, and after Moses received the law
from God, which went over death (and sin that
brought it), who saw the state of man and woman in
paradise: men and women in the time of the law were
meet-helps again to one another, in the work and
service of the holy things about the tabernacle and
sanctuary, and the women had their assemblies.

And it is said, in Joel 2 and in Acts 2 "that
the Lord would pour out of his spirit upon all flesh
in the last days or times."

So this spirit being poured upon all flesh in
the christian times, sons and daughters, handmaids
and servants, old men and young men, that by the spirit of God, all these might have his visions, prophecies and dreams: and this is his spirit, by which all
should profit in the things that be eternal, and to
serve God in the spirit, both men and women, sons and
daughters, old men and young men, handmaids and servants; all offer up to God his spiritual sacrifices.

For all being dead in old earthly Adam, Christ,
the heavenly Adam has tasted death for them all, and
is a propitiation for the sins of the whole world,
and he enlightens all, and his grace hath appeared
unto all, and his spirit is poured upon all flesh,
and his gospel, which is the power of God, is preached
to every creature under heaven.

And now, must not all receive the grace, and

believe in the light, and receive this gospel, and
walk and labour in it, both men and women, sons and
daughters, old men and young, servants and handmaids.

Yea, I say, the gospel being preached to all
nations, and to every creature under heaven, old men
and young, servants and handmaids, sons and daughters;
I say, then must not all these receive this gospel,
and the light and grace? and are they not all to walk
in it? and to offer up their spiritual sacrifices upon the heavenly altar, in the new covenant, and to
walk in the new and living way; and all to receive
the light of Christ, which enlightens all; and to become children of light, and to feel the blood of
Christ to cleanse them from all sin, which they have
in old Adam.

So as the women were to offer, in the old covenant, and in the time of the law, upon the outward altar, their offerings; and God poured out his spirit
upon the house of Israel, that they might understand,
and do what he commanded them: at which time they had
the assemblies of the women, which were not forbidden.

So now, in the time of the gospel, and the day
of Christ, which enlightens all, and in the time of
his grace, which hath appeared unto all men, to teach
them, and to bring their salvation; and in the time
of his gospel preached to every creature, and in the
time of his pouring out of his spirit upon all flesh,
that they might understand, and walk, and live in his
gospel, and by his spirit offer up their spiritual
sacrifices.

So, in this the time and day of Christ, the
captain of our salvation, must not all these labour

in the gospel, and in the word, and in the grace, and
in the light, and know and do God and Christ's work
and service about his heavenly tabernacle and sanctuary? Hath not every one their service that are enlightened? And his grace, that hath appeared unto
them, are they not stewards of it? And must not they
have their assemblies of the women in the time of the
gospel, and of the new covenant, and in the time of
grace, and light, and life, as well as in the time of
the law, and of the old covenant?

And are not all to labour in that which tends
to God's glory, and praise, and honour? For which
end he hath made them all, and for which end he hath
redeemed them, and converted them, and translated and
sanctified them, to make them vessels of his honour,
and of his grace and mercies.

And so now the end of all our men's and women's
meetings in the time of the gospel (the power of
Christ being the authority of them), is, that they
might all labour in his power, and in his grace, and
in his spirit, and in his light, to do his service,
and his business in truth and righteousness.

So the women in the time of the gospel, light,
and grace, are to look into their own selves and
families, and to look to the training up of their
children; for they are oft-times more amongst them
than the men, and may prevent many things that may
fall out, and many times they may make or mar their
children in their education.

So now they come to be exercised in the grace
of God, and to admonish and exhort, reprove and re-
buke, and to keep all their families modest, honest,

virtuous, sober, and civil, and not to give liberty,
nor indulge that which tends to vice, or lascivious-
ness, or any evil, or idleness, or slothfulness, or
the fashions of the world, which pass away; and to
stop all vain words, and idle talking, and stories,
and tales, which are unprofitable; but rather to turn
their ears to godliness, which they should be trained
up and exercised in, and not to fulfill the lust of
the eye; for that being satisfied, brings the pride of
life, and then comes the lust of the flesh; and this
is not of the Father, but of the world.

And if either men or women suffer such things,
they suffer that which defiles their children and
families; and therefore such things are to be reproved
in families, and their children to be stopped from
going into such things.

And therefore they are to have an esteem of
truth and virtue above all such things, and not to indulge any such things as will draw out their minds
from virtue to vice.

Now when the women are met together in the light,
and in the gospel, the power of God; some are of a
more large capacity and understanding than other women,
and are able to inform, and instruct, and stir up
others into diligence, virtue, and rightcousness, and
godliness, and, in the love and wisdom of God, to inform and reform their families, and to help them that
be of weaker capacities and understandings in the wisdom of God, that they may be fruitful in every good
work and word.

So that they may see that all their families
are ordered to God's glory; and that which tends to

looseness or evil, either in words, ways, or actions,
that would corrupt them, either in their lives or manners, may be kept down and reproved.

So that all their children and servants may be
trained up in the fear of God, in the new covenant;
for among the Jews in the old covenant, they that so-
journed amongst them were to keep the sabbath, and if
they did eat of their sacrifice, they were to be cir-
cumcised.

And the women had their assemblies in the days
of the judges and the kings; and old Eli's sons abused
them, and old Eli did admonish his sons, but he did
not restrain them from their wickedness; and therefore
God cut off his sons, and he lost the art of God, and
the priesthood, and his own life also.

So many of you may admonish your children, but
if ye do not restrain them by the help of the spirit
of God, which God hath given to you, you will quench
the spirit of God in you, by indulging them; so by
that you will lose your spiritual offering, and your
priesthood therein; and take heed if you do not lose
your own lives, and your children's also; therefore
mind old Eli for your example.

Now old Eli was not against the assemblies of
the women, who assembled by troops, as (in the margin
of the bible) you may see, I Sam. 2:21, 22, though
some men now-a-days may be against women's speaking
or prophesying, but they are ignorant of the universal
spirit, and of their service and labour to God, in his
grace and gospel, and are of a narrow spirit, and are
not the true servers of God themselves; for if they
were, they would have all people to serve God in his

power, and to keep the true religion, which is to
visit the fatherless and the widows, and to keep themselves from the spots of the world.

And some there have been, that would not have
the women to meet without the men; and some of them
say, the women must not speak in the church, and if
they must not speak, what should they meet with them
for?

But what spirit is this, that would exercise
lordship over the faith of any? And what a spirit is
this, that will neither suffer the women to speak
amongst the men, nor to meet amongst themselves to
speak?

But all this is for judgment, with that spirit
that gives liberty unto all that labour in the gospel,
in the light, and in the grace.

And some men and women there are that suggest,
if women should meet (by themselves) in the order of
the gospel, the power of God, they would be too high:
but such men and women, as so suggest, are too high
already, and would be ruling over men and women's
possessions, and waste their own; for if they were in
the power and spirit of God, they need not fear any
one's getting over them. For the power and spirit of
God gives liberty to all; for women are heirs of life
as well as the men, and heirs of grace, and of the
light of Christ Jesus, as well as the men, and so
stewards of the manifold grace of God.

And they must all give an account of their
stewardship, and are to be possessors of life, and
light, and grace, and the gospel of Christ, and to
labour in it; and to keep their liberty and freedom

in it, as well as the men.

And they are believers in the light, as well as
the men, and so children of the light and of the day,
as well as the men.

And so the assemblies of the women, whom God
hath poured out his spirit upon, are to be in the
time of the gospel, as well as in the time of the law,
that they may be helps-meet to the men in the time of
the gospel, in the restoration, as they were in the
beginning, and time of the law.

So all the women, (in all their assemblies in
the time of the gospel, and of the new covenant of
light, life, and grace,) are to be encouraged, as
they were in the time of the law, and to be stirred
up in the wisdom of God to their diligence and service
of God and Christ, in his new covenant, in his gospel
time, to do the Lord's business about the heavenly
tabernacle, and heavenly garments, as the women were
about the figure in the time of the law.

And now, you that stumble at women's meetings,
had not your women many vain meetings before they were
convinced, and you were not then offended at them,
when they met to satisfy the flesh, and had junketing
meetings to themselves; did you reprove them for such
meetings?

And why should they not now meet in their conversion, in the Lord's power and spirit, to do his
business, and to visit the fatherless and widows, and
to keep themselves from the spots of the world, which
is the practice of the pure religion, wherein the men
and women may be helps-meet in the religion that is
not of the world, that keeps from the spots of the

world.

But some have said, that such meetings must not
be, but as business requires or occasions them. As
much as to say, you must not make up the hedges till
the beasts have devoured your corn; and then the parish overseers must meet together to compute the dam-
age. And here their wisdom is seen, as if it were not
more their duty to meet, to prevent bad actions that
may fall out, and with the power of God to stop up
gaps to prevent evil, or weak places; for when the
evil is entered into, it is too late to meet them,
which rather brings scandal than remedy; and therefore the labourers in the gospel, men and women (being helps-meet), are to see that all walk and live in
the order of the gospel, and to see that nothing be
lacking, then all is well. For the women in their
assemblies may inform one another of the poor widows
and fatherless, and in the wisdom of God may find the
best way for the setting forth of their children; and
to see that their children are preserved in truth, and
to instruct them in the fear of the Lord.

CHAPTER FIVE

WOMEN AS PREACHERS AND PROPHETS

The views on womankind presented in the preceding chapters have not always been flattering to
that sex. But perhaps the least flattering picture
is that which we present here: case studies of actual
women who sought to exercise religious leadership.
Frena Bumenin sitting nude in preparation for giving
birth to the Antichrist, Mrs. Attaway deserting her
husband for one of her followers, other women using
their devotional meetings as an occasion for feasting
and drinking, Lady Eleanor prophesying when on leave
from the mental hospital——all these hardly made a
good case for a female ministry. Of the women in
this chapter, only Sarah Cheevers, the Quaker mission-
ary, conveys an image of sober respectability and fa-
milial devotion.

A number of factors may help to explain this
imbalance. First, at least two of the selections
make no attempt at objectivity. Written by male opponents of female preaching, A *Discoverie of six women preachers* and Thomas Edwards' *Gangraena* are hardly a reliable basis for judging the motivations and
capabilities of women preachers during the Civil War
period. The selection by Johannes Kessler about a
group of Anabaptist women in Switzerland was also

written by a male opponent, but one who opposed the
entire Anabaptist movement. Kessler wanted to point
up the dangerous fanatical tendencies among Anabaptists. Significantly, Anne Hutchinson, who was also
charged with outrageous behavior, gives an impression
of relative restraint and lucidity when allowed to
speak for herself, as in the trial records excerpted
here. No doubt in the other instances as well a different picture would emerge if these women had written
their own stories.

Secondly, it is always true that the unusual
event gains attention. The women who fulfilled ordinary expectations of caring for their husbands and
children and attending church services in silence were
not newsworthy. We may be assured that the vast majority of women among radical Protestant groups were
dutiful wives who fully accepted female subordination.
Some, such as the Anabaptists Soetken Gerrits and
Vrou Gerrets, made a quiet contribution to their religious cause by writing hymns. Others witnessed viv-
idly, yet unspectacularly, to the strength of their
faith by dying as martyrs.

Nevertheless, having made the point that most
radical Protestants were not social oddities, one
must grant that, by definition, those religious nonconformists who did not fit into any organized religious body are classified as radical Protestants, thus
giving the more socially adaptive radicals a bad reputation. Mennonites, for instance, have tried for
centuries to dissociate themselves from the disruptive
Münsterites. And for every notorious female fanatic,
several men could be named. Kessler's Anabaptist

women, for example, follow a long line of medieval
pseudo-prophets posing as Christ.[1]

Yet whereas women may have no monopoly on unusual forms of religious expression, it is no doubt true
that the radical sects provided an outlet for women
dissatisfied with their traditional role. Although in
many ways radical Protestant groups were no less patriarchal than their contemporaries, nevertheless such
groups held certain advantages for women over the
established churches. By denying the tradition of
ordination through apostolic succession, the free
churches made the ministerial office more accessible.
If authority to preach came directly from God, rather
than through a bishop, women could claim the right
along with men. When challenged, the fact that they
had gained a following could be used as a confirmation of their calling.

Radical Protestantism, then, enabled women to
preach and prophesy, not through a willing approval
of such activities but through theological loopholes.
The established churches did not encourage prophecy
from anyone, male or female; but in those sects where
spiritual illumination might be expected to come in
the form of visions and direct revelations, there was
no basis for denying women such experiences. The passage in Acts (2:17) referring to prophecy by women was
well known to the prophetically inclined. Similarly,
for those who denied the authority of the priestly office in favor of the authority of the community of believers, to withhold any religious function from women
was logically inconsistent, even if based on an appeal
to Paul. The male radicals might not have approved of

female preachers or prophets, but their theology had
left the door ajar.

A.   Johannes Kessler, *Sabbata*, ed. Emil Egli and
        Rudolf Schoch (St. Gall, 1902), pp. 154-157.

[Early in his career, Johannes Kessler (1502/3-1574),
one of the leading reformers of St. Gall, had studied for a time in Wittenberg. By chance he had happened to meet Luther in the "Black Bear Inn" in Jena
as Luther was returning, disguised as a knight, from
the Wartburg to Wittenberg in 1522. Kessler was influenced greatly not only by Luther but also by
Melanchthon and, to a lesser extent, Bugenhagen and
Karlstadt. Because St. Gall was still Catholic when
Kessler returned in 1523, he decided against ordination, becoming a saddler instead. Yet he put his
evangelical training to use in informal study groups,
in this way playing a vital role in the reform effort.
Under the leadership of Joachim Vadian, the city
joined the Protestant cause in 1525.

The following account of some Swiss Anabaptist women is taken from Kessler's observations of reform
in St. Gall from 1519 to 1539. Although his opposition to Anabaptism may be discerned in this selection,
he was fair enough in his treatment of the subject to
credit the Anabaptist leaders Conrad Grebel and Felix
Manz with speaking out against these "errors and
fantasies."[1]

Thereafter terrible and presumptuous errors arose
through some Anabaptist women, as for instance a maiden
of Zollikon in the district of Zurich by the name of
Margarita Hattinger.... She lived quite a discreet
life and thus was well liked and respected by the Anabaptists. She came to the point that she said she was
God. And many of the other Anabaptists believed this
and wanted to shield and preserve her from those who
opposed her by citing the saying of Christ, "Have you
not read in the law that you are gods, etc.?" And

"whoever keeps my commandments remains in me and I in
him, etc." Further this Margarita asserted that whoever prays is sinning; and no one wanted to say anything more or offer other instructions but wanted instead to let these words stand. After this she undertook to say things that no one could understand, as if
she were so deeply immersed in God that no one but she
in God could understand her tongue and speech. She began to speak thus: "Is it not written, does the one
who hung from the cross condemn her?" And again no
one would say anything more. In addition she led an
upright life and earned great esteem. Thus it happened that the belief arose among her followers that
whoever could say the most or do anything strange that
no one could understand or decipher was to be considered the most deified and immersed in God.

     There was among us a maiden named Magdalena
Müller, a citizen of our town, a very pretty, honorable, and modest maiden, and an Anabaptist. For the
same reasons as the afore-named Margarita, she proclaimed openly: "I am Christ, the way, the truth and
the life; whoever follows me does not walk in darkness.
Without my asking or desiring, God has brought me out
of hell and set me in heaven." Now this Magdalena had
two comrades, one named Barbara Mürglen, a citizen and
a respectable girl, the other Frena Bumenin, a servant-
girl born in Appenzell. But one day when Magdalena
and Barbara, both seamstresses, were together, they
began to talk about how one of them had become very
sore. Frena Bumenin heard this. She began to speak
with a frightful voice and to shake and foam at the
mouth, saying, "'Tis a lie, if you see a sore; oh, oh

why, why do you grieve the Holy Spirit so?" And after
she had spoken the words with great fury, Barbara fell
down and cried wailingly in a loud voice. "Oh woe,
woe, what have we done!" And she lay there, her body
swelling up, her face burning as bright as a rose,
sweating drop upon drop. So her belt and all her
clothes were undone so that she wouldn't suffocate.
After she had lain there two hours, she came to herself again, and said, "What a voice I heard! How it
penetrated my heart and veins! I thought it would
dissect me completely, for it was the true, living
voice of God. Oh, let us repent and leave off idle
chatter, that we may not grieve the Holy Spirit so
severely." Then they all retired.

On the evening of the following day they came
together again. This time Frena talked until the middle of the night about frightening things and got no
sleep the whole night. She said that she must have
twelve disciples; for she pretended she was Christ,
and the others believed it. There was yet another
comrade by the name of Wibrat. But [Frena] changed
her name and called her Martha. Then she commanded
the others to go to her in the morning and say, "The
Lord has sent me to you that you make ready this moment and follow him." Martha came and was obedient.
And one morning they went away before dawn. As they
left the house, Frena said, "Whoever will follow the
Lord, let him come." So they went out the gate into
the abbot's jurisdiction to a place called Buch, near
Tablat, and went into a house. There, learning to
weave, sat an Anabaptist named Lienhardt Wirt, born
in Lichtensteg in the county of Toggenburg; later he

became the husband of the oft-mentioned Frena Bumenin.
They went down into his weaving room and implored him
by the highest power of God that he should come up
and follow the Lord. He then stood up from his work
and was obedient. Thereafter the others went also
into the houses in the city and before that to all
who were dear to them, saying in imposing as well as
vehement and passionate words: "I implore you by the
power of God to go out to Buch; Christ is there, the
living son of God." Some went out, others received in
their hearts the true warning of Christ when he said,
"There will come false prophets who will say, 'I am
Christ,' or 'he is here or there.' Beware of them
and do not go out, etc." The same booted the messengers out of their houses with rough words and disen-
gaged themselves thereafter from their company.

　　　Those, however, who gathered in Buch confessed
to each other the sins they had committed during their
whole lives, including such things that one would be
amazed and think it preferable to have all one's veins
leeched than to confess such things to oneself.

　　　There occurred also from Frena an amazing confession before all the people. She said she must
give birth to the Antichrist and immediately thereafter she must give birth to the boy child mentioned
in Revelation 12. And after these utterances she
asked to be undressed completely. When Barbara, whom
she called Peter, had undressed her, she sat naked
before all the people, just as God created her. Now
there sat a man across from her who wondered when she
would cover her shame. She perceived this in his
thoughts and punished him for it. If any wanted to

to speak against her, she became as fierce and angry
as if she would tear him to pieces. Now it was late
at night. The others laid down to rest, for they were
tired. But she, Frena, ate, drank, and slept not, but
rather spoke terrible words the whole night. Among
other things she said Judas must hang himself. At
this point it occurred to one that he should go and
hang himself. But as he tried to go out the door with
this conviction and intention, he hit his head so hard
on the door that he turned around and decided not to
do it.

But Frena ran hastily out the door of the room
and said, "Whoever wants to come into the kingdom of
God, let him follow me." Then the others woke up and
soon arose and followed her. But they couldn't find
her and they feared perhaps she had hanged herself.
Then as they were sitting together in great concern
and fear, she came to them, wet up to her waist, for
she had run and tramped in the brook; she was chilling,
for it was cold and snowy in the last month, two weeks
before Christmas.

They told her to sit behind the oven. And after
she had sat there a while they asked her if she wanted
to lie in bed. She said yes. And after she had lain
there for two hours, she commenced to say horrifying
things, such as, "Here lies the great whore of Babylon,
with whom all races of the earth fornicated." After
that she said: "Here lies the true living son of God"
and again soon thereafter, "Here lies the great whore
of Babylon, she, she who, who will give birth to the
Antichrist." She spoke such words throughout the
whole day with such horrible deeds it would be impos-

sible to record and unbelievable to hear. Those who
were lodging her, however, did not want to permit
such conduct in their house. They threw all their
purses and gold into the room and said: "That should
be a sign regarding you, that you have driven out the
Lord." And then they went to another house, also
that of an Anabaptist.

   In this way their actions resounded around the
city and the whole countryside, and many people ran
out to them to see if what they had heard was true.
Their friends and other citizens became concerned
about them, fearing that the abbot, in whose jurisdiction they were, would have them imprisoned and killed.
They requested the abbot's lawyer to let them hand
over these citizens to the authorities of the city to
be imprisoned. This is what happened, and as the
three prisoners were being led through the city to
the town hall, they screamed with a loud voice: "Repent, repent, the day of the Lord, the time of the
uprooting, is at hand." Frena, however, had rent her
hair, her face was distorted, her mouth was foaming,
and her fingers and limbs were twisted as one caught
up in a severe illness. Many, especially pregnant
women, were horrified by her and aghast at her terrible features. And as she came to the town hall, she
ripped her jacket and said, "This is for a sign that
you have imprisoned innocent blood." There the mayor
and honorable council gathered to discuss what should
be done with them. It was suggested that each be
submitted into the hands of her friends and not allowed to see anyone for a while so that perhaps, provided with rest and proper food and drink, they might

return to more fitting conduct. Since Frena was not
a citizen, however, they wanted to release her to go
home to Appenzell. This she didn't want. Someone
suggested that if she would rather stay in town with
a citizen, they should figure up the costs until she
got better. There was, on the other hand, a citizen
who would take her in voluntarily. But she didn't
want this. She said: "I did not come here by myself,
but was brought here, so I will not leave by myself."

Thereupon they commanded her to be led through
the town to the inn and chained up in a special room
as one robbed of her senses. As she lay chained up
she began to act wildly, breaking the windows and
using such unbefitting words with the preachers and
other brethren who came to her (if they wanted to
bring her away from such manners, from [presenting
herself as] Jesus Christ, etc.) that it is better to
leave it unwritten than to sadden the heart of a
Christian reader; she professed, however, that she
had a different understanding.

The first night as she lay there a man came to
her and said, "I am a man sent to you from God to
sleep with you and fulfill my will with you." And
she believed him and let him lie with her that night.
The next night he came again and spoke to her as before. Then she swore to him by the living God, and
he disappeared from her. This she herself later con-
fided secretly to another.

After she had lain there six weeks she decided
to test how firmly she was imprisoned and took the
chain into her hand; thereupon the ring fell off her
hand. When she tried to push the ring back on, she

couldn't get her hand in. Because she was now quiet,
they did not want to chain her up again and would
have been glad to see her go away. She did not want
to leave by herself, however, but had to be led out
of the jurisdiction of the city.

B.   *A Discoverie of Six women preachers, in Middle-*
        sex, Kent, Cambridgeshire, and Salisbury (Lon-
        don, 1641), pp. 1-5.

        [If the male theorists on the question of the female
        role in the church almost uniformly excluded preach-
        ing from the list of permissible activities (see
        chapter four above), nevertheless, as the opponents
        of sectarianism pointed out by way of criticism,
        egalitarianism in the church would have to extend
        to women as well as men. If unordained men could
        enter the pulpit, the logical next step would be
        preaching by women. Although women preachers were
        very rare before the English Civil War period, the
        1640s witnessed the appearance of a large number of
        such women among the sectaries. Needless to say,
        they were greeted with much scorn and rebuke, par-
        tially for the questionable nature of their teach-
        ings, but primarily for their audacity in presuming
        to assume such a high office.]

     The six women Preachers
             Anne Hempstall   Mary Bilbrowe
             Joan Bauford   and   Susan May
             Elizabeth Bancroft   Arabella Thomas

     In ancient times have I read of Prophetesses,
but not until of late heard of women preachers,
their only reason or cause of preaching was, that
there was a deficiency of good men, wherefore it was
but fit, that virtuous women should supply their
places, they were (men they did mean) good for
nothing, but to make their texts good by expounding
the language of the Beast, but they themselves would
preach nothing, but such things as the spirit should

move them.

The first and chief of this female and sacerdo-
tical function, was one Anne Hempstall, living in the
Parish of Saint Andrews Holborne, near London, and in
the County of Middlesex, upon a certain time, she
having a mind, said she was moved to be zealously affected, called an assembly of her bibbing gossips together, whose thoughts were bent more upon the strong
water bottle, than upon the uses or doctrines which
their holy sister intended to expound unto them, but
being come to the house of this Anne Hempstall, zeal-
ous Nan spake to them after this manner.

Beloved sisters, this last night I dreamed a
strange dream, moreover me thought I saw a vision, in
which Anna the Prophetess was presented unto my view,
the splendour of whose countenance did cast me into a
trance, wherein I lay until the next morning, and the
morning being come, I could conceive no interpretation of my dream but this, that I should imitate godly Anna, by preaching unto you, as she prophesied to
others, her speech struck them all into an astonishment, at which, this prophet Anne cried out, "Now
doth the Holy Ghost descend down upon you, wherefore
give ear unto me." Then did she begin to talk, and
speak unto them that which first came into her mind,
but the chief matter of her text was this, that woman's hair was an adorning to her, but for a man to
have long hair, it was a shame unto him, which the
Scripture itself cried fie upon; long did she preach,
and longer I dare avouch than some of the audience
were willing, for some of them had as far home as
White Chapel, wherefore her longitude might cause a

brevitude of her sucking the aquavitae bottle; two
hours being expired, and the bottom of the stool beginning to look open-mouthed with her furious stamps,
she gave them as much peace as in her lay, and so
concluded.

Mary Bilbrowe, one of the audience, being of
the Parish of Saint Giles in the Fields, desired them
to be all with her the next morning, and after Sermon,
they should have a good fat pig to breakfast, besides
a cup of sack or claret to wash it down. They all
agreed unto it, and making use of all the rhetoric
which they were born unto, they gave her thanks, and
so for that time a bottle of ale or two being devoured, they departed every one to their own houses.
The next morning, they met altogether at the house of
Mary Bilbrow, whose husband was a good honest brick-
layer, and so soon as they came within the door of
her house, she brought them all into her parlour as
she called it, and instead of stools and cushions,
she had provided before hand, three bricks a piece
for them to sit upon. Her reason was this, she
thought they would not sit much, because women to
good instructions love standing. Her pulpit was
framed very substantially of brick, so high, that
scarce any thing, but her standing up tippet could be
seen. She began there very devoutly to make an *ex
tempore* prayer, but before she had scarce spoke twenty words, her daughter came running in very hastily,
telling her a gentleman at Bloomsbury stayed to speak
with her about urgent occasions, which hearing, she
leapt out of her prayer into this serious meditation,
I think it be the gentleman I was withal at Salisbury

Court, whom I promised this day to meet withal, whereupon she left her pulpit, spread the cloth, and
brought her gossips in a pig according to her promise,
who fed heartily, and so departed. So much at this
time for Middlesex female teachers.

Now give me leave to take water, and go to
Gravesend, and so further into Kent, where I shall
tell you of one Joan Bauford in the town of Feversham,
who taught in Feversham, that husbands being such as
crossed their wive's wills might lawfully be forsaken.

Then was there one Susan May of Ashford in the
County of Kent also which preached in a barn there,
that the Devil was the father of the Pope, the Pope
the father of those which did wear surplices, wherefore consequently the Devil was the father of all
those which did not love Puritans.

There was likewise one Elizabeth Bancroft in Ely
in Cambridgshire, where Bishop Wren first going to
place altars there, preached behind the minister upon
a Saturday, that it was fit upon Sunday to sacrifice
the Pope's bird upon his own altar.

Then lastly there was an Arabella Thomas, a
Welch woman, which lived in the city of Salisbury,
which preached, and in her sermon said that none but
such painful creatures as herself should go to heaven,
for those ministers which did not preach twice upon
every Sabbath day, she said that very shortly the
black raven by day, and the white owl by night should
scratch out their eyes.

Thus have I declared some of the female acade-
mies, but where their university is I cannot tell, but
I suppose that Bedlam or Bridewell would be two con-

venient places for them.[2] Is it not sufficient that
they may have the Gospel truly and sincerely preached
unto them, but that they must take their minister's
office from them? If there had been such a dearth of
the Gospel as there was in the reign of Queen Mary it
had been an occasion somewhat urgent. But God be
praised it was not so, but that they seemed to be am-
bitious, and because they would have superiority,
they would get upon a stool, or in a tub instead of a
pulpit. At this time I have described but six of
them, ere long I fear I shall relate more, I pray God
I have no cause, and so for this time I conclude.

C.   Thomas Edwards, *Gangraena*, 2nd ed. (London,
        1646), pp. 116-121, Appendix, pp. 120-121.

        [Most virulent in his slanderous attacks against
        female preachers was a Puritan minister of Presby-
        terian leanings named Thomas Edwards (1599-1647).
        It should not be thought, however, that Edwards
        was any more concerned about this evil than about
        any of the other errors he found so prevalent in
        his time. The first edition of his *Gangraena* cata-
        logued 16 sorts of dangerous sectaries, 180 errors
        or heresies, and 28 "pernicious practices." His
        second edition followed soon thereafter with an
        additional list of 34 errors.

        Of Edwards' personality, Jeremiah Burroughs wrote:
        "I doubt whether there ever was a man who was
        looked upon as a man professing godliness that
        ever manifested so much boldness and malice against
        others whom he acknowledged to be religious persons.
        That fiery rage, that implacable, irrational vio-
        lence of his against godly persons, makes me stand
        and wonder."[1]]

        Among all the confusion and disorder in Church-
matters both of opinions and practices, and particularly of all sorts of mechanics taking upon them to

preach and baptize, as smiths, tailors, shoemakers,
pedlars, weavers, etc. there are also some women-
preachers in our times, who keep constant lectures,
preaching weekly to many men and women. In Lincoln-
shire, in Holland and those parts, there is a woman
preacher who preaches (it's certain), and 'tis reported also she baptizeth, but that's not so certain.
In the Isle of Ely, (that island of errors and
sectaries,) is a woman-preacher also. In Hartford-
shire also there are some woman-preachers who take
upon them at meetings to expound the Scriptures in
houses, and preach upon texts, as on Rom. 8:2. But
in London there are women who for some time together,
have preached weekly on every Tuesday about four of
the clock, unto whose preachings many have resorted.
I shall particularly give the reader an account of
the preaching of two women, (one a lace-woman that
sells lace in Cheapside, and dwells in Bell-Alley in
Colemanstreet, and the other a major's wife living
in the Old Baily), who about a month ago, the second
Tuesday in December (as I take it) did preach in
Bell-Alley in Colemanstreet, the manner whereof is
as follows (as I had it from a godly minister of
this city, who was there present an eye and ear-wit-
ness of it): Three women came forth out of an in-
ward room or chamber, into the room where they used
to exercise, and where some company waited for to
hear them. These women came with Bibles in their
hands, and went to a table; the lace-woman took her
place at the upper end; the gentlewoman the major's
wife sat on one side by her; the third woman stood
on the other side of the table; the lace-woman at the

upper end of the table, turned herself first to this
gentlewoman (who was in her hoods, necklace of pearl,
watch by her side, and other apparel suitable), and
intreated her to begin, extolling her for her gifts
and great abilities; this gentlewoman refused to begin, pleading her weakness; and extolling this lace-
woman who spake to her; then the lace-woman replied
again to the gentlewoman, this was nothing but her
humility and modesty, for her gifts were well known;
but the gentlewoman refused it again, falling into
a commendation of the gifts of the lace-woman; whereupon this lace-woman turned herself to the company,
and spake to some of them to exercise, excusing herself that she was somewhat indisposed in body, and
unfit for this work, and said if any one there had a
word of exhortation let them speak; but all the company keeping silent, none speaking. Then the lace-
woman began with making a speech to this purpose,
that now those days were come, and that was fulfilled
which was spoken of in the Scriptures, that God would
pour out of his Spirit upon the handmaidens, and they
should prophecy, and after this speech she made a
prayer for almost half an hour, and after her prayer
took that text, "If ye love me, keep my commandments";
when she had read the text she laboured to analyze
the chapter as well as she could, and then spake upon
the text, drawing her doctrines, opening them, and
making two uses, for the space of some three quarters
of an hour; when she had done she spake to the company, and said, if any had any thing to object against
any of the matter delivered, they might speak, for
that was their custom to give liberty in that kind

(but though there was a great company both of men and
women) yet no man objected; but all held their peace.
Then the gentlewoman that sat at the side of the
table began to speak, making some apology that she
was not so fit at this time in regard of some bodily
indispositions, and she told the company she would
speak upon that matter her sister had handled, and
would proceed to a use of examination, whether we
love Christ or no; and in the handling of it, she propounded to open what love was, and what were the
grounds of our love, and how we should know it; and
as she was preaching, one in the company cried, "Speak
out"; whereupon she lifted up her voice; but some
spake the second time, "Speak out," so that upon this
the gentlewoman was disturbed and confounded in her
discourse, and went off from that of love to speak
upon I John 4 of "trying the spirits," but she could
make nothing of it, speaking nonsense all along;
whereupon some of the company spake again, and the
gentlewoman went on speaking, jumbling together some
things against those who despised the ordinances of
God, and the ministry of the Word; and upon that some
present spake yet once more, so that she was so
amazed and confounded, that she knew not what she
said, and was forced to give over and sit down. The
lace-woman who preached first, seeing all this,
looked upon those who had interrupted her sister with
an angry bold countenance, setting her face against
them, and she fell upon concluding all with prayer,
and in her prayer she prayed to God about them who
despised his ambassadors, and ministers that he had
sent into the world to reconcile the world; whereupon

some fell a speaking in her prayer, "Ambassadors,
ministers, you ambassadors!" with words to that purpose; and upon those words she prayed expressly that
God would send some visible judgement from heaven upon them: and upon those words some of the company
spake aloud, praying God to stop her mouth, and so
she was forced to give over. In brief, there was
such laughing, confusion, and disorder at the meeting, that the minister professed he never saw the
like: he told me the confusions, horror, and disorder
which he saw and heard there, was unexpressible, and
so he left them, fearing lest the candles might have
gone out and they have fallen to kill or mischief
one another. The next Tuesday after there came a
world of people, to the number of a thousand first
and last to Bell-Alley, to hear these women preach
(as an inhabitant of that Alley related it to me) but
these women because of the multitude did not preach
there, but preached in the Old-Baily the same day;
and since have preached in a house near the French
Church; where on Tuesday being the 30 of December,
another minister heard them, and related that he saw
a great deal of lightness and vanity among some that
were at the exercise. And on Thursday the 8 of Janu-
ary near the French Church at one Mr. Hil's, one Mrs.
Attaway (one of the women by all the description of
her spoken of before that preached in Bell-Alley) at
three of the clock in the afternoon preached, where
about fifty persons men and women were present. In
her exercise she delivered many dangerous and false
doctrines: as, 1. That it could not stand with the
goodness of God to damn his own creatures eternally.

2.   That God the Father did reign under the Law; God
the Son under the Gospel; and now God the Father and
God the Son are making over the Kingdom to God the
Holy Ghost, and he shall be poured out upon all flesh.
3.   That there shall be a general restauration, wherein
all men shall be reconciled and saved.   4.   That
Christ died for all; with several other errors and
conceits.   She told them for her part she was in the
wilderness waiting for the pouring out of the Spirit.
When her sermon was done (which was above an hour),
she said, if any one had any exception against what
she had delivered, she was ready to give forth her
light; and if they could demonstrate she had preached
any error, to hear them; she said she was desirous
that all the glory should be given to God, and was
willing to impart or give out that dram of light the
Spirit had given her; that she desired to lay down her
crown at the feet of Christ; and wished that shame and
confusion might cover her face for ever if she had any
confidence in herself.   After she had done speaking,
a sister stood up first and objected what warrant she
had to preach in this manner; the preaching woman interrupted her and said she knew what she meant, that
she ought only to preach to those that were under baptism; and further, she said she disclaimed that she
took upon her to preach, but only to exercise her
gifts; for, she could not be evinced that any in the
world this day living, had any commission to preach.
Then her sister asked her what warrant she had to exercise thus; she answered, her grounds were I Pet. 4:
10, 11.   "As every man hath received the gifts," etc.
and that in the 10. of the Hebrews, "Exhort one

another," and in the 3. of Malachi the 16. and in
Titus, "That the elder women ought to teach the
younger." Further she professed, that when she and
her sister began that exercise, it was to some of
their own sex; but when she considered the glory of
God was manifested in babes and sucklings, and that
she was desired by some to admit of all that pleased
to come, she could not deny to impart those things
the spirit had communicated to her. But still her
sister insisted upon the former objection, and said
she ought not to preach to the world; and said she
would speak more freely, but that there was a multitude there. Then another sister spake to this second
sister, that truth sought no corners, why should she
say so? Then a man stood up and asked the preaching-
woman what she meant by those who were under baptism:
she answered, "under a Gospel order." He replied,
"what was that?" She said, "all that were baptised
being not believers." Then a second was objected,
"who baptised Simon Magus, Ananias and Saphira?" Mrs.
Attaway answered, she doubted whether they did according to their commission in baptising them. In her
prayer this she-preacher prayed God that all those
who were present, and did not acknowledge his weak
ones that spake for the spirit of God, that he would
discover the iniquity of their hearts. She also in
her prayer gave thanks for the occasion of their
meeting, that they had been quiet without distraction, which they were not the former day: and to the
men present that brought an argument for infants'
baptism, she gave an answer to it. He asked her
what baptism was? she answered she was not very fit

to argue those questions, and went from the table to
the fire side: and then another sister said, "You
have heard what was delivered, and may rest satisfied." I was informed also for certain this week by
a minister who came out of Kent, that at Brasteed
where Mr. Saltmarsh is preacher, there is a woman-
preacher, (one at least if not more), in which company besides preaching, 'tis reported (as this minister saith, very commonly) that they break bread
also, and every one in their order.

* * *

Two citizens, godly understanding men related
to me for certain that one of the women preachers
Mrs. Attaway spoken of in this book page 119 and who
upon complaint was questioned by the Committee of
Examinations for her preaching, was run away with
another woman's husband, with whom she had been too
familiar a long time, but about 14 days ago gone
away and that beyond seas (as is commonly reported).
This man [marginal note: Will. Jenney and a preacher
too] with whom she is gone, was one of the society
and company of which Mrs. Attaway was, and one who
used to hear her preach; he left his own wife great
with child, besides other children, and the poor woman (as 'tis reported) was ready to be distracted,
and Mrs. Attaway hath left her children behind too,
exposed to the world at six and seven, and conveyed
away all her goods that are any thing worth. It was
told me also by one of those citizens that 'tis given
out she met with a prophet here in London, who hath

revealed to her and others that they must go to Jerusalem, and repair Jerusalem, and for that end Mrs.
Attaway hath gotten money of some persons, ten pounds
of one young maid, and other money of others towards
the building up of Jerusalem. These two godly citizens not long ago upon occasion of hearing that Mrs.
Attaway preached, went to confer with her, and to dis-
suade her from preaching, and coming thither there
were four or five men with her whereof one of them
was this fellow she is now run away with: and these
citizens speaking with her, one of her company a
sectary said to her, "Sister, speak not to these men
for they are in the flesh," and she discoursing with
them, either the same man or another said, "Sister,
speak no more to them for they being in the flesh you
will but preach them the more into the flesh."

        [Marginal comment to letter of Mrs. Attaway to
William Jenney: This Mrs. Attaway hath a husband in
the army, and the world may see what these women
preachers are, thus to write to another woman's husband and now to go away together.]

D.   The Lady Eleanor, *The Star to the Wise* (London,
        1643), pp. 11-13.

        [One of the strangest female products of England's
        Civil War period was Lady Eleanor, usually known
        under the surnames Douglas or Davies.[4] An apocalyp-
        tic prophetess, she predicted in 1625 the approach-
        ing end of the world and, in a book published in
        Amsterdam in 1633, the execution of Charles I. Nor
        did she display any affection for Archbishop Laud,
        whom she identified with Revelation's beast from the
        bottomless pit. Through a demonstration of anti-
        clericalism in which she sat upon the Lichfield
        bishop's throne, declared herself Primate and
        Metropolitan, and sprinkled a tar-mixture on the

altar-hangings, she earned herself a place in the
mental institution of Bedlam (Hospital of St.
Mary of Bethlehem, London). After her release
and before her next confinement elsewhere, she
wrote this petition to the House of Commons re-
questing, albeit in an obscure way, the licensing
of her book predicting Charles' execution. The
following selection reveals her extraordinary
writing style as well as her penchant for inter-
preting ordinary names and events apocalyptically.]

And so another place belonging to the city, in
these days of such distraction, worthy to be thought
upon, Bethlehem's Hospital, Their House of Bread; for
the witless sent to this, as the Wisemen to the
other, those sages, etc. in some respects to that
not inferior, where some barn or the like, made the
bed-chamber of the blessed Lady; and He there born,
our Bread from heaven, and for a sign given the shep-
herds, of his racking on the cross, that was put into the rack or manger; and by a woman aforehand
anointed; and other like signs and tokens.

Whether these betoken nothing too, appeal to
the wisdom of our age, or to be such an unlikely
thing; that he who wrote that brotherly Epistle [II
John] (going before the *Apocalypse*) to a Lady, saying, He had many things to write unto her. Whatsoever it was which appears not there, but referred to
another time or meeting; that from another Lady, The
Revelation's Interpretation of her writing, should
be sent to Divines for their assent to the same,
written by that Divine, etc. where such a meeting of
theirs, in a time of so much distraction of the
Church.

Where touching or importing an inspiration;
what phrase of speech more meet and proper, than that

of, "Mouth to mouth; that our joy may be full?" for a
full expression of our Lord's coming to be revealed to
a woman; that secret disclosed.

And "the wind blowing where it lists"; wherefore
not serving to bring these about from the Isle of
Patmos, to Great Britain's Islands, when testified he
cometh, he cometh. The Islands may be glad thereof,
etc. Psal. especially at such a time of perplexity and
woe, and for the redemption of wounded prisoners too,
so miserably relieved, and others for their hurts and
maims, disabled ever to help themselves.

Wherefore then not to be revealed to us, before
others in such case: and as soon to his handmaids as
his menservants; the spirit of God to be poured on
them: and so now, as well as then, when she had the
first happy sight of him, after his rising, which was
sent to tell and inform them where they should meet
him first: and what odds between seven Churches visited, or sent unto: and Henry the seventh's Chapel,
in such a Church: and in the seventeenth hundred year
of grace; where the Assembly of Ministers, etc. sitting in that place, dedicated or consecrated to his
memory; whose son's royal issue so soon reedified or
reformed the Church so much gone to decay; renewed in
such a short space of time, the Scriptures buried in
another language, life not only infused into them;
but sent forth as far West, as even East in former
days.

And now in the West, to us since this thing be
revealed, (the mystery of the Lord of Sabbath's Coming)
wherefore to Westminster, not directed too: where the
Kingdom's Great Counsel meeting shewed there where

they shall meet Him coming in the clouds.

E.   "The Examination of Mrs. Anne Hutchinson at
        the court at Newtown," from Thomas Hutchinson,
        *The History of the Province of Massachusetts
        Bay* (Boston, 1767), pp. 482, 484-488, 507-
        509, 513, 517.

> [The case of Anne Hutchinson (1600-43) is well
> known to most students of American history.
> Having immigrated to Boston in 1634, she soon
> began to exercise spiritual leadership in her new
> community, visiting women in childbirth and hold-
> ing meetings in her home to discuss the sermon of
> the previous Sunday. At these meetings the ideas
> which led to the charge of antinomianism were ex-
> pressed. Most Boston preachers, she was convinced,
> were teaching a theology of works, not of grace.
> A sanctified life was generally regarded as evi-
> dence of justification. Mrs. Hutchinson disagreed:
> salvation is by grace alone, and no works either of
> preparation or of sanctification have any bearing
> on God's justifying grace. Closely related to
> this was her belief that the Holy Spirit himself
> dwells in and directs the life of a justified per-
> son. Upon this basis she claimed immediate reve-
> lations from God, a claim which finally brought
> about her banishment. But if her alleged heresies
> were the basis of her conviction, still the issue
> of a woman's right to teach religious matters pub-
> licly loomed large at the trial.]

November 1637

    Mr. Winthrop, governor. Mrs. Hutchinson, you
are called here as one of those that have troubled
the peace of the commonwealth and the churches here;
you are known to be a woman that hath had a great
share in the promoting and divulging of those opinions
that are causes of this trouble, and to be nearly
joined not only in affinity and affection with some
of those the court hath taken notice of and passed
censure upon, but you have spoken diverse things as

we have been informed very prejudicial to the honour
of the churches and ministers thereof, and you have
maintained a meeting and an assembly in your house
that hath been condemned by the general assembly as
a thing not tolerable nor comely in the sight of God
nor fitting for your sex, and notwithstanding that
was cried down you have continued the same, therefore
we have thought good to send for you to understand
how things are, that if you be in an erroneous way
we may reduce you that so you may become a profitable
member here among us, otherwise if you be obstinate
in your course that then the court may take such
course that you may trouble us no further.

Gov. Why do you keep such a meeting at your
house as you do every week upon a set day?

Mrs. H. It is lawful for me so to do, as it
is all your practices, and can you find a warrant for
yourself and condemn me for the same thing? The
ground of my taking it up was, when I first came to
this land, because I did not go to such meetings as
those were, it was presently reported that I did not
allow of such meetings but held them unlawful, and
therefore in that regard they said I was proud and
did despise all ordinances; upon that a friend came
unto me and told me of it, and I to prevent such
aspirations took it up, but it was in practice before
I came; therefore I was not the first.

Gov. For this, that you appeal to our practice
you need no confutation. If your meeting had answered to the former it had not been offensive, but
I will say that there was no meeting of women alone,

but your meeting is of another sort, for there are
sometimes men among you.

> Mrs. H. There was never any man with us.

> Gov. Well, admit there was no man at your meet-
ing and that you was sorry for it, there is no warrant
for your doings, and by what warrant do you continue
such a course?

> Mrs. H. I conceive there lies a clear rule in
Titus, that the elder women should instruct the
younger and then I must have a time wherein I must do
it.

> Gov. All this I grant you, I grant you a time
for it, but what is this to the purpose that you, Mrs.
Hutchinson, must call a company together from their
callings to come to be taught of you?

> Mrs. H. Will it please you to answer me this
and to give me a rule, for then I will willingly submit to any truth. If any come to my house to be instructed in the ways of God, what rule have I to put
them away?

> Gov. But suppose that a hundred men come unto
you to be instructed, will you forbear to instruct
them?

> Mrs. H. As far as I conceive I cross a rule in
it.

> Gov. Very well, and do you not so here?

> Mrs. H. No, Sir, for my ground is they are men.

> Gov. Men and women all is one for that, but
suppose that a man should come and say, "Mrs. Hutchinson, I hear that you are a woman that God hath given
his grace unto and you have knowledge in the word of
God; I pray instruct me a little." Ought you not to

instruct this man?

Mrs. H. I think I may.——Do you think it not
lawful for me to teach women, and why do you call me
to teach the court?

Gov. We do not call you to teach the court but
to lay open yourself.

Mrs. H. I desire you that you would then set
me down a rule by which I may put them away that come
unto me and so have peace in so doing.

Gov. You must shew your rule to receive them.

Mrs. H. I have done it.

Gov. I deny it because I have brought more
arguments than you have.

Mrs. H. I say, to me it is a rule.

Mr. Endicot [one of the assistants]. You say
there are some rules unto you. I think there is a
contradiction in your own words. What rule for your
practice do you bring, only a custom in Boston.

Mrs. H. No, Sir, that was no rule to me but if
you look upon the rule in Titus it is a rule to me.
If you convince me that it is no rule I shall yield.

Gov. You know that there is no rule that
crosses another, but this rule crosses that in the
Corinthians. [I Cor. 14:34-35]. But you must take
it in this sense that elder women must instruct the
younger about their business, and to love their husbands and not to make them to clash.

Mrs. H. I do not conceive but that it is
meant for some public times.

Gov. Well, have you no more to say but this?

Mrs. H. I have said sufficient for my practice.

Gov. Your course is not to be suffered for,

besides that we find such a course as this to be
greatly prejudicial to the state, besides the occasion that it is to seduce many honest persons that
are called to those meetings and your opinions being
known to be different from the word of God may seduce
many simple souls that resort unto you, besides that
the occasion which hath come of late hath come from
none but such as have frequented your meetings, so
that now they are flown off from magistrates and ministers and this since they have come to you, and besides that it will not well stand with the commonwealth that families should be neglected for so many
neighbours and dames and so much time spent, we see
no rule of God for this, we see not that any should
have authority to set up any other exercises besides
what authority hath already set up, and so what hurt
comes of this you will be guilty of and we for suffering you.

    <u>Mrs. H.</u> Sir, I do not believe that to be so.

    <u>Gov.</u> Well, we see how it is we must therefore
put it away from you or restrain you from maintaining
this course.

    <u>Mrs. H.</u> If you have a rule for it from God's
word you may.

    <u>Gov.</u> We are your judges, and not you ours and
we must compel you to it.

    <u>Mrs. H.</u> If it please you by authority to put
it down, I will freely let you, for I am subject to
your authority.

    <u>Mr. Bradstreet</u> [one of the assistants]. I
would ask this question of Mrs. Hutchinson, whether
you do think this is lawful? for then this will fol-

low that all other women that do not are in a sin.

  <u>Mrs. H.</u> I conceive this is a free will offering.

  <u>Bradst.</u> If it be a free will offering you ought to forbear it because it gives offence.

  <u>Mrs. H.</u> Sir, in regard of myself I could, but for others I do not yet see light but shall further consider of it.

  <u>Bradst.</u> I am not against all women's meetings but do think them to be lawful.

  <u>Mr. Dudley, dep. gov.</u> Here hath been much spoken concerning Mrs. Hutchinson's meetings and among other answers she saith that men come not there; I would ask you this one question then, whether never any man was at your meetings?

  <u>Gov.</u> There are two meetings kept at their house.

  <u>Dep. gov.</u> How! is there two meetings?

  <u>Mrs. H.</u> Ey, Sir, I shall not equivocate, there is a meeting of men and women and there is a meeting only for women.

  <u>Dep. gov.</u> Are they both constant?

  <u>Mrs. H.</u> No, but upon occasions they are deferred.

  <u>Mr. Endicot.</u> Who teaches in the men's meetings —none but men? do not women sometimes?

  <u>Mrs. H.</u> Never as I heard, not one.

  <u>Dept. gov.</u> I would go a little higher with Mrs. Hutchinson. About three years ago we were all in peace. Mrs. Hutchinson from that time she came hath made a disturbance, and some that came over with her in the ship did inform me what she was as soon as she was landed. I being then in place dealt with the

pastor and teacher of Boston and desired them to enquire of her, and then I was satisfied that she held
nothing different from us; but within half a year
after, she had vented divers of her strange opinions
and had made parties in the country, and at length it
comes that Mr. Cotton and Mr. Vane were of her judgment, but Mr. Cotton hath cleared himself that he was
not of that mind,[5] but now it appears by this woman's
meeting that Mrs. Hutchinson hath so forestalled the
minds of many by their resort to her meeting that now
she hath a potent party in the country. Now if all
these things have endangered us as from that foundation and if she in particular hath disparaged all
our ministers in the land that they have preached a
covenant of works, and only Mr. Cotton a covenant of
grace, why this is not to be suffered, and therefore
being driven to the foundation and it being found that
Mrs. Hutchinson is she that hath depraved all the
ministers and hath been the cause of what is fallen
out, why we must take away the foundation and the
building will fall.

* * *

Mrs. H. If you please to give me leave I shall
give you the ground of what I know to be true. Being
much troubled to see the falseness of the constitution of the church of England, I had like to have
turned separatist; whereupon I kept a day of solemn
humiliation and pondering of the thing; this scripture
was brought unto me——he that denies Jesus Christ to be
come in the flesh is antichrist [I John 2:18]. This I

considered of and in considering found that the papists did not deny him to be come in the flesh, nor
we did not deny him. Who then was antichrist? Was
the Turk antichrist only? The Lord knows that I
could not open scripture; he must by his prophetical
office open it unto me. So after that being unsatis-
fied in the thing, the Lord was pleased to bring this
scripture out of the Hebrews [9:16]. He that denies
the testament denies the testator, and in this did
open unto me and give me to see that those which did
not teach the new covenant had the spirit of antichrist, and upon this he did discover the ministry
unto me and ever since. I bless the Lord, he hath
let me see which was the clear ministry and which the
wrong. Since that time I confess I have been more
choice and he hath let me to distinguish between the
voice of my beloved and the voice of Moses, the voice
of John Baptist and the voice of antichrist, for all
those voices are spoken of in scripture. Now if you
do condemn me for speaking what in my conscience I
know to be truth I must commit myself unto the Lord.

        Mr. Nowell. How do you know that that was the
spirit?

        Mrs. H. How did Abraham know that it was God
that bid him offer his son, being a breach of the
sixth commandment?

        Dep. gov. By an immediate voice.

        Mrs. H. So to me by an immediate revelation.

        Dep. gov. How! an immediate revelation.

        Mrs. H. By the voice of his own spirit to my
soul. I will give you another scripture, Jer. 46:27,
28—out of which the Lord shewed me what he would do

for me and the rest of his servants. But after he
was pleased to reveal himself to me I did presently
like Abraham run to Hagar. And after that he did let
me see the atheism of my own heart, for which I begged
of the Lord that it might not remain in my heart, and
being thus, he did shew me this (a twelvemonth after)
which I told you of before. Ever since that time I
have been confident of what he hath revealed unto
me.... When our teacher came to New England it was a
great trouble unto me, my brother Wheelwright being
put by also. I was then much troubled concerning
the ministry under which I lived, and then that place
in the 30th of Isaiah [v. 20] was brought to my mind.
"Though the Lord give thee bread of adversity and
water of affliction yet shall not thy teachers be removed into corners any more, but thine eyes shall see
thy teachers." The Lord giving me this promise and
they being gone there was none then left that I was
able to hear, and I could not be at rest but I must
hither. Yet that place of Isaiah did much follow me,
"though the Lord give thee the bread of adversity and
water of affliction." This place lying I say upon me
then this place in Daniel [6:27] was brought unto me
and did shew me though I should meet with affliction
yet I am the same God that delivered Daniel out of
the lion's den: I will also deliver thee. Therefore
I desire you to look to it, for you see this scripture
fulfilled this day and therefore I desire you that as
you tender the Lord and the church of commonwealth to
consider and look what you do. You have power over my
body but the Lord Jesus hath power over my body and
soul, and assure yourselves thus much, you do as much

as in you lies to put the Lord Jesus Christ from you,
and if you go on in this course you begin you will
bring a curse upon you and your posterity, and the
mouth of the Lord hath spoken it....

  Mrs. H. By a providence of God I say I expect
to be delivered from some calamity that shall come to
me.

  Gover. The cause is altered and will not stand
with us now, but I see a marvellous providence of God
to bring things to this pass that they are. We have
been hearkening about the trial of this thing, and
now the mercy of God by a providence hath answered our
desires and made her to lay open her self and the
ground of all these disturbances to be by revelations,
for...all this while there is no use of the ministry
of the word nor of any clear call of God by his word,
but the ground work of her revelations is the immediate revelation of the spirit and not by the ministry
of the word, and that is the means by which she hath
very much abused the country that they shall look for
revelations and are not bound to the ministry of the
word, but God will teach them by immediate revelations
and this hath been the ground of all these tumults and
troubles, and I would that those were all cut off from
us that trouble us, for this is the thing that hath
been the root of all the mischief.

  Court. We all consent with you.

  Gov. Ey, it is the most desperate enthusiasm in
the world, for nothing but a word comes to her mind
and then an application is made which is nothing to
the purpose, and this is her revelations when as it is
impossible but that the word and spirit should speak

the same thing....

    <u>Mr. Harlakenden</u>. I would therefore that the
assembly take notice that here is none that condemns
the meeting of christian women; but in such a way and
for such an end that it is to be detested. And then
tho' the matter of the elders be taken away yet there
is enough besides to condemn her, but I shall speak
no further.

F.   Letter of Sarah Cheevers to her husband Henry
       Cheevers from Malta, November, 1661, quoted in
       William Sewel, *The History of the Rise, In-*
       crease, and Progress of the Christian People
       called Quakers (Philadelphia, 1856), I, 400-
       401.

    [The Society of Friends became involved, at a very
    early stage in its development, in missionary ac-
    tivities outside England. In accordance with the
    generally prominent role of women in the Society,
    a strikingly high percentage of the missionaries
    were women. Of the first ten Quaker missionaries
    to arrive in the American colonies, six were female,
    four male. Wherever they went, their unorthodox
    beliefs and practices brought them into conflict
    with local authorities. While they eventually suc-
    ceeded in gaining a number of converts and setting
    up meetings in the colonies, some ventures to other
    areas were without any apparent gain. Such was the
    mission of Catharine Evans and Sarah Cheevers, who
    set out in 1658 for Alexandria but landed in Malta,
    where they spent four years imprisoned by the In-
    quisition. Continually entreated by the friars to
    accept Catholicism, if only outwardly, they would
    have resisted unto death had they not eventually
    been freed.]

    My dear husband, my love, my life is given up
to serve the living God, and to obey his pure call
in the measure of the manifestation of his love, life,
and Spirit of Christ Jesus, his only begotten Son,

whom he hath manifested in me, and thousands, by the
brightness of his appearing, to put an end to sin and
Satan, and bring to light immortality, through the
preaching of the everlasting gospel, by the spirit of
prophecy, which is poured out upon the sons and daughters of the living God, according to his purpose;
whereof he hath chosen me, who am the least of all:
but God, who is rich in mercy, for his own name's
sake hath passed by mine offences, and hath counted
me worthy to bear testimony to his holy name, before
the mighty men of the earth. Oh the love of the Lord
to my soul! My tongue cannot express, neither hath
it entered into the heart of man, to conceive of the
things that God hath laid up for them that fear him.

     Therefore doth my soul breathe to my God for
thee and my children, night and day, that your minds
may be joined to the light of the Lord Jesus, to lead
you out of Satan's kingdom, into the kingdom of God,
where we may enjoy one another in the life eternal,
where neither sea nor land can separate; in which
light and life do I salute thee, my dear husband,
with my children, wishing you to embrace God's love,
in making his truth so clearly manifest amongst you;
whereof I am a witness, even of the everlasting fountain that hath been opened by the messengers of Christ,
who preach to you the word of God, in season and out
of season, directing you where you may find your
Savior, to purge and cleanse you from your sins, and
to reconcile you to his Father, and to have unity
with him and all the saints, in the light, that ye
may be fellow-citizens in the kingdom of glory, rest,
and peace, which Christ hath purchased for them that

love him, and obey him. What profit is there, to gain
the whole world, and lose your own souls? Seek first
the kingdom of God and the righteousness thereof, and
all other things shall be added to you. Godliness is
great gain, having the promise of this life that now
is, and that which is to come; which is fulfilled to
me, who have tasted of the Lord's endless love and
mercies to my soul; and from a moving of the same love
and life do I breathe to thee my dear husband, with my
children; my dear love salutes you all; my prayers to
my God are for you all, that your minds may be joined
to the light, wherewith you are enlightened, that I
may enjoy you in that which is eternal, and have com-
munion with you in the spirit. He that is joined to
the Lord, is one spirit, one heart, one mind, one
soul; to serve the Lord with one consent. I cannot by
pen or paper set forth the large love of God, in ful-
filling his gracious promises to me in the wilderness,
being put into prison for God's truth, there to remain all the days of my life; being searched, tried,
examined, upon pain of death, among the enemies of God
and his Truth; standing in jeopardy for my life, until
the Lord had subdued and brought them under by his
mighty power, and made them to feed us, and they would
have given us money or clothes; but the Lord did deck
our table richly in the wilderness. The day of the
Lord is appearing, wherein he will discover every deed
of darkness, let it be done never so secretly: the
light of Christ Jesus will make it manifest in every
conscience; the Lord will rip up all coverings that
are not of his own spirit. The God of peace be with
you all. Amen. [*Written in the Inquisition
                  prison by Sarah Cheevers*].

FOOTNOTES

GENERAL INTRODUCTION

[1] Peter Berger, *The Precarious Vision* (Garden City, New York: Doubleday & Company, 1961), p. 103.

[2] Ernst Troeltsch, *The Social Teachings of the Christian Churches,* tr. Olive Wyon, 2 vols. (New York: Harper & Row, 1960). Bryan Wilson in *Religious Sects* (World University Library, n.d.), argues that Troeltsch's categories have limited applicability to the modern, particularly American religious situation. It is true that the disestablishment of churches has made a clear-cut distinction between sects and churches impossible, at least from a political standpoint. Nevertheless, sociologically speaking, it is still feasible to distinguish mainstream denominations, which express the social and political values of the majority of the population, from sect-like denominations, which tend to separate themselves from the majority.

[3] Troeltsch, I, 331.

[4] *Ibid.*

[5] Martin Luther, "Instructions for the Visitors of Parish Pastors in Electoral Saxony," *Luther's Works,* vol. 40 (Philadelphia: Fortress Press, 1958), p. 284.

[6] Claus-Peter Clasen, *Anabaptism: A Social History, 1525-1618* (Ithaca: Cornell University Press, 1972), pp. 51-62.

[7] Sherrin Marshall Wyntjes, "Women in the Reformation Era" in Renate Bridenthal and Claudia Koonz, eds., *Becoming Visible: Women in European History* (Boston: Houghton Mifflin Company, 1977), p. 175.

[8] Elise Boulding, *The Underside of History: A View of Women through Time* (Boulder, Colorado: Westview Press, 1976), p. 548.

[9] Vern L. Bullough, *The Subordinate Sex* (Baltimore: Penguin Books, 1974), p. 204. Bullough admittedly does not label Bohemian Brethren as radical reformers. Their pre-Lutheran origin and their officially recognized status would differentiate them from other "minor Protestant groups." Comenius himself, however, with his eschatological vision of the unity of mankind in one religion was as much an individualistic spiritualist as a representative of the Bohemian Brethren.

[10] Julia O'Faolain and Lauro Martines, eds., *Not in God's Image* (New York: Harper & Row, 1973), p. 194.

[11] Roland Bainton, *What Christianity Says about Sex, Love, and Marriage* (New York: Association Press, 1957), p. 91.

[12] The label "Radical Reformation" as used by George Huntston Williams, author of the most comprehensive survey of the movement (*The Radical Reformation* [Philadelphia: The Westminster Press, 1962]), has generally been accepted as preferable to "left wing of the Reformation," the term advanced by Roland Bainton ("The Left Wing of the Reformation," *Journal of Religion* XXI [1941], 124-134). Another possibility, "Free Church Tradition," has the advantage of extending beyond the sixteenth century, but the disadvantage of having been used rather specifically to refer to English Nonconformists. The fact that Lutheran "free churches" have also arisen in modern times is an indication of the possible confusion to which the term could give rise.

[13] George Williams includes "Evangelical Rationalists" as a third category within the Radical Reformation; this category he describes as "the spirit of reform as it found expression pre-eminently in Romance lands." (George H. Williams, ed., *Spiritual and Anabaptist Writers* [Philadelphia: The Westminster Press, 1957], p. 23). However, because their interaction was primarily with Catholicism rather than Protestantism, they do not fall under the label "radical Protestants," nor are they often studied in the same context as Spiritualists and Anabaptists.

[14] Williams, *Spiritual and Anabaptist Writers*, pp. 28-35.

[15] Troeltsch, II, 773.

[16] See the studies by Fritz Tanner, *Die Ehe im Pietismus* (Zürich: Zwingli-Verlag, 1952), and Gottfried Beyreuther, "Sexualtheorien im Pietismus" (Inaugural Diss., Munich, 1963), reprinted in Erich Beyreuther, ed. *Nikolaus Ludwig von Zinzendorf, Materialien und Dokumente: Band XII: Zweiter Sammelband über Zinzendorf* (Hildesheim: Georg Olms Verlag, 1975).

[17] Quoted in Clasen, p. 317.

[18] Joan Kelly-Gadol, "Did Women Have a Renaissance?," in Bridenthal and Koonz, p. 151f.

[19] See Ruth Kelso, *Doctrine for the Lady of the Renaissance* (Urbana: University of Illinois Press, 1956),

pp. 58-77.

[20]See, for instance, Ellen A. M'Arthur, "Women Petitioners and the Long Parliament," *English Historical Review* XXIV (1909), 698-709.

[21]Short biographies of some of the noblewomen of the Reformation are included in Roland Bainton's volumes, *Women of the Reformation in Germany and Italy* (Minneapolis: Augsburg Publishing House, 1971) and *Women of the Reformation in France and England* (Boston: Beacon Press, 1973). See also Nancy L. Roelker, "The Appeal of Calvinism to French Noblewomen in the Sixteenth Century," *Journal of Interdisciplinary History* (1972), 391-413.

[22]Cf. Clasen, pp. 200-206.

[23]Herbert W. Richardson, *Nun, Witch, Playmate* (New York: Harper & Row, 1971), p. 71.

[24]Marguerite d'Angoulême, "Novel XII," *The Heptameron,* in Lewis Spitz, ed. *The Northern Renaissance* (Englewood Cliffs: Prentice-Hall, 1972), p. 47.

[25]Kelso, p. 267.

[26]The *querelle des femmes* was a literary quarrel on the nature of women which began in the late Middle Ages and continued throughout the Renaissance. See Emile Telle, *L'Oeuvre de Marguerite d'Angoulême, Reine de Navarre, et la Querelle des Femmes* (Toulouse, 1937; reprint Geneva, 1969).

[27]Cotton Mather, *Tabitha Rediviva: An Essay to the Memory of...Mrs. Elizabeth Hutchinson* (Boston, 1713), p. 22. My attention was directed to this passage by Lonna M. Malmsheimer in a paper entitled "Mather's Daughters," presented at the Berkshire Conference on the History of Women, June, 1976.

[28]See, for instance, the titles available in Boston in the late 1600s as listed in Worthington Chauncey Ford, *The Boston Bookmarket: 1679-1700* (Boston: The Club of Odd Volumes, 1917), esp. p. 137.

[29]Anne Firor Scott, "Women, Religion, and Social Change in the South, 1830-1930," in Samuel S. Hill, Jr., ed., *Religion and the Solid South* (Nashville: Abingdon Press, 1972), pp. 92-121.

[30]Their efforts resulted in a commentary on passages of the Bible relating to women: *The Woman's Bible,* 2 pts. and appendix (1895-98; reprint, New York: Arno Press, 1972).

[31]Heinrich Cornelius Agrippa von Nettesheim, *De nobilitate et praecellentia foeminei sexus declamatio* (1529); Lucretia Marinella, *Le Nobiltà et Eccellenze delle Donne* (1600). On the attitude of Anna Maria van Schurman toward Lucretia Marinella's work, see Joyce Irwin, "Anna Maria van Schurman: From Feminism to Pietism," *Church History* 46:1 (March, 1977), pp. 48-49.

[32]Williams, *Spiritual and Anabaptist Writers,* pp. 22-23.

[33]For a discussion of this problem from the perspective of the twentieth-century Church of Sweden, see Krister Stendahl, *The Bible and the Role of Women* (Philadelphia: Fortress Press, 1966).

CHAPTER ONE: INTRODUCTION (pp. 1-8)

[1]Tertullian, *De cultu feminarum,* quoted in George H. Tavard, *Women in Christian Tradition* (Notre Dame: University of Notre Dame Press, 1973), p. 59.

[2]See Rosemary Radford Ruether, "Misogynism and Virginal Feminism in the Fathers of the Church," *Religion and Sexism: Images of Women in the Jewish and Christian Traditions,* ed. Ruether (New York: Simon and Schuster, 1974), esp. pp. 169-176.

[3]Saint Augustine, *The Trinity,* XII, 13, tr. Stephen McKenna (Washington: Catholic Univ. Press, 1963), p. 361.

[4]Lombard, *Collectanea in epist. D. Pauli in Ep. T Ad Cor.,* cap. XI, 8-10 (*PL* 191, 1633); Bonaventure, *Comm. in Sec. Librum Sententiarum Petri Lombardi,* dist. XVI, art. 2, q. 2.

[5]Balthasar Hubmaier, "On Free Will," *Spiritual and Anabaptist Writers,* ed. George H. Williams (Philadelphia: The Westminster Press, 1957), p. 125.

[6]Although Aristotle had identified the male contribution as form and that of the female as matter, it was the medieval mind which made a value judgment of this distinction. Thomas Aquinas saw the superior male generative activity as shaping the imperfect material of the female. (Joseph Needham, *A History of Embryology* [2nd ed., New York, 1959], p. 236.)

[7]Heinrich Cornelius Agrippa von Nettesheim (1486-1535), occult philosopher, magician, skeptic, anti-cleric, did not fit clearly in any religious tradition.

Although attracted by Luther, he nevertheless considered
him a heretic. In spite of beliefs bordering on hetero-
doxy, Agrippa never broke externally with the Catholic
Church. (See Charles G. Nauert, Jr., *Agrippa and the
Crisis of Renaissance Thought* [Urbana: University of
Illinois Press, 1965], ch. 7.)

[8]Agrippa, *The Glory of Women,* trans. Edw. Fleetwood
(London, 1652), p. 10.

[9]Beverwyck refers here to Plato's uncertainty
whether to classify women as rational or irrational animals.

[10]Joh. van Beverwyck, *Van de Uitnementheyt des
Vrouwelichen Geslachts* (Dordrecht, 1639), p. 13.

CHAPTER ONE: SOURCES (pp. 8-41)

[1]Cf. "Handelinge van der disputacie in Synodo te
Strasburch teghen Melchior Hoffmann door de predicanten
derselver stadt," *Bibliotheca Reformatoria Neerlandica*
('S-Gravenhage, 1909), V, esp. 227-258.

[2]On Menno's concept of the Incarnation, see William
Eckard Keeney, *The Development of Dutch Anabaptist
Thought and Practice from 1539-1564* (Nieuwkoop, 1968),
pp. 89-100.

[3]In the seventeenth century, Joh. van Beverwyck
pointed out that the Greek for this passage (Hebrews
11:11) made Sarah the active force in the conception of
her son. Though scholars continue to puzzle over the
wording, Beverwyck saw it as an accurate description
of the process of generation and in accordance with the
Galenic theory which he espoused. *Van de Uitnementheyt
des Vrouwelichen Geslachts,* pp. 13-16.

[4]Verduin's translation is not as precise as one
might wish at this point. Menno's argument hinges on
the use of such prepositions as "of" or "from" (*van*),
"out of" (*uyt*), and "through" (*door*). In this passage
Verduin translates *van* as "of" and *uyt* as "from" but
omits the *uyt* in the repetition of the phrase "out of
thy loins." Thus he misses the point, which is to distinguish the male role in the birth process from that
of the female: the seed, according to Menno, is produced
by the father and is of his substance, whereas the
mother is more like a conduit through which seed passes.
See Keeney, *Dutch Anabaptist Thought,* pp. 217-220.

[5]German *Quall.* The movement of characteristics or
qualities; in the light it is the gentle rising of
powers out of the weave of the Spirit in the Essence of
the will; in the darkness it is the movement of torment.
(This and the following definitions of Böhme's theosophical terms are translated from *Register über all Theo-
sophische Schriften...Jacob Böhmens,* 1730 [*Sämtliche
Schriften,* XI, 9-47]).

[6]*Limbus.* Spiritually it is the heavenly world of
fire, the Father's eternal nature, spiritual heaven and
earth, in which God the Father gives birth in our souls
to his son, the eternal self-sufficient Word. And it is
the principle by which the Son lives in the Father.
According to nature it is the soul of the spirit of this
world in man, which becomes a masculine maiden when
again made whole through rebirth from Christ and spiritual circumcision in the Essence according to both tinc-
tures of fire and light.

[7]*Matrix, matrix naturae,* the eternal mother of the
woman in labour, is in the first principle the harshness,
in the second the gentle mother of the water-spirit.

[8]*Principium, Principien,* the beginning, a world, a
birth, a new life. The first principle is the dark
fire-world, the second the world of light and love, the
third the visible external world. Thus all three are
in each other and in all things.

[9]*Cagastrum,* the fire of nature according to the
fierce sharpness. *Cagastric,* whatever is of the manner
and nature of this fire.

[10]*Tinctura* is something which separates and brings
the pure from the impure. It is the life of all spirits
and brings all essences into their highest degree....
For in the tincture rises the virgin, Christ's heavenly
humanity, the new body of our soul, which clothes the
soul.

[11]*Fiat,* "let there be," the word of creation.

[12]Cf. Keith Thomas, "Women and the Civil War Sects,"
in Trevor Aston, ed., *Crisis in Europe 1560-1660* (London: Routledge & Kegan Paul, 1965), pp. 320-326.

[13]Gulielmus Estius (1542-1613), Biblical exegete,
professor of Sacred Scripture and, from 1595 until his
death, chancellor of the University of Douai.

[14]See his letters to Lady Elizabeth Hartopp and

and Mrs. Edward Polhill in *The Correspondence of John Owen (1616-1683)*, ed. Peter Toon (Cambridge: James Clarke & Company, 1970), pp. 157f., 168f.

CHAPTER TWO: INTRODUCTION (pp. 42-49)

[1]John Calvin, *Opera* (Braunschweig, 1875), XIII, 230, quoted in Williston Walker, *John Calvin* (New York: G. P. Putnam's Sons, 1906), p. 236.

[2]See George Hayward Joyce, *Christian Marriage: An Historical and Doctrinal Study* (London: Sheed and Ward, 1933), pp. 236ff., 406ff.

[3]Cf. Walther Köhler, *Zürcher Ehegericht und Genfer Konsistorium* (Leipzig: M. Heinsius, 1932).

[4]Martin Luther, *Werke* (Weimar Ausgabe), XXX/3, 205.

[5]*Luther's Works,* vol. 54 (Philadelphia: Fortress Press, 1967), p. 31.

[6]Chilton L. Powell, "Marriage in Early New England," *New England Quarterly* I (1928), 323-334.

[7]Reliance on the Old Testament also led Bucer to admit that bigamy, while not advisable, was not morally wrong—a position which led to considerable embarrassment after Philip of Hesse opted for this solution on the advice of Bucer and Luther.

[8]For a discussion of various Anabaptist teachings on marriage, see Claus-Peter Clasen, *Anabaptism: A Social History, 1525-1618* (Ithaca: Cornell University Press, 1972), pp. 200-207.

[9]John Robinson, *A Justification of Separation* (1610); modern edition, *The Works of John Robinson* (London, 1851), II, 466.

[10]James Turner Johnson, *A Society Ordained by God* (Nashville: Abingdon Press, 1970), p. 48.

[11]George Fox, *Concerning Marriage* (London, 1661), p. 3ff.

CHAPTER TWO: SOURCES (pp. 49-122)

[1]"Bekentones des globens und lebens der gemein Criste zu Monster," *Berichte der Augenzeugen über das Münsterische Wiedertäuferreich*, ed. C. A. Cornelius (Münster, 1853), pp. 445-464.

[2]"Stutenbernt" was an epithet applied to Bernhardt Rothmann, one of the leading radical ministers. The term is apparently a combination of "Berndt," a short form of Bernhardt, and "Stute," a kind of flat cake which he used in celebration of the Lord's Supper after he acquired Zwinglian sacramentarian views in 1531-32. (E. Belfort Bax, *Rise and Fall of the Anabaptists* [New York, 1903; reprint, 1966], p. 134.)

[3]See Clasen, *Anabaptism: A Social History,* pp. 207-8.

[4]*Luthers Werke (WA)* LIV, 171-175.

[5]*A godly form of householde government* was published in several editions from 1598 to 1624 with revisions by John Dod, also a Puritan minister. Dod and Cleaver published jointly a number of other works, primarily commentaries on the Old Testament.

[6]Steven E. Ozment, "Marriage and the Ministry in the Protestant Churches," *Celibacy in the Church,* ed. by William Bassett and Peter Huizing (New York: Herder and Herder, 1972), p. 54.

[7]Christopher Hill, *Society and Puritanism in Pre-Revolutionary England* (New York: Schocken Books, 1964), pp. 443-481.

[8]William Gouge, *Of Domesticall Duties* (London, 1622), "Epistle Dedicatory."

[9]Richard Baxter, *A Christian Directory* (London, 1673), p. 533.

[10]Chilton Latham Powell, *English Domestic Relations 1487-1653* (New York: Columbia University Press, 1917), p. 93.

[11]Postscript to *The Judgement of Martin Bucer* (1644), in *Complete Prose Works of John Milton*: Yale University Press, 1959), II, 478-79.

[12]John Calvin, Commentary on Genesis 2:18, from *Commentaries on the First Book of Moses called Genesis,* trans. John King (Edinburgh: Calvin Translation Society, 1847), p. 218.

[13]Paul Fagius (1504-49), John Calvin (1509-64), David Pareus (1548-1622), and André Rivet (1572-1651) were all noteworthy theologians in the Reformed tradition, in whose writings are found statements emphasizing the importance of intellectual and emotional companion-

ship in marriage. For details see *Complete Prose Works of John Milton,* II, 246.

[14]Theodore Beza (1519-1605), Calvin's successor in Geneva, interpreted Mosaic law as permitting women the right of divorcing cruel husbands (*Annotationes Majores* [1594], I, 111).

[15]Baxter, *A Christian Directory,* p. 2 of "Advertisements."

[16]From Baxter's *Breviate,* quoted in Hugh Martin, *Puritanism and Richard Baxter* (London, 1954), pp. 179, 182.

CHAPTER III: INTRODUCTION (pp. 123-130)

[1]Bullough, *The Subordinate Sex,* p. 209.

[2]*The Colloquies of Desiderius Erasmus,* tr. N. Bailey (London: Gibbings & Co., 1900), II, 120.

[3]Agrippa of Nettesheim, *The Glory of Women,* tr. E. Fleetwood (London, 1652), p. 23.

[4]Lodovico Domenichi, *La Nobilità delle Donne* (Venice, 1549).

[5]Lucretia Marinella, *Le Nobilità et Eccelenze delle Donne* (Venice, 1600).

[6]Quoted in Dorothy Gardiner, *English Girlhood at School* (London: Oxford University Press, 1929), p. 196.

[7]Roger Thompson, *Women in Stuart England and America* (London: Routledge & Kegan Paul, 1974), p. 212

[8]Samuel Tuke, *Five Papers on the Past Proceedings and Experience of the Society of Friends in Connexion with the Education of Youth* (York, 1843), p. 12.

[9]See Thompson, *Women in Stuart England,* p. 196.

[10]William Heard Kilpatrick, *The Dutch School of New Netherland and Colonial New York* (Washington: Government Printing Office, 1912), p. 221.

CHAPTER THREE: SOURCES (pp. 130-156)

[1]*The Satires of Juvenal,* trans. Rolfe Humphries (Bloomington, 1958), p. 82 (lines 447-450).

[2]*Euripides* IV, trans. Arthur S. Way (Cambridge, Mass., 1964), p. 213 (lines 640-643).

[3]Williams, *The Radical Reformation,* p. 469.

[4]*Ibid.,* p. 468.

[5]Mrs. Hopkins was the aunt of Elihu Yale, founder
of Yale University.

[6]Preface to *The Tenth Muse,* quoted in Elizabeth Wade
White, *Anne Bradstreet: "The Tenth Muse"* (New York: 1971),
p. 255.

[7]*Ibid.*

[8]On Anna Maria Schurman, Beverovicius (Jan van Beverwyck), and Voetius, see selection G and footnote 17 of
this chapter. Johann Heinrich Hottinger (1620-67) was
an orientalist and Protestant theologian at universities
in Holland, Germany, and Switzerland. In addition to
numerous philological works, he wrote a nine-volume history of the Christian Church.

[9]For a discussion of female education in England
during this period, see Carroll Camden, *The Elizabethan
Woman* (Houston, 1952) and Doris Mary Stenton, *The English
Woman in History* (London, 1957).

[10]Quoted in introduction to Lucy Hutchinson, *Memoirs
of the Life of Colonel Hutchinson,* ed. Harold Child
(London, 1904), p. xxxi.

[11]Samuel Torshell, *The Womans Glorie, A Treatise
asserting the due Honour of that Sexe, and Directing
wherein that Honour consists* (London, 1645).

[12]Anna Maria van Schurman, *The Learned Maid, or
Whether a Maid may be a Scholar?* (London, 1659), p. 32.
(English translation of her original treatise *De ingenii
muliebris ad doctrinam et meliores litteras aptitudine*
[Leiden, 1641]).

[13]Schurman, "Letter to Joannes Beverovicius," *The
Learned Maid,* p. 38.

[14]*Eucleria, seu melioris partis electio brevem
religionis ac vitae eius delineationem exhibens* (Altona,
1673).

[15]Jacob Cats, in addition to his duties as pensionary, was the leader of a school of poetry at Middelburg.

[16]André Rivet, professor of theology at Leiden, was
to carry on extensive correspondence with Anna Schurman
on the topic of women.

[17]Gysbertus Voetius (Gisbert Voet) was rector of
the University of Utrecht and an influential personality
in the Dutch Reformed Church. Although women were not

admitted to university courses, Voetius arranged that
Anna attend his lectures concealed behind curtains.
(Una Birch Pope-Hennessy, *Anna van Schurman: Artist,*
Scholar, Saint [London, 1909], p. 54.) It was under
his guidance that she began to learn Hebrew, Syriac,
and Chaldean.

[18]Frederik Spanheim was professor of theology at
Leiden and later religious advisor of the Elector of
the Palatinate.

[19]Claude Saumaise, or Salmasius, was born in France
but earned his reputation as literary critic at the
Academy of Leiden.

[20]Constantine Huygens was a poet and musician of
the Hague and father of the scientist Christian Huygens.

[21]Jean-Louis-Guez Balzac was a writer who made significant contributions toward the formation of the
French language.

[22]Valentin Conrart, a friend of Balzac, was active
in French literary circles and highly respected as a
writer by his contemporaries though he wrote very little.

[23]Pierre Gassendi, French philosopher, scientist,
and mathematician, revived Epicurean physics but rejected
the Epicurean denial of God and immortality.

[24]Marin Mersenne, French philosopher, theologian,
and mathematician, was closely associated with Descartes.

[25]Samuel Bochart, philologist and theologian, was
considered by Pierre Bayle one of the most learned men
in the world.

[26]*Joh. Beverovicii Epistolica quaestio, de vitae*
termino, fatali, an mobili? (Leiden, 1639).

[27]*Joh. Beverovicii Epistolicae quaestiones cum*
doctorum responsis (Rotterdam, 1644).

[28]*Nobiliss. virginis A.M. a Schurman Dissertatio,*
de Ingenii Muliebris ad Doctrinam...aptitudine (Leiden,
1641).

[29]*Nobiliss. virginis Annae Mariae a Schurman*
Opuscula Hebraea, Graeca, Latina, Gallica, Prosaica &
Metrica (Leiden, 1648).

[30]Jean le Laboureur, *Relation de la Voyage de la*
Reine de Pologne (Paris, 1647).

CHAPTER FOUR: INTRODUCTION (pp. 157-162)

[1] Roger Gryson, *Le ministère des femmes dans l'Eglise ancienne* (Gembloux: Editions J. Duculot, 1972), p. 173.

[2] Joan Morris, in *Against Nature and God* (London: Mowbrays, 1973), speaks of "quasi-episcopal abbesses." No doubt the power of these women has sometimes been ignored, but Morris, looking at them through a magnifying glass, hardly clarifies the situation for the objective reader.

[3] "The Misuse of the Mass," *Luther's Works,* vol. 36 (Philadelphia: Fortress Press, 1959), p. 152.

[4] *Ibid.*

[5] Eduard Freiherr von der Goltz, *Der Dienst der Frau in der christlichen Kirche* (Potsdam: Stiftungsverlag, 1905), pp. 129-132.

[6] Calvin, *Institutes,* IV, xv, 21.

[7] See Richard Hooker, *Of the Laws of Ecclesiastical Polity* (London: Everyman's Library, 1907), II, 257-279 (Book V, ch. 62).

[8] *Ibid.,* II, 379 (Bk. V, ch. 74).

[9] *Mennonite Encyclopedia,* art. "Deaconess."

[10] Hooker, II, 441 (Bk. V, ch. 78).

[11] John Smyth, "Principles and Inferences concerning the Visible Church," *The Works of John Smyth,* ed. W. T. Whitley (Cambridge: The University Press, 1915), I, 259-61.

[12] See Alan Simpson, *Puritanism in Old and New England* (Chicago: The University of Chicago Press, 1955), p. 1.

CHAPTER FOUR: SOURCES (pp. 162-199)

[1] The Brownists were Separatists and followers of Robert Browne (c. 1550-1633), who was exiled to the Netherlands in 1582 for his unconventional beliefs and behavior. Although he later returned to England and served as rector of one parish for forty years, his important treatises setting forth independent church polity (*A Treatise of Reformation Without Tarying for Anie* and *A Booke Which Sheweth the Life and Manners of All True Christians*) were written in 1582 during his exile.

[2]Cf. Katherine Chidley, *The justification of the Independent Churches of Christ* (London, 1641).

[3]See Chapter II, selection G.

[4]An allusion to Cawdrey's *Vindiciae Clavium*.

[5]Cf. Norman Cohn, *The Pursuit of the Millenium,* rev. ed. (New York: Oxford University Press, 1970).

[6]B. S. Capp, *The Fifth Monarchy Men* (London, 1972), p. 82.

[7]*Ibid.,* p. 173f.

[8]Walter of Château-Thierry, 13th-century Parisian theologian, exegete, and reform-minded preacher.

[9]*The Journal of George Fox,* ed. Rufus M. Jones (New York: Capricorn Books, 1963), p. 160.

[10]*Ibid.,* p. 92.

[11]Isabel Ross, *Margaret Fell: Mother of Quakerism* (London, 1949), p. 285f.

CHAPTER FIVE: INTRODUCTION (pp. 200-203)

[1]See Cohn, *The Pursuit of the Millenium.*

CHAPTER FIVE: SOURCES (pp. 203-237)

[1]It should be noted that the beliefs and practices of this circle of Swiss Anabaptists were not continued by later Anabaptist groups but are to be seen much more recently in the Pentecostal churches of our own century. Visitations of the Spirit, speaking in tongues, and physical infirmity as a lack of faith are major emphases among these groups. Furthermore, a leading role in the Pentecostal movements has been played by women, the most notable of whom was Aimee Semple McPherson.

[2]Bedlam was the popular name for the Hospital of St. Mary of Bethlehem in London, an asylum for the insane (see selection D in this chapter). Bridewell, originally a palace built by Cardinal Thomas Wolsey, was used in the seventeenth century for housing political and religious prisoners, vagrants, and prostitutes.

[3]Burroughs, *Vindication* (1646), p. 2, quoted in *Dictionary of National Biography,* art. "Thomas Edwards."

[4]See S. G. Wright, "Dougle Fooleries," *Bodleian Quarterly Record,* VII (1932), 95-98.

[5]John Cotton was subject to a good deal of suspicion during the antinomian controversy. Because Mrs. Hutchinson had credited him with preaching grace rather than works, he was, in the minds of some (e.g., R. Baillie, ch. IV above), tainted with her heresies. Yet, while he defended her, he managed at the same time, as this passage suggests, to appease the authorities.

BIBLIOGRAPHY

CHAPTER ONE

Daly, Mary. *The Church and the Second Sex*. New York: Harper & Row, 1968.

Ruether, Rosemary Radford, ed. *Religion and Sexism: Images of Woman in the Jewish and Christian Traditions*. New York: Simon and Schuster, 1974.

Tavard, George H. *Woman in Christian Tradition*. Notre Dame: University of Notre Dame Press, 1973.

CHAPTER TWO

Bainton, Roland. *What Christianity Says about Sex, Love and Marriage*. New York: Association Press, 1957.

Biéler, André. *L'Homme et la femme dans la morale calviniste*. Geneva: Labor et Fides, 1963.

Eells, Hastings. *The Attitude of Martin Bucer toward the Bigamy of Philip of Hesse*. New Haven: Yale University Press, 1924.

Johnson, James Turner. *A Society Ordained by God*. Nashville: Abingdon Press, 1970.

Joyce, George Hayward. *Christian Marriage*. London: Sheed and Ward, 1933.

Kawerau, Waldemar. *Die Reformation und die Ehe*. Halle, 1892.

Morgan, Edmund S. *The Puritan Family*. New York: Harper and Row, 1944.

Powell, Chilton Latham. *English Domestic Relations, 1487-1653*. 1917. Reprint. New York: Russell & Russell, 1972.

Rockwell, William Walker. *Die Doppelehe des Landgrafen Philipp von Hessen*. Marburg: N. G. Elwert'sche Verlagsbuchhandlung, 1904.

Schraepler, Horst W. *Die Rechtliche Behandlung der Täufer*. Tübingen: Fabian-Verlag, 1957.

Schücking, Levin L. *The Puritan Family*. Trans. Brian Battershaw. New York: Schocken Books, 1970.

Suppan, Klaus. *Die Ehelehre Martin Luthers*. Salzburg: Universitätsverlag Anton Pustet, 1971.

Telle, Emile V. *Erasme de Rotterdam et le septième sacrement*. Geneva: Librairie E. Droz, 1954.

CHAPTER THREE

Camden, Carroll. *The Elizabethan Women*. Houston: The Elsevier Press, 1952.

Cannon, Mary Agnes. *The Education of Women During the Renaissance*. Washington, 1916. (Ph.D. diss. Catholic University).

Cramer, Friedrich, *Geschichte der Erziehung und des Unterrichts in Niederlanden während des Mittelalters*. Stralsund, 1843.

Eby, Frederick, and Arrowood, Charles Flinn. *The Development of Modern Education*. New York: Prentice-Hall, Inc., 1934.

Frost, J. William. *The Quaker Family in Colonial America*. New York: St. Martin's Press, 1973.

Gardiner, Dorothy. *English Girlhood at School*. London: Oxford University Press, 1929.

Goltz, Eduard, Freiherr von der. *Der Dienst der Frau in der christlichen Kirche*. Potsdam: Stiftungsverlag, 1905.

Kilpatrick, William Heard. *The Dutch Schools of New Netherland and Colonial New York*. Washington: Government Printing Office, 1912.

May, Benjamin. *Die Mädchenerziehung in der Geschichte der Pädagogik von Plato bis zum 18. Jahrhundert*. Erlangen diss. 1908.

Richter, Julius, *Geschichte der sächsischen Volksschule.*
    Monumenta Germaniae Paedagogica, vol. 59. Berlin,
    1930.

Strassburger, Ferdinand. *Die Mädchenerziehung in der
    Geschichte der Pädagogik des 17. and 18. Jahr-
    hunderts in Frankreich und Deutschland.* Strass-
    burg, 1911.

Thompson, Roger. *Women in Stuart England and America.*
    London: Routledge & Kegan Paul, 1974.

Tuke, Samuel. *Five Papers on the Past Proceedings and
    Experience of the Society of Friends in Connexion
    with the Education of Youth.* York, 1843.

Watson, Foster. *Vives and the Renascence Education of
    Women.* New York: Longmans, Green & Co., 1912.

White, Elizabeth Wade. *Anne Bradstreet: "The Tenth
    Muse."* New York: Oxford University Press, 1971.

Wood, Norman. *The Reformation and English Education.*
    London: George Routledge & Sons, 1931.

Woody, Thomas. *A History of Women's Education in the
    United States,* 2 vols. New York: The Science
    Press, 1929.

CHAPTER FOUR

Bertinetti, Ilse, *Frauen im Geistlichen Amt.* Berlin:
    Evangelische Verlagsanstalt, 1965.

Goltz, Eduard, Freiherr von der. *Der Dienst der Frau in
    der christlichen Kirche.* Potsdam: Stiftungsverlag,
    1905.

Gryson, Roger. *Le ministère des femmes dans l'église
    ancienne.* Gembloux: Editions J. Duculot, 1972.

Ludlow, James M. *Woman's Work in the Church.* London:
    Alexander Strahan, Publisher, 1866.

*The Ministry of Women: A Report by a Committee appointed
    by His Grace the Lord Archbishop of Canterbury.*

London: Society for Promoting Christian Knowledge, 1919.

Morris, Joan. *Against Nature and God*. London: Mowbrays, 1973.

Ross, Isabel. *Margaret Fell: Mother of Quakerism*. London: Longmans, Green and Co., 1949.

Royden, A. Maude. *The Church and Women*. New York: George H. Doran Company, n.d.

Rupprecht, Walter. *Der Dienst der Theologin—eine ungelöste Frage in der evangelischen Kirche*. Stuttgart: Calwer Verlag, 1965.

Vining, Elizabeth Gray. *Women in the Society of Friends*. Guilford College, North Carolina, 1955.

Werner, Ernst. *Pauperes Christi*. Leipzig: Koehler & Amelang, 1956.

INDEX

Agrippa of Nettesheim, xviii,
5, 6, 7, 125
Ambrose, 38
Anabaptists, iii-vii, x, xi,
xii, xiv-xvi, 3, 7, 21, 44-
46, 49, 63-64, 127, 136, 161,
167, 173, 200-201, 203, 205,
208
Apsley, Sir Allen, 142
Aristotelianism, 4
Aristotle, 5
Ascham, Roger, 142
Ascherham, Gabriel, x
Attaway, Mrs. 200, 218-222
Augustine, 2-3
Avicenna, 5

Baillie, Robert, 165, 167
Bainton, Roland, v, vii, xiv
Balzac, Jean-Louis-Guez, 151, 155
Bancroft, Elizabeth, 210, 213
Baptists, 130, 142
Bauford, Joan, 210, 213
Baxter, Richard, 49, 86, 111-112
Becon, Thomas, 128
Berger, Peter, i
Bernard of Clairvaux, 174
Beverwyck, Jan van, 5-6, 141,
145, 151, 153
Beza, Theodore, 38, 108
Bilbrowe, Mary, 210, 212
Bochart, Samuel, 151
Böhme, Jakob, 6-7, 28-29
Bohemian Brethren, v, 127, 130
Bonaventure, 3
Boulding, Elise, iv
Bourignon, Antoinette, viii
Bradstreet, Anne, 126, 140-141
Brinsley, John, 1, 7-8, 35
Brownists, 45, 167, 168-169
Bucer, Martin, xiii, 46-48, 105
Bugenhagen, Johannes, 128
Bullinger, Heinrich, xiii, 46,
47, 49, 70
Bullough, Vern L., v, 123
Bumenin, Frena, 200, 204-209
Burroughs, Jeremiah, 214

Calvin, John, iii-iv, 43, 46-48,
105, 107, 159-160
Calvinists, v, 127, 159
Castiglione, Baldassare, xv, 124,
126
Catherine de Medici, xiii
Cats, Jacob, 149, 151
Cawdrey, Daniel, 165, 167, 176
Charles I, King of England, 170,
222-223
Cheevers, Sarah, 200, 235
Chidley, Katherine, 168
Christine de Pisan, 124
Christine of Sweden, xiii
Church of England, viii, 160,
161, 165, 231
Cleaver, Robert, 70, 86
Comenius, Jan, v, 132
Congregationalism, 39, 161-162,165
Conrart, Valentin, 151
Cotton, John, 165, 168, 169, 231

Descartes, René, 151, 152
Domenichi, Lodovico, 126
Dudley, Thomas, 140
Durkheim, Emile, i
Dutch Reformed, 45, 130

Ebertz, Catharine, 27
Edwards, Thomas, 200, 214
Eisler, Sibilla, 27
Eleanor, Lady, 200, 222
Elizabeth, Princess Palatine,
151
Elizabeth I, Queen of England,
xiii, 142
Erasmus, Desiderius, 38, 105,
124, 125
Estius, Gulielmus, 36
Euripides, 135
Evans, Catharine, 235

Faber, Gellius, 12
Fagius, Paul, 107
Fell, Margaret Askew (see
Margaret Fell Fox)
Fifth Monarchists, 170